THE BENGAL BOOK

THE BENGAL BOOK

Dola Mitra

"पुस्तकालय कोष्ठक-माध्यमिक शिक्षा विभाग,
उ. प्र. शासन के सौजन्य से प्राप्त"

RUPA

Published by
Rupa Publications India Pvt. Ltd 2021
161-B/4, Gulmohar House,
Yusuf Sarai Community Centre,
New Delhi 110049

Sales centres:
Bengaluru Chennai
Hyderabad Kolkata Mumbai

Kolkata Mumbai Copyright © Dola Mitra 2021

All rights reserved.
No part of this publication may be reproduced, transmitted,
or stored in a retrieval system, in any form or by any means,
electronic, mechanical, photocopying, recording or otherwise,
without the prior permission of the publisher.

The views and opinions expressed in this book are the author's own
and the facts are as reported by her which have been verified to the extent
possible, and the publishers are not in any way liable for the same.

P-ISBN: 978-93-5520-038-9
E-ISBN: 978-93-5520-043-3

Second impression 2026

10 9 8 7 6 5 4 3 2

The moral right of the author has been asserted.

Printed in India

This book is sold subject to the condition that it shall not,
by way of trade or otherwise, be lent, resold, hired out, or otherwise
circulated, without the publisher's prior consent, in any form of
binding or cover other than that in which it is published.

To my God, Anukul Thakur
To my Dad, Prasun Mitra
To my ancestors, whom I invoked
during the writing of this book

CONTENTS

Introduction		ix
I	Bengal in the Beginning	1
II	Sleeping Kings, Slipping Kingdoms	20
III	Treachery Under a Mango Tree	40
IV	Fruitfulness of Flowery Fops	56
V	Of Riches, Romances and Renunciations	73
VI	Casting Shadows in the Soul	90
VII	Mind the Missionary, Hail the Humanist	112
VIII	Genesis and the Generations: They Come and They Go	131
IX	Shining the Light on Love and Learning	148
X	An Ocean of Knowledge and a Sea of Change	169
XI	Fading Memories, Fearless Martyrs	187
XII	Of Breads and Biscuits, Tea and Toast	203
XIII	Those Who Went to Jail So That We Can Be Free	228
XIV	Three Hundred and Thirty Years Later	251
XV	The End	277
Acknowledgements		280

INTRODUCTION

In the vast sea of knowledge that exists on the subject of Bengal, this book is just another wave trying to navigate its way.

It was an honour, to say the least, when Rajan da (Rajan Mehra, owner of Rupa Publications) asked me to write this book. He called it 'The Bengal Book' and I retained that as the title. Speaking to him, I noticed how affectionate he was about Calcutta and Bengal, where I understand he grew up, and his entrusting me with the task of penning its story meant a lot. So, this book is really for him. Besides, Rupa Publications will always hold a special place in my heart because it was the publisher of my first book, *Decoding Didi*, which was on the West Bengal chief minister.

Initially, the idea of writing a book on Bengal was a little daunting. My 'professional' experience of the region was limited to covering it for a national newsmagazine and a regional newspaper (*Outlook* and *The Telegraph*, respectively). I was neither a historian nor an expert on the subject.

In an uncanny coincidence, before writing both the books, I bumped into Gouri di (Gouri Chatterjee, who was the features editor of *The Telegraph* when I worked there) at a Calcutta coffee shop. She suggested that the perspective be 'personal'. That conversation, over cappuccino, cakes and cookies, cleared my mind.

What stirred my soul was a dream in which my father, Prasun Mitra, appeared and steered me in the right direction. I drove on a rain-lashed, storm-struck day to the banks of the river Hooghly, the part of the Ganges that flows through Calcutta and Bengal. I stood there alone, listening to the howling winds whispering in my ear. Rain fell like tears into the flowing river.

Some time before my father died on 2 December 1999, I had visited that spot with him. He had said, smiling, 'Once upon a time, all this had belonged to us.' He was pointing to a vast region on the banks of the river. 'Dad! That is SO embarrassing,' I had said looking around, hoping no one had heard us. But I should have known what he meant. He was deeply spiritual, constantly aware of life's transience, and I had never known him to have much regard for material things, much less for possession of material things. The observation he made was purely for the sake of history and humour. Now that he is gone, I wish I had listened more closely to his stories. His direct ancestor, Gobinda Ram Mitra, was an integral character in the documented history of this region and so many tales trickled down to my father through family lore, undocumented. While writing this book, I borrowed generously from some of these tales told to us by the elders in our family. The legends that did the rounds about Gobinda Ram and were in the public domain included the quirky story of how he wielded a golden cane. But more fascinating for me were the stories in the family that revealed he was a man of deep spiritual faith in private, unlike his public persona.

That day, with the wind whistling and the rain rushing, it dawned on me that indeed, the 'personal' experience of Bengal was much more meaningful to me. The retelling of the known story of a region becomes more interesting if it is sprinkled with bits of the unknown. There is no point, I think, in history just repeating itself, so to speak.

Everyone's story is essentially connected to the history of a place, whether they are the descendants of people who were written about or those who were forgotten. In this book, there are many such descendants who recall titbits about their ancestors, illustrious or not. One man spoke about how his grandfather, a renowned parliamentarian in the country's first cabinet, pointed out to the then prime minister of India that there was a grievous error in the way the national emblem was replicated and how the latter turned down a request for a correction claiming that it would cost too much money. One woman talked about how her great-grandmother, a poor villager, was sent off by the British East India Company to work in sugarcane plantations as a bonded, indentured labourer in faraway Guyana. Their voices enrich the narrative beyond measure and if there is just one valuable piece in this story of Bengal, it is this. They provide the individual fingerprints of a story that is otherwise much-documented, much-thumbed.

Other than this, my research entailed going through existing literature and talking to various experts. During this process, it occurred to me that there is a great deal of debate and disagreement even about some of the seemingly 'established' historical facts amongst historians and that consensus, or even common ground, is not always easy to come by. I tried to bring out, wherever possible, the discussions and divergent views where they exist. In many instances I let the argument stand as disputed or ambiguous. In others, I went by what I thought was the more salient argument.

At some point, I decided that the story of Bengal, like the river that flows through it, is actually in constant motion. Even its past is not stagnant. It is not black and white. Nor is it grey. It is coloured in the many hues of the imaginations and interpretations of many who lived in it and described it. Just like its present.

Today, as a reporter, I can see that the same story can have multiple interpretations. The parts or points of a story that will be highlighted are determined by many factors. It could be based on the political leanings of a media house. It could be the result of editorial policy decisions which, in turn, are based on financial exigencies or marketing compulsions. The tone a story takes on might flow from the writer's personal discernments, predilections, conditionings or even an agenda. Frequently, it is the sincere and good-faith analytical output of one journalist which might reasonably differ from the equally sincere and good-faith analysis of another. Only the naive will insist that 'news' is strictly about incontestable 'facts' though it is certainly—hopefully—the threshold goal of journalism to at least get the 'facts' right.

Likewise, we cannot assume that the writers of history, whether ancient or recent, have not editorialized the narrative to suit their own interests and biases.

Of course, scholars have often disputed or questioned certain 'standard' historical accounts. On many occasions, the scholarly consensus has been revised. I have touched on these disparate views, when relevant to events or people I discuss in this book. Recent studies, for instance, have dismissed British accounts of 'thuggees' as a concoction. Bengal's British rulers formulated laws during the early part of the nineteenth century to criminalize what was considered a cult gang of bandits which preyed on night travellers and even infiltrated groups of pilgrims during the day before robbing and killing them. Ostensibly to curb and crush the menace, hundreds and thousands of tribal people from the jungles and deltas of the region were picked up, jailed and even hanged after cursory trials. Though descriptive accounts of the thuggees and their modus operandi exist from the time when British lawmakers recorded them, as do numerous paintings, drawings and sketches by contemporary artists purportedly depicting them in action, historians today call it a fabrication that was put in place to justify imperial practices.

I am immensely grateful to the experts in many fields who spoke to me for this book. They include historians, economists, environmentalists, politicians, psychologists, sociologists, scholars and journalists, among others. I was fortunate to have been provided by psychiatrist Dr Debashish Ray a description of the psychological disorders which Alexander the Great, the Macedonian emperor and conqueror of the world, may have been suffering from when he failed to get his hands on Bengal. I cannot sufficiently thank IPS officer B.D. Sharma for granting me permission, dozens of times, to go inside the different jails of Bengal and talk to the inmates so that I could write about 'Culture Therapy', the pioneering prison reforms he had initiated, that must find mention in the cultural history of Bengal, which is sometimes known as the 'cultural capital of the country'.

Any retelling of the story of Bengal generates questions and invites conjectures, and there are many throughout this book, some of which are followed compulsively and at length. There are also attempts at filling in some gaps and missing links. Imaginary dialogues appear out of nowhere as though the characters, including some real historical figures, are uttering them. Plausible but fictional situations present themselves in conformity with the sequences of unfolding history. Indeed, delving deeply into the lives of people from the past, even if through the use of invention along with known facts, gives one eerie access to what those people had talked about and what had transpired around them. Secrets seem to want to spill out. There seem to be yearnings in the air for setting records straight. We can never fulfil that task. But we can honour the longings by giving it a voice, affectionately and respectfully imagined by us.

The Bengal Book is a collection of these voices. It is told in glimpses and glances. In reconstructing the tale, I thought it would be interesting to flashback to the 'beginning', when the earliest inhabitants of the region we now call Bengal were alive, and then fast forward to the future when the next state elections will be held, and to tread the time and space in-between. I also needed to recreate events as they were thought to have happened, while filling in gaps. Stray stories that lurk in the background of important historical events often get swept away into oblivion. I tried to bring these out, even if they defy attempts at verification. I think that they add to the intrigue of the story.

For instance, I came across a remarkable story about how, the night before the Battle of Plassey, Bengal's army commander, Mir Jafar, sent out a letter, reassuring the enemy that he would betray his nephew, the king Siraj-ud-Daulah in the next day's battle. The incident is not dealt with in any great detail in the accounts of history and indeed, what transpired on that murky midnight before battle broke out cannot be established with any absolute certainty. But this story was too tantalizing not to find its way into this book.

The story of Bengal in this little book is not really a 'history' of Bengal. If I must give it some kind of a genre label, it would be, as my sister Koli Mitra, editor of my books, calls it, 'part historical fiction, part creative non-fiction'. *The Bengal Book* is a sort of hybrid of the two. I would like to think of *The Bengal Book* as essentially just a story in which imagination interprets a collection of historical incidents. It is an individual story. A single wave, making its way in a tumultuous ocean of facts, evidence, legends, memories and beliefs that make up the 'real' or 'complete'–and never fully knowable—story.

Dola Mitra
2 December 2020

I

BENGAL IN THE BEGINNING

*'You are the original, oh Ancient Power!
The horizons reverberate with the dazzle of your glory.'*[1]

—Rabindranath Tagore

It is a wind-swept, rain-lashed day on the banks of the river Hooghly, which is a long stretch of the river Ganga, flowing now wildly, now mildly, down eastern India. Along the northern stretches of the Hooghly lies Sutanuti which, like ancient memories, tells tales through flashes of lightning on storm-struck days. Through distant rumblings of thunder, like bottled up grumblings, it shares secret stories with those who care to listen.

In the late seventeenth century, Sutanuti was one of the three villages of the region known as Bengal (now divided into the Indian state of West Bengal and the country of Bangladesh) that were merged to create the city of Calcutta, renamed Kolkata. The other two villages were Kalikata, possibly named in deference to the goddess Kali, and Gobindapur.

Today, Sutanuti is a lonely riverside locality, mellowed with age, and housing old residential neighbourhoods and a part of

---

[1]From the Rabindra sangeet *'Prothom adi, tobo shakti'*.

the dusty and long Chitpur Road that once connected north and south Kolkata. The area that corresponds to the erstwhile hamlet of Gobindapur, on the other hand, is still relatively vibrant, housing as it does administrative landmarks such as the secretariat buildings, the general post office and even the courts. Kalikata extends southwards of Kolkata, embracing markets and bustling businesses.

Three hundred and thirty years have passed since Job Charnock, an official of the erstwhile British trading firm, the East India Company, anchored his ship in Sutanuti on 24 August 1690, and reportedly bought the three hamlets and turned them into the thriving settlement that was to become British India's capital city.

However, the claims of purchase that prevailed during the British period and even later have recently been legally quashed. On 16 May 2003, the Calcutta High Court ruled that the villages were not sold but merely leased out to the British East India Company. In the late seventeenth and early eighteenth centuries Mughal rulers in Delhi and Agra (now in Uttar Pradesh) exercised overall control over the land though the local rights to the individual properties were held by regional landlords. The Sabarna Roy Chaudhurys, an influential and landed family of Bengal, held property rights over the three villages. The British East India Company, which had begun the process of negotiations from the 1600s, extracted permission to take the land on rent to do business from the then Mughal emperor Farrukh Siyar but it could not procure permission from the local landlords. The first volume of the authoritative tome documenting this period, *Calcutta: The Living City*,[2] sheds light on these and other intriguing details of the early days of the British East India Company in this region. Other accounts of those ancient times include those of Debashish

---

[2]Sukanta Chaudhuri ed., *Calcutta: The Living City, Vol 1, The Past*, Oxford University Press, 1995.

Bandopadhyay and Alok Mitra,[3] and Purnedu Patree,[4] whose Bengali books, *Bonedi Kolkatar Gharbari* and *Purano Kolkatar Kothachitra* respectively, also point out that the Roy Chaudhurys were apparently not at all keen to let the British settle in their land. In spite of their reluctance and protests, however, the family had no choice but to part with it because the foreigners had bribed the Mughal ruler and ensured that the deal they had struck with him did not fall through.

Three hundred years later, in the late 1990s, descendants of Sabarna Roy Chaudhury discovered documents in various states of decay, some crumbling at the edges, others fraying, stashed away in old cupboards and trunks. The documents were, however, legible enough to clearly indicate that the three hamlets were not sold but had been rented out to the British East India Company for a period of 99 years for a sum of ₹1,300 per annum.

'We were astonished that distorted information had been passed down as historical fact for 300 years,' a member of the Roy Chaudhury family said, 'and we decided to rectify it.' The family formed a committee called the Sabarna Roy Chaudhury Paribar Parishad (or the Sabarna Roy Chaudhury Family Committee) and in 2001, along with a group of nine eminent citizens of Kolkata, which included academics and intellectuals, it filed a public interest litigation (PIL) in the Calcutta High Court. The Calcutta High Court, in its judgment two years later, stripped Charnock of the long-standing honour which had been erroneously conferred on him by the British as the founder of Calcutta, and declared that contrary to British records, Charnock was not responsible for bringing civilization to these parts.

Indeed, the history of civilization in Bengal is traced back to

---

[3]Debashish Bandopadhyay and Alok Mitra, *Bonedi Kolkatar Gharbari*, Ananda Publishers, 1995.
[4]Purnedu Patree, *Purano Kolkatar Kothachitra*, Dey Publishing, 2017.

no less than 4,000 years with human habitation in the region going back even earlier, to over 20,000 years ago. Renowned historian, the late Ramesh Chandra Majumdar, writes that Stone Age tools found in the region indicate that human habitation existed in Bengal for over 20,000 years.

While the earliest known cities date back to the Vedic Age, which spanned six centuries from 1700 BCE to 1100 BCE, archaeologists have traced remnants from the Chalcolithic or Copper Age roughly corresponding to the period between 3500 BCE and 2300 BCE in the Bengal region. Ramesh Chandra Majumdar mentions this in his ancient histories of Bengal and notes that 'Copper Age settlements, including pit dwellings, date back four thousand years.'[5]

Tamralipta, which in Sanskrit means 'filled with copper', was amongst India's most prosperous older cities, its proximity to the Bay of Bengal making it a commercial haven for seafaring traders. The name itself, referring to such a specific geological characteristic of the location, suggests that perhaps it was a time of advanced knowledge in archaeology, metallurgy and other sciences. Though it has now lost its past glory and is merely a dusty town in the remote East Midnapore district of West Bengal, Tamluk, as it is called today, still houses the magnificent ruins of a palace of a king of Bengal.

Considered both a 'thalassocracy', a seaport power, because of its proximity to the sea, and an 'entrepot', because of its many rivers, Bengal was an integral part of the Silk Route, that ancient network of commerce which also connected cultures and civilizations crisscrossing through cities and countries around the world. Not only did Bengal have friendly trade links with the Arabs, Persians and the Mediterranean people who desired its

---

[5]Ramesh Chandra Majumdar, *The History of Ancient Bengal*, Tulshi Prakashani, 1971.

cottons, muslins and silks, according to historian Ghulam M. Suhrawardi,[6] it had established colonies in the islands of the Indian Ocean as well as in Southeast Asia.

According to the anthropological histories of Bengal, settlements in the area took place over centuries with 'consecutive waves of migration' by groups as diverse as the Indo-Aryans to the Dravidians and the Tibeto-Burmans to the Austroasiatics. These references are found in such meticulously-researched works as the series documenting the anthropological histories of the region like *Bangladesh: A Country Study*[7] and *Pakistan: A Country Study*.[8] Richard M. Eaton's *The Rise of Islam and the Bengal Frontier, 1204 to 1760*, further points out that 'by the second millennium BCE the Bengal delta was settled by rice-cultivating communities with people living in systemically-aligned housing and producing pottery'. Delineating Bengal's geographical advantages, which did not just lead to increased migrations and settlements but also to a thriving civilization, these accounts discuss how 'rivers such as the Ganges and Brahmaputra were used for transport while maritime trade flourished in the Bay of Bengal'.[9]

Historians refer to an early fifteenth century group of texts, known as the *Kulopanjikas*, which are essentially compilations of documents tracing family genealogy. These texts seem to suggest another set of settlements in Bengal that reportedly took place in the ninth century. Based on these texts, it is surmised that a local king, Adisura, had brought a group of educated and elite

---

[6]Ghulam M Suhrawardi, *Bangladesh Maritime History,* Friesen Press, 2015.
[7]James Heitzman and Robert L. Worden, *Bangladesh: A Country Study,* United States Government Printing Office (Washington D.C. Federal Research Division), 1989.
[8]Peter R. Blood, *Pakistan: A Country Study,* United States Government Printing Office (Washington D.C. Federal Research Division), 1995.
[9]Richard M. Eaton, *The Rise of Islam and the Bengal Frontier, 1204 to 1760,* Oxford University Press, 1993.

castes, namely Brahmins and Kshatriyas, to the region from what is present-day Uttar Pradesh, for the purpose of imparting knowledge of the Vedas and other religious texts to the locals. Other accounts suggest that they were brought to Bengal to perform religious rites such as yagnas (a ritual usually performed using fire) and were subsequently coaxed to stay on. While there is much debate as to the veracity of the reports of this migration and the circumstances under which it had taken place, a number of Bengal's landed families, which owned entire villages by the river and sea before the arrival of the British, are said to be from this time. These large tracts of land were believed to have been gifted to them as an incentive to remain in Bengal and as compensation for the dislocation.

The exact etymology of the word 'Bengal' is debated, with at least one group of linguists arguing that it has its roots in the name belonging to a tribe called 'Bang' or 'Vang' that had settled in the area no later than around 1000 BCE. Historian Bijay Chandra Mazumdar, in his book,[10] discusses the existence of this tribe, which is supposed to be Dravidian in origin, in the region. That they could have given the land, its people and the language its name is surmised on the fact that references to them occur in some of the earliest literature of the land. The formation and existence of a 'Banga' or 'Vanga' kingdom is mentioned in the ancient text of *Attharvaveda*. Bengal figures in other older literature, notably in the celebrated epic, Mahabharata, which has mentions of kings from 'Banga' or 'Vanga' taking part in the war at Kurukshetra. It must be noted here that the words 'Banga' or 'Vanga' or rather their derivative, 'Bongo', is still in use in Bengali to describe Bengal. The country of Bangladesh is often referred to as Purbo Bongo or East Bengal, for instance,

---

[10]Bijay Chandra Mazumdar, *The History of the Bengali Language*, Kessinger Publishing (Legacy Reprints), 2010 (originally published in 1920).

and the eastern Indian state of West Bengal is called Poshchim Bongo in the Bengali vernacular. In fact, very recently, that is, after the current state government came to power in 2011, it decided to make a bid for an official renaming of West Bengal to 'Poschim Bongo', declaring that since it was its original name it was important to re-establish it for the sake of heritage just as Calcutta was renamed Kolkata in 2001 during the previous regime. The chief minister of the state, Mamata Banerjee, added another argument to the demand, claiming that since West Bengal was alphabetically last on the list of the names of India's states, it was called upon last to speak during meetings of states and it missed out on important benefits distributed by the central government on first-come-first-served basis. Other alternatives suggested by the state government included simply dropping the word 'West' from West Bengal and pushing up the state's name all the way to the top of the list or at least to the fourth position from the top, right after the three names beginning with 'A', that is, Andhra Pradesh, Arunachal Pradesh and Assam. However, last heard, the project is still in the pipeline.

The word 'Bengal' is said to be an Anglicized derivative of the original 'Bangla', which refers both to the region as well as the language. Scholars have pointed out that the word 'Bangla' entered the lexicon of the Urdu-speaking rulers and Persian-speaking people when they came in contact with this eastern region and used it to describe the land (because it was inhabited by the Vang or Bang tribe). Urdu and Persian, as the official language of the courts, gradually influenced other languages, including English. 'Bengal' could also be a variant of the word 'Bangal', used by Bengalis to describe the Bengali-speaking people who have subsequently come to be associated specifically with the eastern part of the region, now in Bangladesh.

One of the most intriguing discoveries in recent times was the unearthing of what seems to be a lost world from the third century BCE. Buried deep beneath the surface in the southernmost tip of Bengal, in the region known as the Sundarbans—which is covered with the earth's longest mangrove jungle, home to the legendary royal Bengal tiger, and is surrounded by the world's largest delta—archaeologists have dug up remnants of a civilization, including items of everyday use such as utensils for cooking. Scholars have mooted the possibility that this region could be linked to a land mentioned in the Mahabharata. The reference occurs in the context of Bheem, one of the Pandav brothers and protagonists of the Mahabarata, engaging the Bengali kings, Chitrasena and Samudrasena in battle. Though Bheem defeats the Bengali kings, he is nevertheless injured when he is struck by the poison arrows shot in his direction by the powerful subaltern rulers. Subsequently, according to the iconic epic poem, the Pandava warrior travels to the southernmost part of Bengal, a region called Patratal, seeking treatment. The description of the area, with its jungles and rivers, infested with wild animals, is uncannily similar to the topography of the Sundarbans and writers have even suggested that the pots and pans discovered in the island could have been cauldrons used for the preparation of herbal medication. Professor (Dr) Rangan Kanti Jana, Curator, Museum Art Gallery at the University of Burdwan in West Bengal, says that such discoveries have opened up the possibility of other excavations in the Sundarbans region. Certain spots, including at a distance of two to three kilometres into deep sea, could be explored and points of the river bed along the wild Matla, which flows through the region to finally disgorge into the sea, could be dug up and investigated.

    Another exciting discovery by archaeologists was the digging up of the lost kingdom of Pundranagar, dating back to no later than the third century BCE. Found in 1808 during an excavation in Mahasthangarh, which is now in Bangladesh, the scientists located a limestone slab inscribed with six lines in the ancient Brahmi script understood to be some sort of royal order in the archaic Prakrit dialect. Interestingly, both the *Attharvaveda* and the Mahabharata describe the formation of a Pundra kingdom. The dates pose a problem though and don't seem to tally, considering that these ancient texts preceded the timeline ascribed to the formation of the discovered Pundranagar. However, it must be remembered that much of the ancient texts in their extant forms had been passed down orally before being recorded in writing and scholars, through the ages, have not ruled out the possibility of these scriptures picking up on current happenings and adding these onto what has come down to us today.

Two hundred years after this discovery, in 2008, evidence that even prehistoric man walked on the soil of Bengal stumbled out of the earth's Pleistocene layer. Way below the Holocene layer, earlier believed to be where human activity in this Gangetic region was limited to, scientists found some 200 Stone Age weapons, including axes, knives and needles, dating back 20,000 years, strewn around at an excavation site in the northern Bengal district of Murshidabad. Of course, Bengal's many indigenous tribes, including the Bhil, Kola, Santhals and the Pulinda, leave little doubt about early settlement in this region but the discovery of remnants from the pre-historic era suggests that this region, flowing between the Ganges in its west, the Bay of Bengal in its east and south and the mighty Himalayan mountain ranges in its north, was inhabited by humans from the time that they first started walking on earth.

Be that as it may, but that Bengal was considered a political and military power to reckon with internationally when human civilization came into being in the ancient world becomes clear from descriptions in Greek and Roman historical records. It is mentioned numerously in Greek and Latin texts as 'Gangaridai', literally meaning 'at the heart of the Ganga', referring to the civilization that had sprung up along the banks of the river Ganga in the east. Diodorus Siculus's *Bibliotheca Historica* is considered to be the earliest surviving text to provide details of ancient Bengal as one with a superior army which even Alexander the Great, was afraid to take on. According to these ancient accounts, the Macedonian emperor, who was unstoppable as he pushed eastward invading every kingdom in his wake since seizing power in Persia in 326 BCE, had to, however, stop short of going to Gangaridai.

Bengal was at that time ruled by the Nanda Dynasty, whose mighty kingdom was known as Magadh. The area stretched from the eastern banks of the river Ganga in its west to the western banks of the Brahmaputra in its east. The Himalayan mountains and valleys were the region's northern boundaries and the Bay of Bengal its southern tip.

Southern Bengal had grown wealthy and powerful through its sea trades and it was the Greek and Latin records of the time which first referred to it as a thalassocracy. Enemies dreaded Bengal's formidable combat force comprising 200,000 infantry, 80,000 cavalry, 8,000 chariots and 20,000 horses. But it was the 6,000-strong 'fighting elephants' that commanded the most fear.

Alexander's army had already had a taste of what Indian elephants could do to them when, at the Battle of Hydaspes, Alexander attacked King Purushottam, known to the Greeks and Romans as Porus, the ruler of the western Punjab province by the Jhelum River. The encounter with the jumbo giants is thus described in an account by Diodorus:

> …the elephants, applying to good use their prodigious size and strength, killed some of the enemy by trampling (them) under their feet and crushing their armour and their bones, while upon others they inflicted a terrible death, for they first lifted them aloft with their trunks, which they twisted round their bodies and then dashed them down with great violence to the ground. Many others they deprived in a

moment of life by goring them through and through with their tusks.[11]

There is some controversy about the outcome of Alexander's face-off with Porus, with most Greek and Latin accounts suggesting that the former, with the help of Ambhi, King of Taxila, who was Porus' enemy, was able to defeat the relatively small kingdom but then relented and gave it back. Skeptics of this theory could scoff at the unlikelihood of such a magnanimous gesture from Alexander. They could observe that such a magnanimous gesture was not just uncharacteristic of a man who has been described in history as a megalomaniacal and ruthlessly power-hungry dictator, but also that he had invested too much money—by some counts he had paid close to 25,000 kilograms of gold to King Taxila to help him defeat Porus—for it all to go to waste. Indeed, it is entirely likely that Alexander fought Porus but beat a hasty retreat; however, since the accounts of the war were written by Alexander's own people, he was shown to have emerged victorious. Those who would defend the earlier theory and argue that Alexander gave it all up in a moment's repentance would perhaps point out that Alexander was also supposed to have been given to bouts of severe remorse. He had been inconsolable for days after he killed one of his closest friends in a fit of rage. Given to drinking, he is said to have often behaved unpredictably. So accounts which describe Alexander as filled with compassion for Porus when the latter, after being captured by the former, was asked how he would like to be treated, replied, 'as a king would treat another king',[12] cannot be entirely dismissed either.

---

[11]John Watson McCrindle (editor), *The Invasion of India by Alexander the Great as Described by Arrian, Q. Curtius, Diodorus, Plutarch and Justin*, Kessinger Publishing Company, 2004.
[12]Guy Maclean Rogers, *Alexander, the Ambiguity of Greatness*, Random House, 2005.

Analysing the incongruous behavioural patterns of Alexander based on existing accounts, clinical psychiatrist Dr Debashish Ray says that these could be symptomatic of deep-rooted psychological disorders or even structural damages to regions of the brain sustained by him during a battle when he was attacked and hit on the head from behind. Dr Ray says, 'Permanent injuries to regions of the brain which determine specific actions and behaviour cannot be ruled out.' However, he suggests that it is most likely that 'Alexander may have been suffering from a multitude of psychiatric problems including post-traumatic stress disorder (PTSD)'.

Could this possibly have been triggered by an unfulfilled desire to conquer Gangaridai? Whatever the case may be, as far as Bengal is concerned, there is unanimity amongst scholars and historians that Alexander did not attempt an invasion of it. That is not to say that he did not intend to. According to the Greek map, which Alexander was following when he set out on his conquest of Asia and the rest of the world, the landmass of the earth that was earmarked for coverage ended at Gangaridai but at the point where it met the Bay of Bengal. In other words, it included the entire landmass of Bengal. This indicated that Bengal was possibly the final destination for Alexander. Certainly, it could not be that a man who was driven by a mission of conquering the world did not nurture some ambition of capturing one of the most powerful regions of the day. The decision in the end to not do so has been put down by historians to a number of reasons. Arguably the most prominent of these is that Alexander's men were horrified at the prospect of facing such a formidable enemy as the one which Gangaridai possessed, especially the 6,000 elephants. They put their feet down, quite literally, and straight out refused. When an unrelenting Alexander rebuked them and insisted that whatever its might, they must take on the region, his soldier planned a mutiny. They had decided to kill their leader in case they were forced to comply with his wishes. On the advice of his trusted general, Coenus, Alexander eventually gave in and abandoned his desire to proceed towards Gangaridai and turned back. But he is understood to have been so deeply demoralized by this that he possibly considered it the biggest failure of his otherwise extraordinarily successful 10-year-long expedition which he had begun at the tender age of just 22. Three years after his retreat, he died in Babylon, at age 32, under mysterious circumstances, including the possibility of death due to liver disease caused by excessive drinking. It has been suggested that he was morbidly depressed ever since his return from India, heartbroken that he could not set his eyes, forget get his hands, on Gangaridai.

No, Alexander never did get a share of Bengal. Ironically, however, in the years and centuries that followed, the region was subjected to one successive invasion after another with emperors, kings and rulers establishing their respective kingdoms, after fighting great battles or sometimes after mere petty skirmishes. As they did so, they transported into the land their religions, languages, cultures and customs. All of it has left its imprints and played a part in the evolution of Bengal as we know it today.

One of the most prosperous periods for Bengal was when it was ruled by the Maurya Dynasty from 321 BCE to 185 BCE. Its founder Chandragupta Maurya, whose reign lasted 23 years from 321 BCE to 298 BCE, was an exceptionally able administrator who, after wresting power from the former Nanda Dynasty, built up an empire that stretched from Bengal to most of the Indian subcontinent, with the exception of the southern regions which now corresponds to Andhra Pradesh, Tamil Nadu, Telengana, Karnataka and Kerala as well as the eastern region of Odisha. Chandragupta had initiated diplomatic ties with other nations, including from the Macedonian region. This was a clever strategy, no doubt thought up in order to keep the powerful Mediterranean empire from entertaining thoughts of any strikes against Bengal.

Alexander's exploits and his designs on the region were well-known and still fresh in the memory of the political rulers of Bengal. When the previous Nanda regime had prepared for war in anticipation of Alexander's attack, the news had spread like wildfire. The Mauryas pre-empted any such possibility by extending a friendly hand. Commercial trade and cultural exchange, instead of mutual suspicion, became the buzzword between the two ancient civilizations. Of course, the brain behind Chandragupta's masterful political, economic and military strategies was the legendary kingmaker, Chanakya. How the pious Brahmin, with a razor-sharp intellect, shaped the political career of his most famous protégé is well-documented in history. He had picked up the orphaned and abandoned infant, giving him shelter, clothing, food and a family but most importantly, training him in the art of governance. Some have compared Bengal's Maurya period to the earlier Magadh era, dating back at least to 600 BCE, which having originated in present-day Bihar, spread throughout the east including in Bengal. During the Magadh rule, Buddhism and Jainism were said to have developed. Similarly, Chandragupta's reign was not only marked by economic, military and political strength and stability but it was a time of great religious tolerance. Chandragupta later renounced his kingdom, as well as the world in general, following in the footsteps of his spiritual inspiration Lord Buddha, though formally it was the Jain religious order that he embraced. Eventually he chose the path of death that the Jain community call Santhara, in which the spiritual soul is supposed to leave the body by depriving it of food and nutrients, a form of fasting, except that it is accompanied by meditation and chanting of mantras. Chandragupta's grandson, Ashoka, whose empire stretched from modern Afghanistan in the west to the present-day Bangladesh in the east, continued the Maurya tradition of peace and prosperity but only in the later years. His earlier reign was characterized by an emphasis on expansion which saw bloody wars of conquest. He waged war against Kalinga, now in Odisha, a region his ancestors could never capture, and though he won, he is said to have been heartbroken to see the massive scale of death and destruction. More than 100,000 people had died in the war and many more wounded and others displaced. Filled with remorse, Ashoka reflected on the pointlessness of it all. Eventually he too, like his grandfather, turned to spirituality for solace and embraced Buddhism. During his reign Ashoka had erected his trademark pillars, stone columns between 40–50 feet high, weighing 50 tons each and inscribed with his edicts, throughout his kingdom. The most famous of these columns was one which had been placed at Sarnath, in what is now Uttar Pradesh, where Buddha had travelled to after achieving Enlightenment to teach his disciples. This pillar was capped with a stone sculpture, now known as the Lion Capital, depicting four lions sitting back-to-back atop a circular base embossed with motifs of an elephant, a bull, a horse and a lion, each separated by intervening 'chakras' or wheels with 24 spokes, symbolizing the Buddha's 24 'acharidharmas' or ways of life. What influence that particular period in Bengal's glorious past had on the future of India is indicated by the fact that more than two millennia later, parts of the Ashoka pillar has been chosen to symbolically represent the nation's ethos of courage, symbolized by the lions and spirituality, symbolized by the wheel. While the Indian flag bears at its centre a graphical representation of the 'chakra', the country's currency notes carry watermark images of the lions.

On the subject of India's adopting a replica of a part of the Ashoka pillar as the national symbol, there is an interesting anecdote. That the Ashoka Chakra would be adopted as the national emblem was decided during the Constituent Assembly debate of 1949. The first Indian prime minister, Jawaharlal Nehru, had presided over the debate. Though there were a few voices of dissent by those who felt that it had too much religious connotation when the 'chakra' was suggested, Nehru argued that it was also an integral symbol of India's freedom movement and hence should adorn both the national flag and emblem. This was also the majority view in the house. But eight years later a member of the Indian Parliament's upper house from Bengal named Radha Kumud Mookherjee wrote a letter to Nehru expressing concern that the symbol that the country had adopted was not based on the original Ashoka pillar but that of a distorted one. Dated 27 August 1957 and signed by nine other MPs, the letter said, 'We are concerned to find that our state emblem, known as Ashoka Chakra, is not an accurate replica and what is more important, distorts the significance originally sought to be conveyed.' The letter then went onto point out, 'It appears that a "chakra" with 32 spokes was, in the original, placed atop the shoulders of the four lions. The basic idea was that the wheel of righteousness, representing spiritual forces, should be above the four lions, representing material strength. However, there is evidence to show that this top wheel fell off the shaft on which it rested and so in the Sarnath Museum one sees the lion capital without the top.'[13] The letter ends by urging Nehru to take action and rectify the mistake. Nehru replied in a terse letter that no change was needed and the material cost involved in correcting the minor error outweighed the significance of the matter.

It is commonly held that though ostensibly Ashoka's reasons for erecting these pillars throughout his kingdom was for the spreading of the message of spirituality, namely Buddhism, compulsions of assertion of power and domination too played a part. But there seems to be a more complex motivation. It is interesting to note that the great rulers of Bengal and India have

---

[13] Radha Kumud Mookherjee in a letter to then Prime Minister Jawaharlal Nehru, dated 27 August 1957. Photocopy of the original letter was provided to the author of this book by Mookherjee's family.

struggled with the idea of how much power to exert, how much domination to exercise. Wars of conquest, invasions for expansion of kingdoms have left in their wake untold misery and sorrow and have given rise to feelings of futility in these emperors and conquerors. And yet, kingdoms needed to be strong, fortified and ready for battle if attacked. Sometimes the adage, 'offence is the best defence' was true for these rulers. But it was also that in youth, they must have been driven by the passion for power and then, once achieved, it lost its sheen. Like children who throw away the toys for which they fought tooth and nail, these conquerors and invaders, once wisdom dawned after experiencing the transience of the high of victory, renounced it all. Ashoka's pillars perhaps delineate this silencing of the brute forces within as the wheel of life turns.

The first and second millennia CE were times of immense tussle for power in Bengal with the fight to establish religious dominance being a key feature of this era. Before the arrival of the Mughals and then the British, Bengal was ruled by three other main dynasties in quick succession, the Gaudas, the Mallas and Palas. The Gauda Empire, which lasted only 36 years from 590 CE to 626 CE, saw the persecution of Buddhists, especially during the reign of King Shashank, who was otherwise considered an extremely efficient administrator. The Mallas, who ruled Bengal for approximately two decades, roughly between 694 CE and 710 CE, were supposed to have arrived from present-day Nepal and established themselves in the jungle-covered areas, now known as Jungle Mahal which stretches across the districts of Bankura, Birbhum and parts of West Midnapore in the state's western border with Jharkhand. They were of the warrior caste, Kshatriyas, and were known for their proficiency in wrestling and warfare. In fact, the term 'malla' in Sanskrit means 'wrestling' and with 'juddha' meaning 'war', the phrase 'mallajuddha' (or wrestling warfare) has entered the Bengali lexicon and is used to define a particular type of 'combat wrestling'. It is also often used in Bengali to connote a quarrel or squabble which degenerates into a scuffle or physical fighting. The Pala Dynasty, which ruled from 750 CE to 1200 CE, is credited with ushering in the atmosphere of intellectual advancement and cultural refinement that has come to be associated with Bengal and Bengalis. It was a time when literature, art and music were promoted in the courts and philosophical discourses encouraged. Most significantly, the development of the Bengali language in its present form is deemed to have taken place during this period.

It was into this land, thus seasoned for hundreds and thousands of years by a succession of advanced civilizations, that Charnock had set foot. So the claim that has gone down in history that he had brought civilization to these parts did indeed need to be quashed. Nevertheless, his and the East India Company's arrival and setting up of business in this port did change the course of Bengal's history, becoming a turning point which eventually ushered in India's colonial era.

Interestingly, Sutanuti, perhaps defiantly, in retaliation for having become the unwitting gateway to a period of forced colonization, shows little sign of the changes brought on by British rule. Even three centuries and three decades later, on this windswept, rain-lashed day, the vast expanse of the gray riverbed and the gray sky above could just as well have been the landscape of that day when Charnock's ships landed in Sutanuti. A painting depicting their arrival shows people spilling out of canoes, rowed by turbaned 'natives', to clamber up the slippery slopes of the river banks. Charnock, exhausted after the arduous sea journey, is supposed to have rested under a tree by the river. The tree still stands. It is as though the intervening years, when the story of the Bengal of today unfolded, have not even made a dent in the eternal time flowing through it.

The snazzy malls and swanky multiplexes that have cropped

up all across the Bengal of now, especially Calcutta, the capital city, are nowhere to be spotted here. Sutanuti still clutches on to the ancient past, deliberately obliterating the transition—the transition that is known as the colonial era. The river bank today is still lined on either side with tiny ancient temples and forlorn burning ghats (crematoriums), which could have been here for hundreds of years, conveying the perpetual paradox, delineating their existence as timeless temples of transience, as immortal institutions of mortality. In between flows a river, which too has passed through here for hundreds and thousands of years, carrying in its tides many memories of the transient transpirations of human happenings. The only permanence, clearly, is the transience.

II

SLEEPING KINGS, SLIPPING KINGDOMS

'If your destination is East, never take the road going West.'

—Sri Sri Ramakrishna

Siraj-ud-Daulah, the Nawab of Bengal, had gone to sleep early that evening on 20 June 1756. Or that's what his soldiers told the prisoners of war. He had been exhausted. In the past days the Nawab, royal ruler of the entire region of Bengal, had travelled down to Calcutta from his official residence in Murshidabad, some 240 kilometres northeast of the city, and led his army into a bitter battle against the soldiers of the British East India Company, who had been gathering in the fort it had set up near the river. Recently, the Company had started constructing additional fortresses around it, ostensibly to defend their growing trade interests in Bengal, but the Nawab, who did not authorize the building of the structures, knew better.

He knew that the British East India Company had long ceased to be just a commercial enterprise. It had increasingly been making inroads into the foreign lands where it had, over the past century and a half, established trading ports and started to interfere in their economy and politics. It had designs which were more than just the innocuous buying and selling and importing and exporting of merchandise associated with a trading organization. It had been building up a military and Siraj-ud-Daulah was not going to rule out the possibility that the Company was mulling a takeover. With its headquarters in London, the Company was made up of shareholders comprising Britain's aristocracy, called 'directors' and it was headed by a 'governor'. But so lucrative was the trade and so unprecedented the revenue it was generating from its foreign ventures and the mercenary expeditions it was leading around the world that it had begun increasingly to gain the favour of the British Crown and the British government, which took an active interest in the workings of the Company. In fact, the Company had become a middleman of sorts, carrying out the diplomatic missions between its country of origin and the countries where it was doing business.

In India, the bonds of friendship between Britain and the Mughal rulers remained tenuous for the most part, though it also intermittently oscillated between the extremes of friendliness and hostility throughout the seventeenth and the early part of the eighteenth centuries. The Company was trying desperately to establish itself in the land and it faced both utter resistance as well as brief spells of royal treatment from the Mughal rulers, who still held sway. While the phases of open confrontation lasted for long periods, the Company cleverly manipulated the times of stronger ties. So much so that by the early eighteenth century they had managed to get the Mughal rulers to virtually waive off all export and import duties. In 1717, the Mughal emperor Farrukh Siyar granted the Company duty-free trading rights in all of Bengal.

But within about four decades, things began to change. Bengal had undergone a regime change. And the new rulers expected the Company to start paying taxes. The Mughal rulers in Delhi too started imposing stiff taxes on import and export, increasing it to the tune of some three and a half percent, which, the British Company claimed, was not a part of the original agreements known as 'firman'. But the Mughal kings, who had established their dynastic rule in the land since the end of the Pala era and a brief period of Muslim Sultanates, were in no mood to continue to subsidize the British enterprise which, as far as they were concerned, had been steadily draining the country of its resources. The Indian rulers felt that they had been more than generous and that for over a century and a half their taxation of the British was so lenient it needed an overhaul.

British East India Company officers first disembarked in India in 1608 in the western port of Surat in Gujarat. At that time the emperor was Nuruddin Salim Jahangir, the fourth generation Mughal king, after Babur, Humayun and Akbar. Beset by competition from Dutch and Portuguese merchants, who had put a spanner in the works by engaging them in bloody battles at sea, the British traders decided that the only way to crush their rivals and monopolize the Indian business would be to get the country's rulers on their side.

That was easier said than done. The Mughal rulers had little reason to be interested in giving the British a smooth passage. James I, then king of England, intervened on behalf of the Company and sent an officer, Sir Thomas Roe, to Jahangir to try to negotiate trade prospects. Eventually, Jahangir accepted the British proposal to sign a mutually beneficial commercial treaty in which the Company would shower the emperor with rare gifts from the European market in return for the freedom to do business in the land. He extended such a warm welcome to the British merchants that perhaps they themselves could never have imagined it. In a letter he sent to the English monarch through Sir Roe, the Mughal king wrote:

> Upon which assurance of your royal love I have given my general command to all the kingdoms and ports of my dominions to receive all the merchants of the English

nation as the subjects of my friend; that in what place soever they choose to live, they may have free liberty without any restraint; and at what port soever they shall arrive, that neither Portugal nor any other shall dare to molest their quiet; and in what city soever they shall have residence, I have commanded all my governors and captains to give them freedom answerable to their own desires; to sell, buy, and to transport into their country at their pleasure. For confirmation of our love and friendship, I desire your Majesty to command your merchants to bring in their ships of all sorts of rarities and rich goods fit for my palace; and that you be pleased to send me your royal letters by every opportunity, that I may rejoice in your health and prosperous affairs; that our friendship may be interchanged and eternal.[14]

Jahangir was 43 years old in 1612, when he thus opened India's doors to the British. He was considered a bit of a romantic. He had many wives, mistresses and concubines and had, in his youth, fallen head over heels in love with a beautiful court dancer, Anarkali, who reciprocated his infatuation. According to the legend, she was buried alive by the young lad's incensed father, the emperor Akbar, for her audacity. Other accounts claim that Akbar himself had feelings for her and could not bear the thought of her falling for the younger man. Though the historical veracity of this doomed love story has been questioned, it is a fact that Jahangir, though he did succeed to the throne, had fallen out with his father on a number of issues. The two are supposed to have had very different personalities, the elder a more serious administrator and the younger, though as efficient, more of a

---

[14]The text of this letter appears in Paul Halsall's 'Internet Indian History Sourcebook Project' located in, though independent of it, at Fordham University, New York.

dreamer. Jahangir is also believed to have been addicted to opium and had a fondness for drinking.

Soon the British East India Company spread to other parts of the country, opening trading posts in every direction. In the west, it was of course already present since inception, having arrived in Surat in 1608 as stated earlier and then establishing its port 11 years later, in 1619. After the death of Jahangir in 1627, his son Shah Jahan ascended to the throne and continued the imperial patronage. In fact, it was during his reign that the British received the green signal to set up factories along the eastern and north-eastern coasts.

The intriguing story behind Shah Jahan's decision to allow the British East India Company to set up trading centres in Bengal, at that time the richest province in the land, goes back to a dark evening in Agra nearly 400 years ago in 1641. Shah Jahan's favourite daughter, 27-year-old Jahanara Begum was walking back to her room through the dimly-lit corridors of the palace when she slid too close to a burning lamp and her silken garments caught fire. Though there were male guards nearby she did not holler for help as it was not the custom of the time to let strange men see women of her stature from so close. She ran to the female quarters and her attendants eventually doused the flames. By then however, she was badly burnt. Her charred clothes clung to her. The flames had leapt up to her face too and singed her skin. The burns she sustained did not just disfigure the princess who was celebrated for her beauty, but her very survival was in question. Shah Jahan was grief-stricken. It was hardly a decade since he lost his favourite consort, Jahanara's mother, Mumtaz Mahal, with whom he had been married for 19 years, since she was 19 and he was 20 years of age. He had 13 children with her and it was during the birth of their fourteenth child that Mumtaz developed post-natal complications and passed away. Mumtaz was not just Shah Jahan's constant companion, even though the emperor had other wives and concubines, she was also an astute advisor to him whom he consulted on state affairs. Her death, at 38, devastated him. He built her the most magnificent memorial, made completely of marble, and named it Taj Mahal after her. He declared a two-year mourning period, forbidding any kind of public celebration, even dancing, singing or merry-making. He remained inconsolable. Finally, he found solace in Jahanara, who looked like her beautiful mother and reminded him of her. Shah Jahan bestowed the title of 'Malika-e-Hindustan Padishah Begum' or the First Lady of the Indian Empire on the 17-year-old Jahanara. These accounts are documented by several historians, including Edward Henry Nolan in his *History of the British Empire in India and the East*. Nolan writes:

> Shahjahan, the great Mogul, had a favourite daughter, named Jahan Ara: on one occasion, after spending the evening with her sire, when retiring to her own apartments, she passed too closely to one of the lamps that lit a corridor of the palace, and set her dress on fire. Fearful of calling the attention of the guards—oriental ladies of her rank regarding any exposure to the gaze of strangers as a calamity to be avoided at whatever cost—she rushed to the harem, her light apparel in flames, which the rapidity of her flight of course fanned. She fell insensible into the arms of her attendants, who extinguished the fire, but the princess was severely and even perilously injured.[15]

According to these accounts, though the country's best physicians, doctors and even quacks were summoned, who prescribed dozens of ointments, lotions and creams to soothe the burns, they could

---

[15]Edward Henry Nolan, *The Illustrated History of the British Empire in India and the East, from the Earliest Times to the Suppression of the Sepoy Mutiny in 1857*, Nabu Press, 2012 (reproduced from the original which was published prior to 1920).

not cure her. Eventually, a British physician, Dr Gabriel Boughton, who was the resident doctor of the East India Company and was reportedly stationed at a ship in Surat, was called in. He successfully treated the princess, who lived to be 67. Interestingly, when the emperor, out of sheer gratitude, offered him any reward that he wished for, the English doctor did not ask for any personal favour. He requested that Shah Jahan grant his company trading rights in the east, which had thus far been difficult to achieve. This act of altruism by Dr Boughton has been a topic of discussion in contemporary and subsequent writings. He has been praised not just by his Company and his peers but also by the Mughals, especially Jahanara, who was so impressed by his selflessness that she convinced her father, who did have some initial apprehensions. Others have suggested that the doctor acted on the orders of his employers, the Company, and did not really have much choice but to toe the line.

At any rate, the British East India Company now had trading rights in Bengal. It was a big achievement. By the time Shah Jahan's son Aurangzeb became emperor in the year 1659, the Company had established several trading centres in the eastern region. But while it had its eyes focused on Bengal, the Company continued to grab, with both hands as it were, prime land in other eastern ports. It was able to start a commercial centre in the most coveted spot in the entire land from the perspective of seafaring business and that was at the south-eastern tip of India, in a place called Madras, now Chennai, where the Indian Ocean met the Bay of Bengal. By 1669, the Company's trade increased so much that it opened another western business centre, this time in Bombay, now Mumbai. And by the time Job Charnock created the Calcutta centre of the East India Company in the 1690s, it was operating 23 factories in India. In another two and a half decades, roughly around 1717, when the central rulers completely waived off customs duties as earlier pointed out, the British Company had been trading in cotton, silk, tea, indigo and saltpetre.

Trouble started a couple of decades later, in the mid-1700s, when the Company's Bengal unit started to clash with the local administration. Since the death of Aurangzeb in 1707, the Mughal Empire had begun to crumble. The descendants of the once mighty dynasty led a series of weak and ineffective governments, marked by greed for power, deception, betrayal and wars of succession. The resultant void made the central throne vulnerable to attacks and invasions from foreign enemies. The new rulers in Delhi loosened their grip on the regions that saw the increasing rise of local nobles as governors. Of course, even during the time that the East India Company enjoyed friendly central policies through the 1600s and early 1700s with the emperors intermittently rolling out the red carpet to the foreign traders, the Company, with some exception, experienced strained relationships with the local lords and leaders, from whom its officials faced stiff resistance. In Bengal, before Job Charnock could finally set up business in the 1690s, he had been driven out a number of times in spite of having a central clearance. Amongst those to have strongly objected to giving the East India Company unrestricted trade freedom, and to have given Job Charnock a very hard time, was Shaista Khan, governor of the Bengal province from 1664 to 1688. In a sense that was surprising, considering that Shaista was Aurangzeb's own maternal uncle and supposedly very loyal to his nephew. However, the two did have a brief falling out when Shaista Khan, who was sent by Aurangzeb to the western province of Pune to fight a war against the Maratha king Shivaji and invade the Maratha kingdom, returned defeated. What made it worse for the Mughal kings was that initially Shaista's army did manage to seize the western province, driving out Shivaji's men completely from the city. However, Shivaji's army outsmarted them by re-entering the city camouflaged as wedding guests and then, during the night, in a surprise attack they crept into Shaista's camp killing the guards, many soldiers as well as one of his sons. Shaista, who was sleeping in a secret chamber, had survived the attack but Aurangzeb was apparently so humiliated and angry by the defeat that in a punishment posting, far from Delhi, he transferred Shaista Khan to Bengal as its governor without so much as a meeting with him, as was customary before any new appointment. Shaista Khan's defiance of Aurangzeb's order granting the East India Company easy passage could be related to this.

Or, perhaps, the dual voices with which the Mughal emperor Aurangzeb and his provincial representative in Bengal spoke could just be an early indication of the shrewd and machinating ways of the politician perceptible even today. For political exigencies, they can play the good cop, bad cop roles with aplomb.

The political dynamics of the transitional phase between the end of the Mughal era and the beginning of the British period was marked by a conflict of interest between the central rulers and the regional leaders. In fact, it must be remembered that though the Mughal rulers controlled a centralized empire, in many instances, the land was ruled regionally by independent and individual kingdoms, princedoms and local leaders who did not necessarily even owe allegiance to the central power.

It is therefore unlikely that the regional rulers and local leaders during Jahangir's time would have been entirely happy with the magnanimity that the emperor had extended to the British. They would almost certainly not have been pleased that he granted the British company free access to the land and expected them to cooperate with the foreigners because, not only did it clearly undermine their authorities, but the pact hardly had any material benefits for anyone other than the emperor himself. Moreover, such unbridled freedom was in danger of allowing the British company monopolies which would (and eventually did) hamper competitive trade and this would have given rise to considerable consternation and resentment amongst the regional leaders.

And yet, others would perhaps have welcomed the decision, arguing that being in the loci of foreign trade would mean development for those regions. Whatever the case may be and whatever it is that would have gone through the minds of the local leaders of the land when Jahangir threw open the country's doors to the foreigners, eventually they had little choice but to accept it. Not that they did not put up a fight. They did and often put their feet down. There are innumerable instances of how regional rulers of the time often refused to cooperate with East India Company officials even though the latter had extracted permissions from central rulers. Not just the regional rulers, but local landlords of Bengal too objected to the British East India Company setting up businesses in their areas. The Sabarna Roy Chaudhury family, as pointed out earlier, reportedly did not willingly rent out the three villages to the East India Company officials but had to do so because the Mughal emperor had granted it permission after having accepted a bribe.

In short, the local landlords and regional rulers in Bengal gave Job Charnock a harrowing time before he could set up shop. After being repeatedly denied entry at the local level, he finally demanded that the central Mughal rulers intervene. He declared that only on the condition that he would not be disturbed by the area's regional rulers would he venture into Bengal again. The Mughal rulers, possibly because of quid pro quo deals which were common, responded to the ultimatum and did grant him such a reassurance. And so, he agreed to return to Bengal in 1690. Not that he didn't want to, of course. Bengal had been his most favoured destination to begin with. Initially it was another port, in the northeast of Bengal, that he had set his eyes on and that was Chittagong, now in Bangladesh. Reports of how the Portuguese, Dutch and Spanish had been disembarking in that port for decades, trying to set up shop, made the British traders even more eager to get a share of the pie. But on his way there, a storm struck and Charnock diverted his fleet to southern Bengal instead. As far as Job Charnock was concerned it turned out to be better than Chittagong.

Sutanuti was not yet at the centre of a competitive tug-of-war between other European traders and so Charnock was left alone to build his business empire. From a personal standpoint too, he preferred the relatively easy-going pace of this remote region in Bengal. He was getting on in years. In 1690 he turned 60. He had spent an entire lifetime in a foreign land. He had arrived in India in 1659, when he was just 29-years-old and though he had contemplated returning to England after four years of service at the factory, the directors of the company in London felt that he was indispensable for the Indian operation and wanted to retain him. He was promoted to the position of chief 'factor'—as the factory in-charge was called—so that he wouldn't leave. He stayed on. But after all those years, the ceaseless sea travel, not to mention battles with enemies, was taking its toll on him. Charnock was disliked by his colleagues. He was a reticent and morose type of a man, but he was also ruthlessly honest and did not tolerate corruption in his subordinates. He is supposed to have put an end to smuggling amongst his workers, which was quite rampant in other company offices around the country. Moreover, because his integrity and efficiency made him a favourite with his bosses in London, it bred envy and resentment amongst his competitive co-workers. Though he would still be engaged in company work, unlike in Madras, where he had been stationed thus far, in Bengal he was free to do his own thing.

About the time that Charnock had been contemplating returning to England way back in the early 1660s, another factor, other than the promotion and incentive from his company that he received, may have influenced his decision to stay back in India. Around 1663, he got married to a Hindu woman, a widow. At that time, he was heading the factory in Patna, Bihar where he was entrusted by the company with the responsibility of procuring saltpetre, one of the raw materials for making gun powder. One day, he saw a procession of people leading a young girl to her husband's funeral pyre, where she was to be burnt alive as per the now obsolete and banned custom of sati. Taking pity on her, and by some accounts, 'smitten by her beauty', Charnock snatched her away and took off, unmindful of the danger that he had put himself in from orthodox Hindus, who could have had him killed for interfering in their religious ritual. Somehow, they didn't and both Charnock and the girl were safe. She was later found to be a Rajput princess and only 15 years old. Charnock, who was then 34, nevertheless married her and renamed her Maria. The couple had three daughters. The information about Job Charnock marrying a Hindu widow after rescuing her appeared in a book called, *Thackerays in India: And Some Calcutta Graves*[16] written by the noted Scottish historian William Wilson Hunter. First published in 1897, two and a half centuries after the incident is said to have taken place, the authenticity of the account, like so much information that is passed down as history, has been questioned by cynics. However, the information also finds mention in an earlier account and that is in the journal of a seaman named Alexander Hamilton[17], who had been an employee of the East India Company for a brief period in the early 1700s. In his work, Hamilton wrote about Charnock having taken a Hindu widow as his bride and adopting the country's customs as his own. Charnock is said to have even 'been accused' of converting to Hinduism. Hamilton was born sometime 'before 1688', which would make him only a toddler when Charnock died in 1692, at age of 62, and so he was

---

[16]William Wilson Hunter, *Thackerays in India: And Some Calcutta Graves*, General Books, 2012 (originally published in 1897).
[17]Alexander Hamilton, *A New Account of the East Indies: Being the Observations and Remarks of Captain Alexander Hamilton*, Cambridge University Press, 2013 (originally published in 1727).

no contemporary of Charnock's. But the fact that he worked in the East India Company and, therefore, would have been familiar with the life of one of the company's most high-profile generals, lends credibility to the account. If Charnock paved the way for the British East India Company to get a foothold in Bengal, the process by which it gradually began to capture political power in the region and subsequently the rest of the country, was set in motion around the mid-1700s.

Since the late 1600s the Company had constructed walled fortresses ostensibly for the purpose of protecting their commercial enterprises. But by the mid-1700s its real motives had begun to be suspected by local lords.

With the Mughal rule virtually crumbling from within and without an efficient administrator at the center, not to mention a strong military to defend it, the land had become a magnet attracting foreign invasions. In 1739, Punjab, Delhi and other parts of the northwest had been sacked by Nadir Shah, the tyrannical ruler of Persia who captured the Mughal emperor Mohammad Shah and imprisoned him as Nadir Shah's army went on a killing spree, massacring thousands of people on the streets. Eventually they left after plundering Delhi, taking with them the priceless diamond that had been passed down through generations of royals across the world since time immemorial: the Kohinoor. Meaning 'mountain of light', Nadir Shah himself first called it that. They had also stolen the Peacock throne of Shah Jahan though they could not hold on to the loot for long. Legend had it that the diamond had a curse that if a man were to wear it, though he would be the owner of the whole world, he would also inherit all its evil. Nadir Shah was assassinated in 1747. After that the diamond made its way back to India and eventually fell into the hands of the British rulers who then took it back with them to their country. Their queen, Victoria, had it cut to size and added to the royal collection of jewellery known as the Crown Jewels, even wearing it on occasion. In her will she had left instructions that it should only be worn by a female member of the royal family. Never by a male. On display at the Tower of London along with the other gems of the royal collection, it is today at the centre of a dispute between Britain and India, with India pointing out that the Kohinoor was stolen from this country and should be returned to its rightful owners.

In the mid-1700s, the land having become thus vulnerable to foreign attacks, the rulers of Bengal, understandably, had become wary about the presence of the forts constructed by the British. To make matters worse, the East India Company had begun to reinforce its fortress in Calcutta, which was named Fort William after the English king. It must be noted here that by this time Bengal had virtually seceded from the central authority in Delhi, just as several other regions had done, taking advantage of the total political disarray that the Mughal dynasty now faced. From 1717 to 1756 three successive rulers of Bengal, Murshid Quli Khan, his successor Shuja-ud-Daulah and his successor Alivardi Khan, maintained a policy of encouraging foreign trade but all of them kept strict control over the dealings of the merchant companies.

What these rulers perhaps didn't bargain for, however, was that the English company was gradually gathering an army of its own and the forts had become more than just the protective enclosures guarding their commercial enterprises.

In April 1756, Alivardi Khan's grandson from his daughter's side, Siraj-ud-Daulah became the Nawab of Bengal. He was against allowing the British East India Company to continue to use walled enclosures which were out of bounds for even the rulers of the land. It was tantamount to letting the foreigners create independent zones in another sovereign country. So, as far as he was concerned, additional reinforcements were out of the question. However, the British justified further buttressing of their fortresses, citing, interestingly, the same volatile political situation in the country, which they argued, exposed their trading ports to the dangers of plunder and loot. On the face of it, it was a legitimate enough reason.

But the new ruler of Bengal was convinced, with good reason, that the Company had been building up a military base, not usually associated with a commercial enterprise and that it had other motives than just the protection of its costly assets. Siraj-ud-Daulah was sure that the British company was going to launch an attack on him. Two months into taking charge of Bengal, on 20 June 1756, he led his troops from Murshidabad to Calcutta and seized Fort William, which had been built on the eastern banks of the river Ganges.

More than the capture of the fort itself, the incident is remembered in history and has gained notoriety for the way that the prisoners of war were reportedly treated by Siraj's troops. Referred to as the Black Hole Tragedy of Calcutta, it was a turning point for the British East India Company's already strained relations with Bengal's rulers. According to the accounts of one of the British East India Company officials named John Zephaniah Holwell, who had been amongst the captured, 146 British troops which included Anglo-Indian as well Indian soldiers who had fought on the Company side, had been crammed into a dark cell measuring not more than 14 feet by 18 feet and left there—in the 'black hole', a slang used by the soldiers—overnight. Between eight on the previous night, when the iron door of the prison cell was reportedly slammed on their faces and locked up from outside and six in the morning when it was opened again, most of them had died of suffocation or dehydration. Others were reportedly crushed to death in a stampede when one of the guards took pity and tried to pour drinking water through a tiny window on the opposite end of the room. Only 23 were found to be alive.

It has been claimed in some British accounts, including that of Holwell that Siraj-ud-Daulah himself neither ordered the imprisonment nor was informed of it. The diabolical deed was said to have been carried out by vicious and vindictive enemy troops, in connivance with guards, still fired-up from the just concluded battle. Holwell, who had survived the ordeal, had written in his account—which was published in the 1758 issue of the yearly publication, *Annual Register*—'It was the result of revenge and resentment in the breasts of the lower sergeants, to whose custody we were delivered.' Siraj's soldiers are understood to have told the prisoners, who had pleaded with them to request the Nawab to shift them to a more spacious room, that he was asleep and could not be disturbed. According to Holwell, who was in-charge of his troops and had met the Nawab after Fort William fell, to discuss what will happen to the prisoners of war, Siraj had assured him, 'On the word of a soldier,' that, 'no harm would come to us.' But then Siraj had retired to bed early that day.

Since Holwell, several others, including scholars and historians, both of the time and later, have recreated the sequence of events that reportedly took place that fateful night, pieced together from various sources including, in the earlier narratives, survivor and witness accounts and subsequently by evaluating the various disparate reports.

Of these, Holwell's account is considered the definitive source.

Holwell begins the narrative, which was written as a letter to a friend, by explaining that it was initially difficult for him to find the words to express the sheer horror of what transpired in the dungeon known as 'black hole' on that fateful night and that the memories were painful and psychologically disturbing. He then goes on to describe the ordeal by stating that the prison cell was a tiny room with only two windows and not fit for the confinement of so many prisoners. The windows were barred with thick iron rods and the ventilation was extremely poor. Fumes from fires in different parts of the fort which were still burning after the battle, caused the inmates to choke. Holwell writes that he offered a guard a bribe of ₹1,000 if he shifted them to another, more spacious room and later doubled that to ₹2,000 but to no avail. The prisoners were told that permission could not be obtained because the Nawab was sleeping and that no one dared awaken him. The prisoners, dehydrated and in various stages of asphyxiation, were crying out for water. A sympathetic sentry brought them some but it worked to the prisoners' detriment as it generated a stampede with the thirsty men trying to rush from across the room towards the window through which the water was being passed. Most of the water was wasted as it spilt in the desperate attempt by the prisoners to grab the hats in which Holwell had poured it. Several prisoners died after being crushed underfoot. By late evening others died of dehydration, exhaustion or suffocation. Those who still survived were delirious, raving and ranting or had lost consciousness. The Nawab woke up at dawn and ordered that the doors to the dungeon be opened. Holwell was one of the 23 survivors.

Explaining why, in spite of the pain of doing so, he decided to write about the incident, Holwell writes, 'I cannot allow it to be buried in oblivion.'[18]

When Holwell, as prisoner of war, was taken to the Nawab as was the custom, Siraj apparently did not express any regret about what had happened though he did offer him a glass of water and asked that a chair be given to him to sit.

The question arises then that why would Holwell and others exempt the Nawab from any culpability?

One could conjecture that since Holwell and the others were still prisoners of war in the Nawab's court—after being produced

---

[18]Holwell, John Zephaniah, *A Genuine Narrative of the Deplorable Deaths of the English Gentlemen and Others who were Suffocated in the Black Hole in Fort William in Calcutta in the Kingdom of Bengal in the Night Succeeding the 20th Day in June*, (originally published in the 1758 issue of the yearly publication, Annual Register), 1758.

before him the day after the night of the Black Hole, they were promptly shifted to a jail in Murshidabad—they feared for their personal safety and lives and made public declarations absolving Siraj. Public declarations, of course, were statements made in the presence of administrators of the royal court. It must be remembered that while Siraj-ud-Daulah was the ruler of Bengal, which acted independently in many matters, he was still bound by central laws which provided prisoners of war with basic rights, even in those days of relative barbarity, torn as they were by wars and plunder. Indeed, the Mughal Emperor had developed a highly evolved legal system, particularly designed to hold in place effective collection of revenue and tax, but it also emphasized governance that promoted human dignity. Siraj-ud-Daulah would no doubt have wanted to evade questions about the incident in Calcutta, because if he was asked, he would be hard put to explain such a flagrant violation of the prisoners' rudimentary rights. If Holwell and others publicly declared that Siraj was party to the incident while they were still his prisoners, there could be, or they must have feared that there would be, repercussions. That leads us to the question, why would Holwell and the others continue to lie about Siraj-ud-Daulah's involvement or the lack of it, even after being freed by the British East India Company troops the following year? It could have been political exigency—Mughal rule, though on its last legs, continued in Delhi and Agra, and the British could ill-afford to embarrass the central rulers, who ultimately were still responsible for the law of the land. Or it could be that Holwell and the others were compelled by honour to stand by their comments even after being freed rather than appear to have spoken out of cowardice earlier. Or it could be that they were telling the truth and Siraj-ud-Daulah really did not have a clue about the cruel act reportedly committed by his army men.

The British East India Company cited the Black Hole incident as the trigger for the subsequent aggression in which it set its troops hot on the heels of Siraj-ud-Daulah. By that logic, the Black Hole incident was the root cause of the colonization of India by the British because, the pursuit and defeat of Siraj eventually led to the capture of power and establishment of Company rule and later Crown rule. But the Black Hole incident was perhaps only the justification that the British East India Company was looking for so that it could launch an attack.

Indeed. Perhaps for this very reason—that it justified an attack on Bengal by the British East India Company—a controversy rages about whether or not the incident took place at all. Suggestions that it was a fabricated or at least a highly exaggerated tale can be substantiated by a number of arguments. First and foremost is that the British East India Company, as has been mentioned earlier, had been building up an army and it was constructing reinforcements around its fortresses in Bengal. This indicates that the Company had in all probability been planning an attack on Bengal long before the Black Hole incident but was just looking for an excuse to do so. The Company could not just strike without a reason because it was answerable not just to its directors, governors, owners and shareholders in London, but it had also to report to the British Crown. Any interference with the politics of any of India's provinces would be taken serious exception of by the English monarchs, considering that it would strain or even jeopardize diplomatic relations between Britain and the Mughals. This in turn would have serious economic repercussions as trade would be affected.

But as far as the Company was concerned, it had been present in the soil of the land for over one and a half centuries. It had practically established dominance over all the strategic points of the country, including the sea and river ports. It had strengthened its economic base by building up a virtual monopoly in commercial trade. All that was missing was political power. It was a time, as mentioned earlier, of regular tussle for power in

Delhi and Agra, with battles of succession and more significantly, wars of invasion. The time was rife and, the Company reasoned, it had as legitimate a right to rule over the land as any other foreign intruder.

Building up the reinforcements around Fort William in Calcutta, in this context, was nothing but a bait to engage Siraj-ud-Daulah, who had demanded that these be immediately demolished, in a skirmish. It was on the Company turf and travel-weary Siraj was not expected to win. Had Siraj lost the battle for Fort William, that would have been the decisive moment of the British East India Company's takeover of Bengal.

But when Fort William fell and was captured by Siraj's troops, it was an unexpected twist in the tale for the British. They did not expect to lose. Later, however, the Company still managed to turn the incident to its advantage. If the theorists who claim that the Black Hole story was a concocted one are to be believed, it created the biggest excuse for the British East India Company to wage a war on Bengal.

And so, one year later, on 23 June 1757, the British East India Company troops descended on the Bengal capital, Murshidabad, and drew Siraj-ud-Daulah into battle. It took place in the Nawab's mango groves by the river in a place called Polashi—or Plassey—meaning an orchard of the Polash or Palash flowers.

That night Siraj-ud-Daulah did not sleep at all.

III

TREACHERY UNDER A MANGO TREE

'Treachery is a sin for which it is hard to find redemption.'
—Sri Sri Thakur Anukul Chandra

Siraj-ud-Daulah didn't get a wink of sleep on the night of 22 June 1757. Over the past year, since his capture of Fort William, his spies had been bringing him word that the British East India Company was planning to directly attack him in his royal headquarters in Murshidabad, the then capital of Bengal. Prisoners of war from Calcutta were still holed up in the jails there. The Company's troops would try to free them. But that was not all. They would attempt a siege of Murshidabad itself. The Nawab had been aware of the British design. Like his grandfather, the former nawab of Bengal, Alivardi Khan, initially he too had no problem with the Company doing business in Bengal. Import and export trade was economically mutually beneficial. Bengal, with its sea and river ports, had grown to be the richest part of the country. It was considered richer than all of Britain put together. After he came to power in April of the previous year, Siraj had, in fact, tried to maintain cordial relations with the Company's officials in Calcutta and other parts of Bengal. There were some serious issues though and he tried to solve these diplomatically with the British Company. He had sent his messengers at least three times between April and June to request them to demolish the additional reinforcements that they had been putting up around Fort William. Earlier, they had erected fortifications at their factory in Cossimbazar, near the Nawab's royal court in Murshidabad. These were constructed without even intimating the Nawab, least of all gaining his permission. Nor was consent obtained from Alamgir the Second, the Mughal emperor at that time. It was as though the British were deliberately baiting Siraj, flouting his orders and ignoring his authority as administrator of Bengal.

The British East India Company had been using the 'defence' pretext for long. Other than the threat of plunder and loot from invaders from other provinces, the Company justified its fortifications to keep attacks from its main competitor, the French East India Company, at bay. By the middle of the eighteenth century, the Portuguese and Dutch traders had been all but pushed out by the British. The French remained but with much less control over territory in India than its British counterpart. Also, as far as the French were concerned, the competition with the British was driven not simply by compulsions of commerce but it was an extension of a major war being fought between the two countries—England and France—in Europe, the chief cause of which, among other issues, was imperialistic control over colonies. There were frequent clashes between the French and British East India Company for domination of trading posts in Indian port cities that resulted in battles being fought and respective fortifications being breached. The fortresses were walled enclosures, which in the case of the British East India Company were deemed 'presidencies', directly lorded over by a president and his council, which was elected by the Company's court of directors in London. These became like mini kingdoms. The British Company had long exercised a policy of diplomacy with local kings and rulers but by the mid-eighteenth century, though it continued to outwardly practice this, its officials based in India had begun to nurture ambitions of gaining power themselves. The 'protection' excuse was bandied about by the British East India Company. But secretly it had been building up a huge force comprising not just its own European, Eurasian and Armenian soldiers, but men recruited from across the land in the Indian subcontinent, training them to fight, especially as matchlock soldiers, paying them just enough to retain them. It was not difficult for the Company to employ Indian youth from poorer families who would oblige even for a pittance. They were valuable additions to the British army because they knew specific terrains and its people, customs and traditions well, considered vital information in launching attacks. As the British Company's army grew, it started offering its uses to the local kings and rulers as 'security' from foreign invasions in exchange for privileges like duty-free trade.

The Bengal Nawab was not impressed. He had a huge military force of his own and he also regarded the British Company's growing interest in local politics and governance, as reflected in its hobnobbing with kings and rulers, with suspicion. Disturbing news had also been reaching Siraj-ud-Daulah that the British East India Company army had been hiring people—dissenters—who had earlier served in his army but had escaped due to harsh punishment for various misdeeds or other reasons and were given shelter inside the British-controlled Fort William. Siraj was incensed when he learnt that the Company provided refuge to Krishna Das—son of Dhaka aristocrat, Rajballav—who had supposedly duped the Bengal government of large sums of money and fled to Calcutta. These direct provocations were further exacerbated by the British Company's gross violation of trading rights, which had started becoming a point of contention even before Siraj came to power. The Company refused to pay revised custom duties, claiming that they reserved the right to follow only the rules of the original trade licences agreed upon by the earlier Mughal rulers, especially a 1717 contract, which all but exempted it from paying taxes. The Company argued that it was not obliged to accept rates of business transaction determined by Bengal's changing establishments. But the new rulers found these earlier contracts too lenient, allowing the British company liberties such as unlimited access to ports and the freedom to move about and trade anywhere in the land along with a host of other privileges. The Company had been taking full advantage of these rights by not just depriving the provinces, especially Bengal, of millions of rupees in revenue, but individual officials had been depleting the land of its rare treasures by sneaking out of the country with priceless jewels including diamond, gold and silver jewellery, amassing untold personal wealth at the cost of the people of Bengal. As far as Siraj was concerned, the foreigners seemed to have lost all respect for the laws of the land to the point where it got detrimental for Bengal. No amount of warnings by the Nawab was working. The siege of Calcutta and Fort William was the only option for him. What else was he supposed to do? Sit back and wait for an enemy attack for the possession of Bengal? Siraj didn't pay too much importance to reports of prisoners of war in Fort William being crammed into a tiny cell on the night of the siege. But while returning to Murshidabad, from his palanquin coach he had noticed that a few of the prisoners who had been brought back by boat—among whom he recognized the British commander Holwell—were being dragged through the streets with chains tied to their legs and hands. He immediately ordered that they be freed from the shackles. He felt that he had been gracious enough but the British had been trying to bait him. He had heard that they had been instigating dissent in his people.

Of particular concern was an agent of the British East India Company named Robert Clive. He had been sent from the

Company's offices in Madras and had been appointed to lead its army to Bengal. The Company army along with its naval fleet, which too it had been slowly building up, had already recaptured Calcutta and Fort William since Clive took over. Siraj had heard about this Clive fellow's sly ways. The Nawab's spies brought him information that he had befriended many of Bengal's influential aristocrats, including wealthy businessmen and well-respected landlords of the area around Calcutta.

Siraj had also taken note of how one such member of the region's powerful gentry, a man by the name of Umi Chand, had been making frequent visits to the house of Mir Jafar, his granduncle, the brother-in-law of his maternal grandfather and former Bengal ruler, Alivardi Khan. Jafar also happened to be the commander-in-chief of Siraj's royal army. Siraj and this relative, Mir Jafar, had always regarded each other with a certain amount of contempt. Siraj was disdainful of the old man whom he considered too hungry for power, having supposedly hankered after the throne ever since the days of Alivardi Khan. And Mir Jafar is supposed to have resented the fact that the young Siraj, at just 23, bypassed him to become nawab. At 65, Mir Jafar was 42 years his grandnephew's senior and hated having to serve under Siraj, not just because he felt humiliated by his role as subordinate to a boy whom he practically saw being born, but also because he found the Nawab to be too arrogant and brusque.

One of Robert Clive's biographers, Mark Bence-Jones, in his book, *Clive of India*,[19] writes about the last independent nawab of Bengal:

> Siraj-ud-Daulah has been pictured as a monster of vice, cruelty and depravity. But though he may have suffered from the demoralizing effects of too much wealth and power at too early an age, he was in fact no more cruel than most Eighteenth

---

[19]Mark Bence-Jones, *Clive of India*, Constable, 2016 (first published in 1974).

Century Eastern despots. His main fault was weakness, which caused him to be fickle and indecisive; he was also arrogant, of changeable temper and lacking in courage.

But then, as other historians have observed, most of the extant accounts of Siraj-ud-Daulah, are those culled from the reports of his enemy, the agents of the British East India Company. There are almost no historical documents from the time, written by someone who could be expected to provide a more objective description of the ruler of a province which, due to its enormous wealth, was under constant threat of invasions, plunder and war. Not the least of these contenders for Bengal of course was the British East India Company itself. And not only did Siraj-ud-Daulah's action—such as launching an attack on and destroying the forts erected illegally by the British East India Company in spite of his requests, orders and threats, in that order—within 60 days of his ascension to the throne indicate that he was not 'indecisive' but within a year of that incident, it became amply clear that it was not Siraj but rather Clive, who was severely 'lacking in courage'. In fact, the British Company commander is perhaps amongst world history's most cowardly army chiefs who, instead of taking the enemy head-on and fighting a battle as a brave soldier, resorted to duplicity and bribery to weaken the opposition.

There are differing versions of how exactly Clive connived with Siraj's granduncle and army chief, Mir Jafar, to betray the Nawab. From his association with Bengal's aristocracy, the British agent was said to have become aware of a clique, comprising influential members of the region's wealthy landlords and trading community, who were conspiring to overthrow Siraj-ud-Daulah.

The first volume of *The Cambridge History of the British Empire*, a scholarly text spanning over three decades of research from 1929 to 1961, and published in eight volumes, seems to attribute this partly to powerful Hindus of the time rebelling against what appeared to be Siraj's orthodoxy and intolerance of other religions.

The Cambridge History of the British Empire states:

> It was...becoming apparent that many persons besides the English...desired a revolution in the government. The chief people in this movement were Hindus. Ali Wardi Khan had favoured them and promoted many of them to high places in his administration. Siraj-ud-Daulah did not share his predecessor's feelings and he succeeded in alienating all the principal men of the 'durbar' (royal court). The great Hindu bankers, the Seths, who had contributed largely to the establishment of Ali Wardi Khan, had been threatened with circumcision.[20]

However, judging by the fact of the involvement of several non-Hindu aristocrats, including Mir Jafar, the revolt against Siraj is unlikely to have been driven so much by religious sentiments as by the Nawab's hubris. *The Cambridge History* itself further notes that Siraj had gained the wrath of his officers by his distrust and his disregard for their authority. It observes, 'Rai Durlabh, who had held the office of diwan, had been placed under the orders of a favourite of Siraj, called Mohan Lal and Mir Jafar, who had held the office of 'bakshi' had been dismissed with insult and cannons were planted against his palace.'

But there were other compelling reasons than wounded egos of the Bengal aristocracy leading them to hatch a conspiracy to overthrow their ruler. With the growing involvement of the Centre, in the collection of local taxes and the introduction of more stringent tariff laws, it was becoming particularly difficult

---

[20] *The Cambridge History of the British Empire, Vol. 1: The Old Empire from the Beginnings to 1783*, Cambridge University Press, 1929.

for the wealthy merchants and landed gentry to do business with the British on individual basis. The Jagat Seths, literally the world bankers, who had held sway over the commercial profits of the international trade, which dominated Bengal for over a century, were losing their grip. The mutually beneficial monetary arrangements between the aristocrats and the British, when the laws were less structured or at least less minutely controlled or monitored, were crumbling. In short, Siraj's economic policies were directly and adversely impacting the commercial interests of both the Bengal aristocracy and the British.

But Clive did not simply go by the accounts of his close circle of friends in the Bengal aristocracy. That there were elements of dissent within Siraj's inner coterie was confirmed to him by the British East India Company representatives at the royal court of Siraj. In an atmosphere of distrust, Clive wanted to tread carefully. And only when he became absolutely certain that a mutiny was indeed being planned that he decided to begin the process of negotiations.

It was not difficult for the British commander to identify a leader within the rebellious group. Mir Jafar, with his known dislike for his grandnephew, was the weakest link, much more so than any of the other aristocrats. Well aware by now of Mir Jafar's lust for the throne of Bengal, Clive promised him that he would make him king. It would be mutually beneficial. The British Company preferred the more malleable, mild-mannered and elderly granduncle to the young and uncooperative Siraj.

By most accounts, Umi Chand, a rich merchant, was used as the go-between to hold talks with Mir Jafar. The negotiations themselves were fraught with treachery. Convincing Umi Chand to take on the dangers of performing this onerous task, which involved the risk of being intercepted by Siraj's spies, was not easy. According to several reports, Umi Chand made it clear that he would only perform this duty if he was promised a heftier share of the post-defeat plunder than what was being offered to him and even threatened to reveal the secret plan to Siraj unless this demand was met. Irked by his haggling, Clive and the other conspirators tricked him by drawing up two separate written agreements, one of which mentioned him as the recipient of the sum he quoted in case of a victory over the Nawab and the other which completely left him out as a beneficiary, monetary or other. The document which was shown to Umi Chand was not signed or endorsed by all the other signatories. Umi Chand noticed this much later. By then it was too late.

But it was Umi Chand who had perhaps first conveyed to Mir Jafar the British Company's detailed plan to lead its army to Murshidabad and attack Siraj. All that Mir Jafar would have to do would be to turn his forces against the Nawab during the siege.

Siraj had heard the murmurs of a betrayal for long. He just didn't know who in their midst would turn traitor. He had grown so suspicious over the past year that he didn't trust anyone. He had sentries placed in every nook and corner of the kingdom. Even the inner chambers where the women stayed were guarded by his spies.

But on the night of 22 June 1757, they failed to intercept a figure slip out of the quarters. According to some accounts, Mir Jafar had sent word through a messenger conveying his full support to Clive.

Clive had already arrived in Murshidabad. He had led his army to a mango grove in Plassey where they camped. He was desperately waiting for a green signal from Mir Jafar. He would not, could not strike without it. On the black night of 22 June 1757, as Siraj-ud-Daulah tossed and turned in his bed, insightfully aware of some ominous doom, Robert Clive received the reassurance he was awaiting.

The story goes that Clive faced a huge last-minute dilemma. The strength of Siraj's army was more than 10 times greater than his own. The Nawab had close to 50,000 soldiers, including infantry, cavalry and artillery as well as cannons and reinforcements from the trained army of the French East India Company. In comparison, Clive's total military force of some 3,200 was no match. His only hope was Siraj's military commander Mir Jafar betraying him, as he had agreed to do earlier, even signing a joint contract with Clive and a few of the aristocrats. But at that point, Clive could not be sure whether Mir Jafar would honour that contract. Clive was aware that just a few days earlier, Siraj, having gotten drift of a conspiracy, had launched a military attack on Mir Jafar in the latter's palace, following which Mir Jafar is understood to have pacified his grandnephew and pledged his support to him. Whether that was a ruse or whether Mir Jafar did really change his mind, was something that Clive was completely clueless about. He didn't know how far to trust Mir Jafar.

So uncertain was Clive at that point that he and 12 others of his generals are understood to have decided against launching an attack even though they had come prepared to do so. There was a vote and only one was in favour of going ahead with the battle. Clive overruled it. But disturbed and restless, he extricated himself from the rest of the group and walking over to a mango tree, stood under it, immersing himself in deep, solitary thought, contemplating the course of action.

What made Clive change his mind after an hour's reflection, has been a mystery. By some accounts it was the letter of reassurance from Mir Jafar.

By then the sun had set over the Bhagirathi River and darkness had descended over Murshidabad. No one had noticed the dark clouds that had been gathering over the horizon. Across the river, boatmen hollered the warning signals of an approaching storm. A distant thunder rumbled as winds swept through the mango forest. And as the messenger, having handed over the chit of paper to Clive, scuttled away into the night, back towards the palace, the retreating figure lit up momentarily in a flash of lightning.

And then it began to rain.

In spite of being severely disadvantaged in terms of the strength of his forces, Clive's decisive victory the next morning in what has come to be known in history as the Battle of Plassey is attributed as much to Mir Jafar's betrayal of Siraj as to the sudden downpour.

British East India Company agents had called it divine intervention and manna from heaven. But essentially it was superior preparation. Clive had brought tarpaulins to cover the cannons to keep the gunpowder dry in case of rain. Siraj's army did not. Their cannons and gun powder were completely drenched. They had been taking up position behind their entrenchments facing the mango groves over the past few days. Siraj-ud-Daulah had been aware of the approach of Clive's army to Murshidabad. While the European, Eurasian and Armenian soldiers of the British had mostly arrived by boat, Clive's Indian foot soldiers had taken the land routes. Siraj's spies had been keeping track of the enemy movement. His own troops had formed themselves into an arc behind entrenchments across the mango grove, led by two of his loyal military generals, Mir Madan and Mohan Lal. But they did not take into account Robert Clive's preparedness in case of rain.

In the midst of the ensuing chaos and confusion, when Siraj's forces began to drop dead or flee with the smell of dank gunpowder filling up the air, it was further noticed that one side of the army arm, the formation made up of Mir Jafar's 14,000 soldiers, was neither attacking nor retreating.

Generals who were faithful, rushed to Siraj's enclosure and advised him to abandon the battlefield and run for his life. He fled, heading towards what is now the capital city of the state of Bihar, Patna. Down the river, on a tiny boat, camouflaged as a commoner, he felt he had escaped but he didn't realize that Mir Jafar had sent out his spies all across. Eventually when he reached land, he was intercepted by Mir Jafar's son. Siraj was arrested and brought back to Murshidabad.

On 2 July 1757, Siraj was stabbed to death in a house in Murshidabad on the orders of Mir Jafar. The ruins of this building, a rain-damaged red-bricked structure, which is one of the main tourist attractions of this historical province in Bengal, has come to be known as '*namak haram deorhi*' or the 'the hallway of traitors'. The words 'namak haram' literally means someone who betrays the person who has given him his 'salt' or sustenance.

Whether Siraj stood for the symbol of 'salt' or sustenance to his subjects and contemporaries is, however, a moot question. Sure, he was the ruler of Bengal and this entitled him to the title of 'salt-giver'. But did he truly fulfil his duties towards his land and its people? The fact that his nemesis Robert Clive was an unscrupulous usurper who not only bribed his way to power but also plundered the country which had given him the right to live in it and earn his livelihood from it, virtually rendering its people pauper—Clive is held responsible for creating the conditions which led to the great famine in Bengal in the 1770s, when hundreds of thousands of people starved to death—does not by default make Siraj an exemplary ruler without his faults. While reiterating the arguments put forth earlier in his defence—that he was certainly not the 'indecisive' or 'cowardly' or even 'insensitive' ruler as he has been portrayed by several of his detractors—it would be a fallacy not to review him also in the light of the many allegations of 'vices' that stand against him. These include reports of his 'despotism'.

He has not only been accused of humiliating his contemporaries, as mentioned earlier, stripping them of their powers and positions, thereby antagonizing them to the point that they wanted to remove him at whatever cost, but stories of lasciviousness and extreme cruelty when he was denied his will have been attributed to him.

A similar tale of unrequited love, to that of Mughal Emperor Akbar burying alive the beautiful court dancer, Anarkali, who fell in love with his son rather than himself, has been ascribed to

Siraj-ud-Daulah too. He supposedly got so incensed by news that one of the courtesans, Faizy, whom he had bought from Delhi for a cost of ₹100,000, had fallen for his cousin Syed Muhammed Khan, that he had her placed in a closet, which was sealed by building a wall over the door. Three months later, her skeleton was removed from it.

History, by and large, is strangely forgiving of such acts of untold horror when they pertain to those figures who have gone down as 'the greats'. That is because they are judged not on the basis of the indiscretions or excesses they committed in their personal lives but for the achievements in their respective fields in the public domain. This is as much true today as it was in the bygone days. Artists who are worshipped for their art have often led notoriously 'debauched' lives which would stigmatize lesser mortals but have not come in the way of them being catapulted to the heights of adulation. Scientists who are revered for their path-breaking discoveries have been known to be unkind and insensitive. Political leaders who are held in high esteem for running able administrations, or simply for having the ability to rule over people, did not always follow the rules set for the rest of humanity and sometimes, got away, quite literally, with murder. Examples galore and there is no need to mention specifics because world civilization is replete with such men and women, who command history's respect but if one digs deeper into their lives and times, skeletons tumble out of the cupboards.

That said, Siraj-ud-Daulah is celebrated in the Indian subcontinent because he was a martyr, who had had the courage to defend his own land against treacherous and unscrupulous British imperialists. He commands, as he ought to, the admiration and worship of the people of Bangladesh and India because he was a young man who gave up his life in honour of his country. Nor can he be singled out for the brand of cruelty that had seen a young woman murdered in such a grotesque manner. Just as the Mughal emperor Akbar is held in high regard for the peace and prosperity he brought to his people despite his private acts of injustice against a helpless court dancer, so Siraj and countless others before and after him have commanded respect despite their endless acts of cruelty.

The betrayal of Siraj-ud-Daulah has, in recent studies, been scrutinized from a point of view that challenges the idea that the treacherous acts committed against the Nawab were acts of 'treason' per se. Before delving into the shortcomings of these arguments and pointing out that these arguments and challenges come from a set of scholars who have a stake, an emotional one, in defending the 'indefensible' (at the risk of taking the less neutral and more established patriotic view) Mir Jafar, it is necessary to review the merits of these arguments and challenges. These argue that patriotism as we know it today is vastly different from what it was 250 years ago and Siraj-ud-Daulah was hardly defending a unified country against the aggression of a separate nation. It was not a fight of the Indians against the British. It was a thwarting of an attack on the ruler of the province of Bengal by the army of a foreign trading company, which had, it must be remembered, already established itself, as a military force which often enough lent its support to particular sides in wars between the rulers of the land. Those who seemingly sided with the foreign traders were actually being aided by its army in their goal of removing Siraj. That is not the same thing as wanting the foreigners to get instated. In fact, Mir Jafar believed that the foreign army was helping him ascend to the throne for more lenient tax structures. The compulsions of the other men were different, though equally driven by self-interest. The Jagat Seths or world bankers, namely Mahatab Chand and Swarup Chand, who controlled much of the economy of Bengal and the trade with the British East India Company, feared that Siraj's scrutiny of and tightening control over the tax system were endangering their monopoly over the revenue generated from international businesses. Those like Umi Chand are believed to have been driven by lucre and were bribed by the British. Rai Durlabh and other Hindu kings, as mentioned earlier, were possibly driven by religious sentiments. Whatever the vested interests of the conspirators, two and a half centuries ago, their intention was not to put the foreigners in power. The conspirators within the Bengali aristocratic community did not consider that they were helping the foreign trading company to gain power, whether political or economic. It is difficult to say whether they would still do what they did had they any inkling that eventually the overthrow of the nawab of Bengal would result in the British colonizing the whole of the subcontinent for two centuries. But at that time, as far as they were concerned, by providing support to the British East India Company, they were not helping the foreign company gain any sort of power, political or economic; rather, they were helping themselves secure freedom from Siraj-ud-Daulah whom they considered an unfriendly force. Therefore, terms such as 'nationalism' or 'patriotism' did not apply. Indeed, these terms had not yet become the concepts that they are now.

It was one of Mir Jafar's descendants, Syed Mohammad Reza Ali Khan, who had analysed his ancestor's treachery in the context of that era. A history professor based in Murshidabad, he had conducted extensive research on his ancestor of eight generations ago and concluded that Siraj-ud-Daulah's granduncle did not set out to sell his country to the British. Khan's research spanned over five decades from the 1970s until his death in 2020 at the age of 73. He argued that the 'traitor' title became attached to him later after the British established dominion over the Indian subcontinent and Mir Jafar's role in making their entry into the power politics of the land started being reviewed in that context. The frustration of freedom fighters during movements of Independence of the later centuries, which tried desperately to get rid of the British rulers, further reinforced the idea that if it had not been for Mir

Jafar's betrayal of Siraj in the Battle of Plassey, the British may have never been able to gain access to Bengal and subsequently India. Nationalists decried Mir Jafar's treachery and put the onus of their predicament on him. According to Khan, Mir Jafar only wanted to overthrow his grandnephew because the young ruler was becoming increasingly despotic and had unleashed a reign of terror, heaping scorn and humiliation on his own officers. Khan argued that at that time of kingdoms ruled by dynasties, it was not uncommon for family members, even sons and brothers, to fight each other in order to claim the throne. Mir Jafar, insists his descendant, had the courage of his conviction to act on his sense of revenge.

There are however, flaws in that argument. Mir Jafar may not have known that the British would turn their victory in the Battle of Plassey into the entry point through which to eventually takeover India, but the fact remains that he had made it possible for the foreigners to take control of the politics and economics of the land even at that time. Indeed, he had signed pre-war documents promising the British East India Company not just large sums of money from the Bengal exchequer but also virtually gifted to the foreign traders' rights of political power in certain provinces in exchange for helping him ascend to the throne. Had Mir Jafar confronted Siraj-ud-Daulah, taking him on in the battlefield and fought a war with him to ascend to the throne, he would perhaps not have earned the dubious epithet. But he abandoned his grandnephew in the battlefield, conniving with foreign forces to mislead him. As chief of his army, he betrayed his trust and resorted to insidiousness. And cowardice. And that is what justifies the title of traitor. Maybe Mir Jafar was prepared to do whatever it took, even treachery, to oust Siraj towards his goal of becoming king, but no one can claim that it was not the work of a 'traitor'. Especially since it resulted in 200 years of enslavement to a foreign power.

IV

FRUITFULNESS OF FLOWERY FOPS

*'They like to snack on dainty candles and they sip soups
made of soap, using spoons with delicate handles.'*

—Sukumar Ray[21]

Within less than a decade after the Battle of Plassey, the East India Company had gained complete economic control over Bengal when in 1765 it extricated the rights of the collection of taxes—referred to in the local language as 'dewani'—from the then Mughal emperor, after defeating him and his allies in the Battle of Buxur, the previous year, in 1764. The British financial plunder of Bengal, of course, had unofficially begun immediately after the Battle of Plassey, when the East India Company started to extort huge amounts of money from Mir Jafar in exchange for the favour it had done him. The new nawab of Bengal, practically a puppet in the hands of the Company, was forced to dish out more than ₹17,700,000 in instalments as compensation for the attack that Siraj-ud-Daulah had launched on its Calcutta forts, with an additional two million rupees to Robert Clive and one million rupees as 'bribe' to other officials. The riches that the Company officials thus arm-twisted Mir

---

[21] The lines, *'Shabaner soup aar mombati khay shey'* from the rhyme 'Tash Goru' in *Abol Tabol*, Sukumar Ray's book of humorous and satirical poems.

Jafar into parting with went mostly into individual coffers and each eventually carried the treasures back to their homelands in England where they became owners of fortunes.

One wonders if Mir Jafar had ever felt regret, even fleetingly, and wished he could turn back the clock and undo that moment in time when he took the decision to betray his own. Was his situation, during the reign of his grandnephew more unbearable than it was now, when he was virtually a prisoner in the hands of the foreigners? Did he not command more power as the leader of the army of his own people than now, when he was a king who was ruled by foreigners? And what glory was there in being the nawab of Bengal when his subjects knew how he ascended the throne? Did these questions not often creep up in the mind of the treacherous man as he acquiesced to the Company officials' endless demands during the day as he held court? And did these thoughts not haunt him as he retired for the night and perhaps paced the long, narrow corridors of his palace in the dark, reflecting on what it would be like had he not done what he did? Did he realize during that time that he had almost single-handedly changed the course of history?

Finally, unable to cope with the demands made on him constantly by the British East India Company, two years into his reign, he entered into a secret pact with the Dutch, enlisting their help to ward off the British. Getting drift of the plan—Dutch warships had been gathering on the Hooghly River, near the French-dominated port of Chinsurah (Kolkata suburb now) which, the British reasoned, would not have been possible without clearances from Mir Jafar—the British swung into action and thwarted the imminent attack in a battle that has come to be known as the Battle of Chinsurah of 1759.

The Company removed Mir Jafar from the throne and installed his son-in-law Qasim as the new nawab.

But the younger man proved to be more independent than

his father-in-law and less tolerant of British interference in the governance of Bengal. With the aim of getting rid of the British, he formed an alliance comprising the then Mughal emperor of Delhi, the ruler of Awadh. However, the force was defeated by the British in a battle in the year 1764 in Buxur, a province which is today a part of the state of Bihar.

This resulted in the Mughal emperor having to abdicate authority over Bengal to the British East India Company in a treaty the following year.

If a semblance of Mughal rule over Bengal had still remained, if only in name, after this defeat, it ceased to exist completely.

And by 1793, the British East India Company was governing the entire province.

After a point, it ceases to matter how power is wrested. History is replete with examples of brutal aggression in the conquest of kingdoms, countries and states. It does not stop the people of the conquered region from eventually accepting the new rulers, and not simply because they have little choice but to do so. With the passing of time, as new regimes settle in, people grow accustomed to them and life goes on. This is true even when the new rulers are as different from the masses as the British imperialists were from the locals.

The culture of the British, their customs, traditions, religions, rituals, language, cuisine, habits and their values, had little in common with the natives over whom they now had imposed governance.

What almost always ensues in such cases is that the rulers either inject the imported culture into the lives of their new subjects or the process is gradual and the ruled begin to adopt, gradually and even willingly, the ways and manners of the new rulers.

The reverse is also true, often with the rulers too gradually adopting the cultures and customs of the colonized.

The period—during the transition from the Mughal period to the British era—was for Bengal a time of unprecedented change. Perhaps at no other time had the region experienced such a schism in terms of the differences between the rulers and the ruled.

Yet gradually the differences did fade and fusion began to take place. And the fusion created a new set of people, who did not fit the description of any earlier category and who were defined by a set of unique characteristics, emerging as a result of the changed social, political, economic and cultural circumstances and the assimilation.

Amongst them was a class of people who came to be known as the 'babus'. There are discrepant accounts as to when exactly the first babus came into being with a section of historians arguing that it was not before the middle of the eighteenth century because they were essentially products of the British takeover. Most have pointed out that it is difficult to specify precise dates. However, there is general consensus that they played a significant role both in sustaining the period of British colonial rule in India as well as in eventually rebelling against the foreigners and finally chasing them out. It is because of the initial support of the babus that the British could make deeper inroads into Indian soil and it is also because of the babus, who ultimately withdrew that support and lent it squarely to the mass resistance movements for freedom, that the British had to leave.

It is therefore difficult to put a tag on what exactly defined a babu. Their characteristics changed over nearly 250 years. These did not remain static. Who he was, what he did and why he did what he did, underwent vast changes. The 'types' of babus evolved, mutated and eventually came to represent qualities which were as diametrically opposed to each other as hedonistic consumerism and spiritual renunciation.

Broadly speaking, while it was indeed the mid-eighteenth century, post-Plassey scenario, after the Company took over

Bengal's economic rule that 'babudom' or 'babuana' as it was called, really flourished, the babus started to come into existence much earlier, around the late seventeenth to early eighteenth centuries; that is, soon after the British East India Company set up shop in Bengal. Most of the babus were associated with the British East India Company as employees.

In fact, as early as 1698, eight years after Job Charnock landed in Sutanuti, the induction of Indian employees into the Company had started. That it would be on the lookout for cheap, local labour to carry out the myriad work associated with conducting business, especially business in a foreign country, is entirely logical to assume. But the foreigners also appointed 'equals' and even 'superiors'—in terms of economic status, education or social strata—in spite of the obvious possibilities of ego clashes and power tussles which would and did ensue. The babus were not the menial workers, poor or illiterate. They had necessarily to be from the existing upper-classes, already economically comfortable, educated enough to carry out accounting or oversee the businesses and really stand in for the foreign officials, as substitutes, if that was the requirement.

They were deputies, authorized to collect taxes on behalf of the Company and, by virtue of this, had gained control over large sums of money. But though they have, therefore, been described by a section of historians as 'nouveau riche', this is in fact an inaccurate description of the babus, who as discussed earlier, came from the upper crust and were not new to money or wealth. Having said that, the unprecedented opportunities in employment and international trade resulted in drastic improvements in their incomes too, with them acquiring and amassing more riches than they had ever previously possessed. The babus were, more accurately, Indian versions of the British 'gentlemen', which in vernacular Bengali translates to *'bhadralok'* (literally, 'a civilized man'), a term which has been widely used to describe them.

The earliest records of the British East India Company engaging Indian deputies is traced back to the 1690s. Gobinda Ram Mitra (or 'Mitter' as the British named him, based on the informal Bengali way of pronouncing 'Mitra' as 'Mittir') was considered Calcutta's first Indian 'zamindaar' or landed gentry ('zamin' meaning land and 'daar' meaning 'holder') and certainly the British East India Company's most powerful deputy collector. The job of the deputy collector or 'black zamindaar', as the British referred to them, was to assist the collector, who was usually a Briton, in collecting taxes and rents. As far as the position or designation was concerned, Nand Ram Sen, Mitra's predecessor, was the first. However, Sen did not wield the kind of influence or could amass the kind of wealth that Mitra did.

Eventually Mitra went onto found a dynastical house of nobles which gained renown in Calcutta as the 'House of the Mitras of Kumortuli'. Nestled along the banks of the river Ganga in Sutanuti, not far from the port where Job Charnock had disembarked, Kumortuli was a vast area housing colonies of potters (the word 'kumor' means potter and 'tuli' signifies a space where groups of people are concentrated).

Potters who sculpted idols of deities for worship would take the soft clay from the shores of the Ganga which is considered holy and auspicious. Gradually Kumortuli came to be known for the magnificent clay statues of the gods and goddesses which they built as commissioned by the houses of the babus during various religious festivities. To this day, Kumortuli is associated with 'the Pujas' especially 'Durga Puja', Bengal's biggest religious festival, when the Goddess Durga is worshipped and it is from the narrow lanes crisscrossing this ancient neighbourhood that most of the idols are still supplied to the rest of Calcutta and West Bengal.

Interestingly, for the construction of the Durga idols, it was the tradition that priests would go to the red-light districts and collect soil from the doorsteps of a prostitute, which he would then hand over to the potter for preparing the clay mixture. This consisted of mud from the banks of the holy river, cow dung, cow urine and this soil from the brothel. How and why this ancient practice started is not known but several conjectures have been made by generations of theorists.

Anath Taran Ghoshal, a Hindu priest and scholar, explains the different theories. He says,

> One of them suggests that when men entered the room of a courtesan for carnal pleasure, he left his virtues at the doorstep which made the soil there virtuous, if not literally, at least, figuratively. Another hypothesis is that while asking, or begging as it were, for the soil from a prostitute, a priest recites holy mantras at the doorstep, turning the land sacred.

Yet other suggestions attribute the ritual to patriarchal guilt or even to feminist practices of the day which did not want to leave out sex workers, who were stigmatized and marginalized throughout the year, from the Durga Puja celebrations, which marks the worship of female power. Calcutta's largest red-light district, Sonagachi, which is less than 10 kilometres from Kumortuli, is said to have thrived during the time of the babus, many of whom had a coterie of concubines and courtesans. In fact, there are suggestions that the tradition of mixing soil from the red-light areas into the clay with which Goddess Durga is made was a way to keep them appeased. The tradition continues to be practised to this day.

The babus competed with each other in hosting the biggest religious celebrations. Indeed, the ostentatious public displays of their enormous wealth and their lavish lifestyles earned them as much social prestige and respect as it did resentment and envy. Discrepant economic standings between the babus and the common people, India's masses, bred ill-will. They were, moreover, feared and hated for what was considered their mercilessness as tax collectors, no less 'cruel' than their British employers who were not known to spare even the most poverty-stricken from paying dues. Gradually, in the later years, with the waning of their powers, the babus started to be vilified and caricatured as comical characters in the days' theatres, books and works of art and later, in the twentieth century, even in cinema.

Two nineteenth century novels stand out for their brilliance in satirizing the babus. One of these was *Alaler Gharer Dulal* (that can be translated to mean, 'The Darling of the House of Alal') by Peary Chand Mitra, who wrote under the pseudonym Tekchand Thakur[22]. It depicted the follies of the babus through the protagonist Motilal. The book, which was first serialized in Mitra's own monthly magazine, *Mashik Patrika* was the first Bengali novel to use colloquial language in print. The novel opens with a tongue-in-cheek description of the protagonist who has, 'through sheer dint of competence and adequate amounts of boss-pleasing, earned a great deal of wealth within a short period of time.'

The other great work of satire on the babus of yore was *Hootum Pyachar Naksha* (roughly, 'The Night Owl's Designs'), by Kaliprasanna Singha[23], who, being from a famous zamindaar family himself, knew the babus inside out. It was published when Singha was 21 years old, nine years before his premature death, and has, over the past one and a half centuries, gained almost iconic status as a caustic commentary on a cross-section of Calcutta's people during his time.

In his review in *The Telegraph*, of a recent English translation of the book, historian, editor and author Rudrangshu Mukherjee writes:

---

[22]Peary Chand Mitra (Tekchand Thakur), *Alaler Gharer Dulal*, Createspace Independent Publishing Platform, 2018 (first published serially in a Bengali monthly magazine, *Masik Patrika*, 1857).

[23]Kaliprasanna Singha, *Hootum Pyachar Naksha*, Sundar Prakashani, 2018 (originally published as a series of sketches in 1861).

Hootum Pyanchar Naksha, published in 1861, is in many ways a unique text in the annals of Bengali literature. The *nom de plume*, Hootum—not a secret in the writer's own time—belonged to Kaliprasanna Sinha, a remarkable individual in spite of his short life of thirty years, 1840 to 1870. He translated with the help of several Sanskrit pundits the *Mahabharata*; was actively involved in the social reform movements of his time; he wrote and produced plays; he offered to pay the fine that had been imposed on Reverend James Long for publishing the English translation of *Nil Darpan*; he was a well-known philanthropist. His early death may have been linked to his consumption of alcohol; he was hugely in debt when he died. His colourful personality was reflected in the manner in which he decided to depict the social life of Calcutta, the city in which he lived. He chose to do this through a series of sketches…Hutoom's prose reflected the way the common people spoke in their everyday lives. The prose was earthy, colloquial, playful and occasionally bawdy. He mocked the new rich and parodied their lifestyle and manners without mercy.[24]

The babus generated so much derision, in fact, that they virtually spawned an entire genre of writing. And this writing was done by those who clearly had a keen knowledge and understanding of the subtle nuances of the cultures that were overlapping to create these new individuals with their unique idiosyncrasies.

Another sardonic take on the babus is found in *Ekei Ki Boley Sabyata?*[25] (meaning, 'Is this what they mean by civilization?'), by Michael Madhusudan Dutta, who is celebrated today as a visionary

---

[24]Rudrangshu Mukherjee, 'An Owl's Eye View of Calcutta.' *The Telegraph*, 14 December 2012.

[25]Michael Madhusudan Dutta, *Ekei Ki Boley Sabyata?*, Kalikata Bangiya Sahitya Parishad, 1955 (originally published in 1860).

poet but had faced censure when he converted to Christianity despite a great deal of opposition, even from his parents.

In the twentieth century, the babus continued to be satirized and perhaps no other writer has captured their comic idiosyncrasies more incisively than Sukumar Ray in his humorous rhymes for children.

In a rhyme called 'Tash Goru' (a phrase implying a fake person with the word '*tash*' connoting a Bengali pretending to be English or European and the word '*goru*' meaning cow) Ray pokes fun at a babu-type office clerk. The poem begins with the words:

> *Tash goru, goru noy*
> *Asholey te pakhi shey*
> *Jaar khushi dekhey esho*
> *Hadu der officey.*[26]

It means, '*Tash Goru* is not a cow at all, but is actually a bird. Whoever wants to take a peek, go and check him out at the office where Hadu works.' Ray also laughs at their eating habits, influenced no doubt by their colonial masters and he writes, 'they eat soap soup and candles'. Ray, who was the son of famous writer of children's literature, Upendra Kishore Roy Chaudhury, and father of renowned filmmaker Satyajit Ray, like Singha, died a premature death. Born on 30 October 1887 he died on 10 September 1923, when he was only 36 years old. He had contracted '*kala jar*' or 'black fever', as the severely infectious Leishmaniasis parasitic fever which spread through the bite of certain types of sandflies was called and which did not have a cure at that time.

Singha and Ray were both geniuses of the humour genre. Had they continued to live beyond the three to three-and-a-half

---

[26]Sukumar Ray, *Abol Tabol* (the individual rhymes were first published in the magazine *Sandesh* edited by Ray between 1915 and 1923 and the collection was first published in book form by U. Ray and Sons Publishers in 1923).

decades into which their short lives were contained, they would no doubt have continued to enrich Bengali literature with their critical glare and sometimes indulgent glance on the changing times. The wit inherent in their writings remains unmatched.

Nevertheless, the babus continued, and still continue to be portrayed in dozens of literary works as those known for a host of vices including promiscuity, debauchery, decadence and arrogance.

A number of descriptions of babu culture of the eighteenth and nineteenth centuries depict them as a social class which was unscrupulous and unprincipled, devoid of ethical, moral or even humane values. Though many babus were engaged in charity, the 'generosity' was, in most cases, more an outward show of compassion rather than any genuine concern for the beneficiaries. Indeed, just as they did during festivities, the babus of different houses competed with each other in an attempt to outdo one another in the demonstration of their so-called magnanimity.

It has been pointed out that this trait of the babus was a classic example of the concept of 'conspicuous compassion', a phrase coined in 1899 by the Norwegian-American economist Thorstein Veblen to describe the very public displays of donation-making and alms-giving by the rich to the poor. The express purpose of such charity by the wealthy, pointed out the philosopher, was drawing respect unto themselves by highlighting their economic power and social status. It has also been noted that the theory of 'conspicuous consumption' which Veblen introduced in his book, *The Theory of the Leisure Class: An Economic Study in the Evolution of Institutions*[27] too fits the description of the expenditure habits of the babus to a tee, applying as it does to the ostentatious

---

[27]Thorstein Veblen, *The Theory of the Leisure Class: An Economic Study in the Evolution of Institutions*, Macmillan, 1899.

public displays of money-spending by the nouveau riche classes on luxury goods and services. It had more to do with impressing others than for any necessity or utility.

The shallowness and superficiality of the babus continue to be written about even today. The following delineation of 'babu culture' by an online portal called Sapasgroup[28], which throws light on various aspects of Bengali life, for instance, provides a humorous glimpse into the way these Bengali fops were, and still are, generally perceived. Dripping with sarcasm and often punctuated with politically incorrect commentary, the satiric account nevertheless perfectly captures and conveys the general impression of the babus of yore as a bunch of foppish dandies, who were referred to, pejoratively as 'phool babu', or 'flower fops' because of their fanciness. Here is an excerpt:

> They (babus) were half-baked in terms of education and upbringing, partially 'Anglicized' and partially 'Sanskritized' which had earned them the satiric title of 'ejuraj' or 'educated raja'. They spent most of their time and wealth on consorting with women of ill-repute (sic) and throwing lavish parties.
>
> They not only had palatial houses and mansions built in and around the city of Calcutta but owned property in the villages which included sprawling bungalows and farm houses with ponds.
>
> The babus loved to dress up. They wore linen dhotis and silk kurtas and carried handkerchiefs made of soft, white 'malmal' cloth. They wore shiny footwear, referred to as 'palm' shoes (though this can be a distortion of the English 'pump' shoes) which were always polished. They wore perfumes. They liked to carry canes with handles made of ivory.

---

[28]Paramita Mandal, Shib Sankar Das. 'Babu Culture: An Era in Medieval Calcutta.' *Sapas Group*, https://sites.google.com/site/sapagroup1/babu-c. Accessed 21 July 2010.

The babu used to go out in the evenings in his decorated landaulet, drawn by milky-white horses and driven by a coachman. The guards would throw open the huge gates of their residences with a loud shout of '*Hushiaar Ho*' (or 'Attention All') to alert outsiders that the babu is about to go out and that all must move out of the way. The sentinel would then close the gate behind him and remain standing until the babu returned, which would be sometime in the wee hours of the next morning.

Whether it was at midnight or early morning when the babu returned, servants would immediately attend to him. He would usually be very drunk and would have to be carried indoors with the help of his assistants, his arms thrown around their shoulders for support. Once in, he would at once fall asleep in the drawing room where a cozy bed, covered in silk and satin sheets and pillow cases, which had been made for him earlier in the evening, usually awaited him. Babus seldom went inside their bedrooms, where their wives slept.[29]

The babus' promiscuity and neglect of their wives or 'bibis', as they were called, was notorious and has been documented in literature and films. The popular Hindi song 'Na jao sayyan' (don't go darling), from the 1962 film *Saheb, Bibi aur Ghulam* (Master, Missus and Knave) sung by Geeta Dutt and lip-synced to the character of a desperate Meena Kumari clutching on to the hand of her husband in a vain attempt to stop him from going off to meet his courtesans, captures the plight of the wives of babus.

The online account says about the bibi:

> Ultimately in most cases, the husband returned to her in old age, either after getting rejected by his 'kept' or because he himself left the latter.

---

[29]Ibid.

The wives are a prime example of the helplessness of an upper-class Indian woman of that era: trapped in a gilded cage, expected to uphold family honour and spend her time in waiting endlessly for her husband to come home... (for diversion) going for pilgrimages, usually to pray for the wellbeing of her husband.[30]

Paintings, drawings, sketching and art in general, of the time, too reflected the babu culture that had been flourishing in Bengal. 'Patachitra', a traditional Bengali genre of scroll painting, which uses long strips of cloth tied to tiny bamboo rods on either end, which is rolled down to tell tales of mythological characters, started showing stories on the lives of babus and their bibis. These themes were especially popular in the Kalighat Patachitras, a particular type of these scroll paintings found in the locality of the ancient Kali Temple of Kolkata, inhabited by artists who are adept at this art form. These Patachitras depict scenes such as bibis clutching the hands of their babus in desperate gestures as though pleading with them not to leave; babus in dalliance with their courtesans, babus falling at the feet of their bibis asking for forgiveness perhaps or even bibis hitting their babus with broomsticks in a gesture of anger. Humorous Kalighat Patachitras include scenes such as a courtesan holding a babu, depicted as a sheep, on a leash possibly in an attempt to convey his helpless dependence on her. A number of English and European painters of the time too painted scenes which depicted aspects of the babu culture of the time such as the paintings of Baltazard Solvyn. The well-known uncle-nephew duo Thomas and William Danielle, who painted landscapes, buildings, etc., didn't necessarily focus on the topic of babus as a theme. However, the lives of babus were so integral to India, that it would be impossible to avoid touching, even if inadvertently, on them. These, however, were

---

[30]Ibid.

less deliberate depictions of babu culture with a view to mock or satirize them than delineations of life in Bengal. Scenes such as the opulent houses of Kolkata's rich or the bejewelled dancers at a musical gathering were more incidental reflections of babu culture rather than any intentional focus on them as a particular people. The perspectives were vastly different and were devoid of the biting satire of Bengali artists poking fun at members of their own clan who had started to identify with the colonizers. The satiric delineations of the babus were usually the works of their own kin and kind.

Whether literature, cinema or art, babu culture had clearly fired the imagination of the creative people of the land.

From many such accounts of babu cultures, emerges a tale of an extreme decadence. Babus squandered away their wealth in trivial pursuits, including litigation over insignificant matters. Not that their expenditures were necessarily always on unworthy causes. They did patronize the arts and donate generously towards cultural activities. However, they often spent with unbridled abandon, even going beyond their means. They extended invitations to the country's most celebrated and expensive dancers and musicians (namely the court dancers of the time known as 'baijis') for night-long musical soirees and the performances often stretched on for days, weeks and even months. They lavished gifts, which comprised everything from gold, diamond and silver jewellery to brocaded and embroidered silk saris to garden houses in the districts, on these courtesans and, not to mention, their mistresses. The babus spent extravagantly on hobbies such as collecting exotic birds, imported from foreign lands and planting rare flowers and fruit trees. Babus were known to often oscillate between fits of anger directed at their errant servants (who could reportedly even be thrashed mercilessly for as little a fault as delaying to open a door) and bouts of guilt when he was prone to gifting away anything from jewellery to property out of remorse.

Eventually, the babus' complete dependence on servants and support staff, which extended to them entrusting them even with responsibilities of looking after their finances, is said to have caused their downfall. Indeed, the role of the 'domestic helpers'—the menial household labourers of the babus, who were usually treated with a significant amount of feudal contempt—too deserves highlighting. (Especially so, because in the intervening two centuries the equations between 'servants' and 'masters'—or the poor and the rich—have undergone, if not vast, at least some changes and it reflects on the churning that took place since those early days. The poor of West Bengal today have a voice and the rich have conceded, if not defeat, at least a deference.)

The babus and bibis were dependent on servants almost to the point that they lived—in the context of performing daily chores—vicariously through them. Even tasks of personal hygiene, whether bathing or shaving not to mention the beauty rituals of the bibis, including combing their hair and applying scented oils on their tresses every evening, was the job of the maids and servants. They usually came from poverty-stricken families, of course, and were at the mercy of the masters and their wives and were expected to be at their beck and call and do their every bidding in return for the succour that they provided, which was desperately required by them for looking after their own families.

Thus, the predominant image of the babus who ruled eighteenth and nineteenth century Bengal as the deputies of the British is one of decadence and depravity which inevitably led to their decline.

But hidden within the depths of such apparent degradation lurked other compulsions for the babus of Bengal to behave the way that they did. Thousands of years of history and heritage—including social and spiritual—had conditioned them, defining what they thought and determining how they acted. To dismiss them as merely equivalents of the British fops would perhaps disregard the complex layers which enveloped them and from which they emerged.

The Bengali bhadralok classes were also keenly aware of their ancientness compared to the British gentlemen and they knew that their identities were separate from the foreigners who influenced their decadent lifestyles and they gradually grew tired of it.

And so, it is from this babu class that emerged the leaders who would rebel against it all—questioning themselves and the foreign rulers—and at the same time, embracing those values in either culture which they deemed worth nurturing to usher in the new era of Bengal.

If evolution is about progress and not degeneration, then this new mutant was a combination of all that which would lead the way ahead.

V

OF RICHES, ROMANCES AND RENUNCIATIONS

'Oh Divine Mother, I know that all comes to naught/ Yet with desires my heart is fraught/ My hopes refuse to die/ Though I know that the end is nigh/ I have shed endless tears/ And it has been many years/ Let me in your lap now lie/ I cannot any longer cry.'

—Kamalakanta Bhattacharya[31]

The year was 1720. A storm may have been brewing over the vast river bed at Sutanuti, darkening the horizon. As the waves of the Ganga crashed wildly against the banks at Kumortuli, a vast rural area in the vicinity, a lone figure could have been spotted, silhouetted against the grey sky, staring out, his hands folded in prayer, deep in meditation. Or wrapped in a silken shawl, with his soft, white cotton dhoti blowing in the wind, he may have been clutching the gold handle of a cane, tapping it gently on the unpaved clay, deliberating. He may have been brooding, torn by dilemma. Should he hear what his heart was telling him or should he listen to his head?

Gobinda Ram Mitra has gone down in history not just as

---

[31]From the Shyamasangeet 'Amar shaadh na mitilo, ashaa na phurilo, shokoli phurayey jay, Maa.'

the first 'black zamindaar' or 'black prince' of the British era (as mentioned in the earlier chapter) but also as the prototype of the babus. It has been said about him, that 'Mitter' (as he was referred to by the British) earned fabulous amounts of money. He had a sprawling house at Kumortuli spread on 50 bighas (around 16 acres) of land. He also had a famous villa, Nandan Bagan, in rural Bengal. He is also credited by some as being the first Bengali to drive a coach. And, 'It was he who fired the urge for conspicuous consumption in the society of his time.'[32]

But while Gobinda Ram did indeed earn the reputation of being amongst the wealthiest and most extravagant of the babus, the founder of the House of the Mitras of Kumortuli was also a deeply spiritual man, who was haunted by thoughts of transience. He was a devotee of Lord Shiva and Goddess Kali, according to his direct descendants, and he built temples dedicated to them. These included the famous 'Pancharatna' or five-turreted 'Pagoda', which finds mention in the detailed and descriptive texts of Jaya Chaliha and Bunny Gupta in the chapter 'Chitpur' of the fascinating first volume of *Calcutta, the Living City*.[33] Flanked by two smaller, 'Navaratna or nine-turreted towers, its spire, in its original form, stood at 165 feet high and reportedly became a navigational aid for boatmen and sailors.' The temple complex, which had sprawled along the Chitpore Road, then a main thoroughfare of Calcutta, was built in 1730 (there are discrepant accounts about the exact date with the years 1725 and 1731 also mooted), a decade after Mitra assumed the position of deputy collector of the British East India Company.

The grandness of the temple complex and the resultant

---

[32] These mentions are found in the first volume of the authoritative biographical dictionary edited and authored by Anjali Basu and Subodh Chandra Sengupta, *Samsad Bangali Charitabhidhan*, Shishu Sahitya Samsad Pvt. Ltd, 2016.
[33] Professor Sukanta Chaudhury ed., *Calcutta, the Living City, Vol. 1, The Past*, Oxford University Press, 1995.

costs the construction had clearly incurred, have been cited as an example of Gobinda Ram's opulence as well as his profligacy. The *Samsad Bangali Charitabhidhan* says about him,

> His celebration of the Hindu festivals was marked with lavishness and extravagance. The entire image of Goddess Durga was wrapped in gold and silver leaf. Thirty to 50 maunds (one maund is about 37 kilograms) of rice was offered to the deity and a 1,000 Brahmins were fed and given gifts.

But there was more to these expenditures on religious symbols than just the eagerness to publicly display his wealth and ability. It was certainly also an indication of his willingness to expend his worldly wealth for the attainment of heaven or the heavenly at any rate. It was a reflection of his growing detachment from the life of decadence and his gradual search for divinity.

In fact, there were indications of Gobinda Ram Mitra's intrinsic detachment to the wealth he had acquired as the powerful deputy of the British Company right from the onset. Unlike many of his contemporaries, he was not servile and did not do anything to try to hold on to his job by pleasing the employers. On the contrary, he is understood to have constantly rubbed them the wrong way with his insouciance. And yet he was indispensable. It has been said about him, 'He was so powerful that his boss Holwell could not remove him.' Indeed, the British frustration with and dislike for him is reflected in the accounts of British historians and politicians of the British era. Harry Evan Auguste Cotton (24 May 1868 to 7 March 1939) writes[34]:

> The 'Zemindar' was a collector of revenue as well as a judicial officer; and it is on record that it was part of his duty to 'make

---

[34] Harry Evan Auguste Cotton, *Calcutta Old and New*, Creative Media Partners, 1907.

roads and repair drains'...The President and Council, or any three of them, the President being one, were empowered to hold a court in revenue cases, but the real power lay with the Zemindar, and, it may be added with the Indian deputy, who went by the name of 'Black Zemindar'. This office was filled during whole of the period from 1720 to 1756, by the famous Gobindram Metre (Mitter), of whom John Zephaniah Holwell, Zemindar of Calcutta from 1752 to 1756, wrote that by reason of the many changes in the headship of the office, 'a power in perpetuity devolved on the standing deputy who was always styled the 'Black Zemindar,' and such was the tyranny of this man and such the dread conceived of him in the minds of the natives that no one durst complain or give information.

As mentioned earlier Mitra constructed the Pancharatna and Navaratna temples a decade or so after he started working with the British East India Company. The assumption that the money that he spent on the temples was an indication of conspicuous consumption is faulty because it does not take into account the possibility that since he had ample opportunity to publicly display his power and wealth over a decade of decadence, he may have actually outgrown those initial propensities. The argument that he continued to demonstrate the same tendencies throughout his life as when he started his career as a young man, is flawed because it is tantamount to disregarding the reality that as life progresses, individuals grow, evolve, change. Their beliefs, their ideas, their perspectives and their thinking undergo transformations.

It is entirely likely that the abundance of power and wealth led Mitra to gradually grow disillusioned with the material world. It is possible that he realized that the happiness he ever hoped to gain from his material power was limited to the physical plane. He had reached the peak of the worldly world. He had experienced it all. According to his direct descendants, as late as the 1930s and '40s, before Independence, the Mitra households, by then spread out in different parts of Calcutta, were still in possession of riches that trickled down from the era of Gobinda Ram Mitra. Kalyani Mitra says[35]:

> Not just gold and silver, gems and jewels; there were all these exquisite antiques from the Mughal period, like chandeliers and rare musical instruments, including violins imported from European markets during the British East India Company era, which were strewn around the house. Our ancestor had a taste for the exclusive, the exotic, the expensive and the exquisite. The enormous wealth he had collected had got distributed as the family started to branch out. But even thus divided, the opulence was remarkable. The individual units owned land, houses with gardens and bungalows with orchards across Calcutta and the rest of Bengal. There was the practice of purchasing a place if it was found to be pleasing during the time of Gobinda Ram Mitra and the tradition continued for 200 years. Another custom was to acquire a new cow each time a child was born so that the infant would have a designated one and would never be deprived of adequate amounts of milk. The one that I was gifted was a robust red one whose milk was very sweet. I am talking about the 1930s and 1940s.

After Independence, with the collapse of economic, social and political status quo, zamindaars gradually ceased to exist and their properties were often confiscated by the state. The descendent continues:

---

[35]Kalyani Mitra, daughter of Kailash Chandra Mitra, granddaughter of Gobinda Ram Mitra's great grandson, Dharmada Charan Mitra, in conversation with the author.

> We had taken the wealth for granted, in fact, not only were we not interested in these as children, even as we grew older and pursued our individual interests trying to make our mark in the modern world we did not want to delve into the past. We did not bother much about the treasures. Antiques, utensils, often plated in silver, were treated with as much neglect by us as say a plastic plate would be today. Once we lost everything, we realized their value. And learnt that these lost treasures cannot be measured in money, but in exclusivity.

One of the last vestiges of the zamindaari in the Mitra family was the use of palanquins to convey the women folk of the family. Kalyani Mitra describes the opulence of her grandmother's palanquin,

> When my grandmother got married to my grandfather (paternal), a palanquin, its interiors covered in silk and gold, was sent to fetch her. Sixteen bearers, eight carrying the front and eight carrying the back handles, were employed to ferry the palanquin.

If wealth was in abundance, so was amorousness. Gobinda Ram Mitra is understood to have had several mistresses. Three of them were said to have been such favourites that he had them put up in his rural garden houses and provided for them. The names 'Rattan', 'Lolita' and 'Mati' figure in a list of applicants for compensation which the British East India Company had prepared for submission to the court of Siraj-ud-Daulah after his attack on Calcutta and Fort William. Journals dealing with Calcutta's history of this period suggest that they would have been Mitra's mistresses.[36]

---

[36] Chitra Deb, 'The Great Houses of Old Calcutta', *Calcutta, the Living City, Vol 1, The Past,* Oxford University Press, 1995.

It has also been said about Gobinda Ram Mitra that, 'Mitter became a legend in his lifetime.' He owned a 'chhari' or cane either made completely of solid gold or, according to some accounts, it was gold plated, with a handle made of solid gold. Others suggest that the cane was simply a figurative idea explored in a rhyme composed at the time to conjure up the power that he wielded. However, considering that the three other mighty 'lords' mentioned in the poem are brought up in the context of the proverbial tangible objects for which they were known, it is unlikely that only Mitra's would be in the realm of a symbol. Consider the 'chhara' or rhyme which mentions the 'chhari':

Banamali Sarkarer bari
Gobinda Ram Mitrar chhari
Umi Chander dari
Huzoori Maler kori
Ke na janey?

In English, it translates to:

Banamali Sarkar's house
Gobinda Ram Mitra's cane
Umi Chand's beard
And Huzoori Mal's money
Who hasn't heard about these?

Indeed, this rhyme has been passed down through the generations of Mitra's descendants, with families often reciting it, especially during get-togethers. With children growing up hearing it, it has helped in keeping alive the memories of their ancient, awe-inspiring ancestor.

Mitra may have wanted to eschew the hollowness of a life of power or physical pleasure and in later years yearned for spiritual knowledge. Each individual, in his or her quest for truth, charts out his or her own path for the journey. It is entirely likely that

Gobinda Ram Mitra, in his search for enlightenment, decided to build altars to the gods and goddess. Often associated with what historians have called his 'tyranny', he may have felt that constructing temples was his only penance, his way to seek salvation.

The majesty of the structures of these temples, especially the Pancharatna and the Navaratna, and the magnificence of their architecture, have inspired artists to paint, draw and illustrate them. The temples have been captured in the brilliant brush strokes of Thomas Daniell in his 1787 painting, 'Gentoo Pagoda and House', James Baillie Fraser in his painting of 1826 and Charles D'Oyly in his painting 'Hindoo Mutt in the Chitpore Bazar'.

Seven years after the construction of the temples, in 1737, however, a cyclone ripped through Calcutta, knocking off the tower of the temple. It was as though the fates were giving Gobinda Ram Mitra an affirmative glimpse into the true nature of life—that it was nothing if not transient. What was there one moment could and did eventually and inevitably disappear into nothingness the next.

These thoughts of the ephemeral nature of life must have made him want to live intensely, passionately, desperately and in the moment. The first flush of power and wealth for him would have been joyous. And once he had had his fill, he would have grown thirsty for knowledge of what lay beyond. He would have wanted to reach out, or upwards, to the Gods and the Goddesses.

The blueness of Shiva and blackness of Kali drew him. It was the nothingness from which life sprung and then disappeared back into, in death.

Clearly, for Mitra, in his later years, life had become as transient as the changing colours of the day and night. The same blackness becomes light. And then goes back to being blackness again. Gobinda Ram Mitra must have known that he could not get attached to any of it.

His direct descendant Prasun Mitra (1929–99), who went on to become a writer, journalist and international broadcaster for the Voice of America in the United States, had extensively researched on his famous ancestor, especially whether he played any role in the 'betrayal' of Siraj-ud-Daulah and concluded that Gobinda Ram Mitra did not participate in the conspiracy and was not one of the 'traitors'.

It is acknowledged in the records of the British that Gobinda Ram Mitra did not bow to British diktats. 'He was extremely independent and was a constant source of unease for the British,' says Mukul Mitra, one of Mitra's descendants.[37] 'He was straightforward and the underhanded approach of the plan of betrayal against Siraj-ud-Daulah did not suit him. This further incensed his bosses and earned their wrath but he was so indispensable that they did not dare remove him. In fact, they could do nothing. However, as a punitive tactic, the British, who otherwise recorded contemporary history exhaustively, virtually blacked out the name of Mitra. There are only cursory documentations of him even though he played an extremely important role in building Calcutta. By not giving him his due exposure in their writings, the British believed that they were depriving him. But Mitra's legacy has been passed down through his lineage, which is proud that he did not participate in the conspiracy.'

Indeed, Mitra's name does not figure in any of the records of the time which document the conspiracy against Siraj-ud-Daulah. Questions arise as to what prevented him from joining in when so many of his contemporaries were involved in the treachery. If his contemporaries considered Siraj-ud-Daulah a difficult, dictatorial ruler, whom they wanted to remove and replace with a more

---

[37] Mukul Mitra, son of Kailash Chandra Mitra, grandson of Dharmada Charan Mitra, who was a great grandson of Gobinda Ram Mitra in a conversation with the author.

malleable Mir Jafar, what made him think and act differently? Unlike the other conspirators, did he realize that dethroning the then nawab of Bengal would become synonymous with ushering in the British rule? How would he know that when the others did not?

As far as Mir Jafar was concerned, even though the British East India Company led the battle, the premise was that the land would still be ruled by the established dynasty to which he belonged. The others hatching the plot too would not have had any inkling that the East India Company would eventually snatch power and rule Bengal and the rest of India for 200 years. They perhaps did not consider that what they were doing was tantamount to committing treason.

But that is what happened. And it is entirely likely that Gobinda Ram Mitra knew. He had been associated with the British for long. He would not have been on the side of the British. His strained relationship with his boss Holwell (who, it must be remembered, was Siraj-ud-Daulah's enemy), indicates that he treated the foreigners with a certain amount of disdain and contempt. Mitra would not have sided with the British against the nawab of Bengal. And he did not.

Indeed, he would even have been in deep dilemma just *joining* the foreign Company as an employee. That day, by the banks of the river Ganga in Sutanuti, close to his house in Kumortuli, he would have been deliberating, deciding. His heart would have rejected the idea of working as a subordinate to the foreigners, who were known to upper-caste and upper-class Bengali families of the time, such as the one to which Mitra belonged, as 'mllechho'—or those who did not follow the strict codes of conduct as far as Hindu pedigree was concerned.

'In upper-caste, upper-class Hindu households of the time mllechho's were considered to fall way below the exacting Hindu standards of every aspect of life,' says Anath Taran Ghoshal,

Hindu scholar and temple priest.[38] 'The Hindu way of life, even in ordinary Brahmin or Kayastha households, was determined by regulations. There were rules for everything. The list of dos and don'ts was long. They could not only not eat particular types of food but they could not eat food cooked by those of "lower" castes. They were forbidden to marry members of other castes. Even rudimentary "hygiene" fell into the ambit of regulation with foreigners being considered "unclean" because they didn't take holy dips in the river Ganga perhaps or didn't bathe as many times a day as say a Hindu man or woman was expected to do. Under the circumstances, it was challenging for Hindus from upper-castes and upper-classes to take up offers, no matter how lucrative, from foreign firms.'

Yet there was no denying that the foreigners brought in a new approach to life. A new world of possibilities opened up and opportunities for trade and travel presented themselves to the Bengalis, especially the younger generations who were not yet too set in their ways to embrace change. Though the exact year of Gobinda Ram Mitra's birth is not documented (all that is recorded about his infancy is that he was born in Chanak Village, which is located near present day Barrackpore, a Calcutta suburb), he could not have been more than a young man in the year 1720 and would have been considered fit enough by the British East India Company to take on the physical rigours of the job of a deputy collector. They offered it to him. After much internal debate and dilemma, Mitra listened to the voices in his head and took it up.

In the distance, it thundered. The storm struck. Winds howled. River rose. Rain fell. The silhouetted figure disappeared across the Ganges. And it was as if it was never there. It was as if nothing was ever there.

---

[38]During an interview with the author.

It is interesting to note that generations of the direct descendants of Gobinda Ram Mitra, who died in 1776, would continue to display the same traits as their forefather and even as late as the twentieth century, Prasun Mitra, his father Kailash Chandra Mitra and grandfather Dharmada Charan Mitra would all, in their own way, renounce worldly pursuits, drawn by the spiritual path.

Gobinda Ram's son, Roghoo or Raghu Mitra had constructed, by the Ganges, a ghat and named it after his father. The ghat still exists today and is a famous landmark in north Calcutta, Baghbazar Ghat.

Gobinda Ram Mitra's other descendants too gained illustriousness and roads, streets, lanes and neighbourhoods have been named after them. A main thoroughfare in Kumortuli is named after Abhay Charan Mitra, Gobinda Ram Mitra's great grandson. It is said that three portraits of three generations of the Mitras of Kumurtuli hang from the hallowed walls of the Calcutta High Court as testimony to the continued eminence of the descendants of their illustrious forefather. And a mark of the power that the distinguished babu of 300 years ago wielded, is the still existing old Calcutta neighbourhood of Jorabagan (meaning Double Garden) which, close to the river at Sutanuti, is so named because the road that cuts through it connects with two sprawling gardens, one of which had belonged to Gobinda Ram Mitra.

But if Gobinda Ram Mitra was a zamindaar who reigned before the British East India Company took over the governance of Bengal, most of the other famous babus came into the picture later, during actual British rule.

They belonged to and were descended from upper-class or upper-caste families who were pujaris or priests, rajas or princes, dukes or zamindaars, byaparis or merchants, as well as local kings and even court assistants known as dewans.

They built themselves magnificent mansions, often modelled

after architectural marvels of Europe. The residential home of the family of Gokul Chandra Daw, for instance, resembled London's Royal Albert Hall, with the balconies facing the inner courtyard made to look like galleries. His adopted son Shib Krishna Daw was counted amongst the most prominent babus of this era, though much like Gobinda Ram Mitra before him, Gokul Chandra Daw himself was more spiritually inclined and had reportedly even turned down a lucrative offer of a top position in the East India Company because he felt that the demands of the job would interfere in his carrying out his religious practices.

He had instituted the family Durga Puja possibly around 1840, but it was Shib Krishna Daw, who was much more worldly-wise, who introduced the glitz and glamour to its celebration. P. Daw, one of his descendants writing on their famous ancestors, had pointed out how Shib Krishna Daw, his great grandfather, on a trip to France and Germany, had stumbled upon a set of metallic decorations in floral motifs which appealed to him so much that he immediately decided to use them for the ornamentation of their family deity. He placed an order for around 500 pieces and returned to India, leaving instruction that they be shipped to him.

Eventually they arrived by *daak* (post) just in time for the festivities. Traditionally, the backdrop on which the idols of the gods and goddess are buttressed are made of *shola* (thermocol). Intricate designs are carved into it and a decorative bling, *chumki*, is sewn into it. This is called '*sholar saaj*' or thermocol decoration. Daw's metal canvas, constructed out of a copper and brass plate and decorated with the exotic designs imported from abroad reportedly became an instant hit, attracting throngs of visitors from far and wide. It was the start of another tradition in deity-decoration, which is still followed today and is called '*daaker saaj*' or the postal decoration.

It is said that the Daws' Durga Puja was matched only by one other family in Calcutta with whom they had a running competition on who could outdo the other in grandeur. That family, their neighbours in the north Calcutta cultural hub of the time, Jorasanko, was none other than the Thakurs, the illustrious ancestors of their even more illustrious descendant Nobel laureate Rabindranath Thakur (or 'Tagore', as he is known internationally).

The Thakur family's Durga Puja is supposed to have started much earlier, in the year 1784, and it had immediately gained popularity for the pomp and show with which it was observed. The idol of the Thakurs' deity was dressed up every year in the finest clothes and pure gold jewellery that was always immersed into the river along with the statue of the Goddess. Fishermen, boatpeople, bathers, swimmers and street urchins, splashing around in the river would dive in and grab the treasure before it was permanently lost in the water. It was considered a form of giving to the poor during the holy festival.

The Daws' Durga deity was decorated in precious stones and other gems such as pearls, diamonds and ruby imported from Europe that they removed before the immersion and reused.

The story goes that since the Thakurs did not repeat the jewellery, they always considered themselves to be one up on the Daws.

'Commoners' circulated many myths about the babus amongst themselves. A popular proverb, perhaps philosophically trying to resolve the zamindaars' conflicts from a distance, was about how Durga herself did not distinguish between her devotees, irrespective of the grandeur of the worship. When the Goddess descended on earth—or Bengal as it were—from her heavenly abode in the high mountains of the Himalayas, she first dropped in at the house of the Daws', went the nineteenth-century oldwives' tale. She put on her clothes and jewellery there and then went for her holy supper to the house of Abhay Charan Mitra, scion of the Mitra household, who worshipped her every year, lavishing her with the sweetest of fruits and the most fragrant of flowers and offering her the most aromatic of rice and the most intoxicating of incense smoke. And thus, she hopped, riding on the back of her mascot, the lion, from one zamindaar home to the other.

Legends sprung up around the larger-than-life 'black princes'. They built castles sometimes quite literally in the air, with towering ivory pillars shooting through the skies. And often, the fairy tales came true, as with the magnificent 'Marble Palace' built by Raja Rajendra Mullick Bahadur in 1835. One of the few mansions of the Bengal zamindaars to still exist and that too almost in its full former glory (descendants still inhabit a part of the palace and maintain it well), the sprawling riverside palace with its marble walls, floors and roofs, not to mention the large collection of Greco-Roman marble sculptures, which are housed there along with other rare works of international art from two centuries ago, is testimony to the kind of luxurious lives the babus led. Far from the reach of the ordinary citizen, as inaccessible and held in as much awe as were the kings and princes of yore, the zamindaars would not have it any other way.

And so babu Pradyumna Mullick of the ancient family of traders and art collectors, who owned 34 cars, 10 of which were Rolls Royces, is supposed to have compulsively gone about buying up property in different parts of Bengal and every palatial building in the region that he could get his hands on. He could not stop. But neither could he sustain the huge expenditure and apparently became a pauper. It is said that he eventually killed himself and his wife (shooting her to death before taking his own life).

The babu Krishna Mullick, on the other hand, was eager to put the spotlight on the one house he owned—a grand, palatial building. He tried to convince the administration to have it recognized as an official government building—more specifically the Governor House—but his plea was rejected. He even moved court in order to push his agenda. When that was also denied, he took the matter to the Privy Council in London where he won the case but ended up spending so much money on litigation that he too became penniless. If their decadent lives led the babus to penury, pride prevented them from declaring it.

The babus went to extraordinary lengths to decorate, beautify, clean and maintain their properties. Ramtanu Dutta, a descendant of the famous merchant family, the Duttas of North Calcutta, reportedly had his entire house rinsed, twice a day, with pure rose water imported from Mirzapur in present-day Uttar Pradesh.

The babus came to be associated with bizarre habits and hobbies. Khelat Ghosh, grandson of famous babu, Ram Lochon Ghosh—who had served as a personal 'dewan' of Warren Hastings and his wife and who was also a scholar and musician—started the trend of having dancers dance on huge sweets which were made to order. The balls of sweets were supposed to be so tightly bound by the adhesiveness of sugar syrup and clarified butter that these would not crumble even under pressure from the dancers' feet.

Then there was the eccentric babu and one of the richest merchants in Bengal, Bhuban Mohan Niyogi, who belonged to the late eighteenth century and is widely considered to be the last of the flamboyant babus. In order to publicly demonstrate his wealth, power and perhaps also generosity (or rather, conspicuous compassion) he used to distribute Benarasi sarees, (the specialty of which is silk cloth, brocaded with threads of gold), to nearly 2,000 sex workers living in the brothels nearby. Ironically, this carefully cultured image of a magnanimous man was undone by his own attempts to showcase his enormous wealth by another means: he used to light his cigars by holding lit currency notes to them instead of matchsticks. This made it apparent that showing off his wealth and his ability to spend money was what drove him rather than any genuine concern for the needy.

However, that babuana continued to live beyond the eighteenth and nineteenth centuries and spilled over to the twentieth became amply clear when in the year 1936, Calcutta's

The Statesman newspaper published a report and a black and white photo of a gentleman being carried in a coach that was driven not by horses but by a zebra. The story goes that Manmath Nath Mullick, youngest son of Jadulal Mullick and nephew of hapless Pradyumna Nath, had gotten so tired and bored of being drawn around by horses (of which he owned some of the best breeds that were permanent fixtures in his stables) that he bought two zebras from the zoological society for the price of ₹6,000 rupees each. One of these died but that did not stop Mullick from being driven around by the other.

However, the later babus, many of them at least, ceased to squander their money and power in wasteful extravagance and trivial pursuits, putting their enormous wealth and influence to better use instead, namely the upliftment of the underprivileged. Many babus became patrons of devotional songs and classical music and the arts and subsidized talent.

If some were led by overabundance to eventually eschew worldly ways and embrace enlightenment in the spiritual space, others devoted themselves to the pursuit of justice in the material world, diving headlong into philanthropy, charity and the amelioration of the sufferings of the impoverished masses. They stood by those who belonged to the economically and socially lower strata and came to the rescue of the starving multitudes during famines and draughts. They further engaged themselves with significant social causes, raising their voices against social evils and fighting for their exorcism.

Of them, one of the most prominent was Raja Ram Mohan Roy (1774–1833), who is credited with ushering in the pioneering nineteenth century movement of intellectual, religious, social and cultural reformations that came to be known as the Bengal Renaissance.

VI

CASTING SHADOWS IN THE SOUL

'In this world so bountiful/ There is a land most beautiful/ Of dreams and memories it is made/ In comparison all the others fade/ She is the queen, she is the best/ Oh Motherland, on your lap, let me rest.'

—Dwijendralal Roy[39]

European imperialism had another side to it. On the flip side of the coin of power, domination and oppression imposed on the people of the colonized land by the British rulers was, of course, unprecedented international trade and business. This resulted in a massive churning of the economic status quo of the land.

The feudality of the wealthy was gradually disintegrating as Bengal's lower classes and castes began to emerge from under the weight of the economic monopoly of the upper-classes and castes. For these ever-exploited, chronically-deprived lot of poor people, however, it turned out to be more like a journey from the frying pan to the fire.

While the British East India Company was employing the educated Indian upper-castes and classes for the bulk of their

---

[39]From the patriotic poem which became an iconic song, 'Dhono dhanney pushpey bhora, amader ei boshundhora', by the poet, dramatist, academic and musician, Dwijendralal Roy.

official work, they were also recruiting large numbers of people from the lower castes and classes to work as menial labourers. Hundreds and thousands of poor people were hired and sent off to work in distant British colonies as slaves. By 1833, when slavery was officially abolished by the British government, the Company started the infamous 'Indian Indenture' system, when it shipped millions of workers from India to the colonies to labour in its plantations, especially for sugarcane cultivation, under cruelly exploitative conditions. They were recruited from different parts of the country but with high concentrations from the eastern region, especially Bihar and Bengal. The indentured system was more regulated but instead of working out to be beneficial for the workers, it bound them to inescapable servitude through legal documents, contracts and agreements.

'Most of the contracts were for five-year terms and periods, following which we were supposed to have been sent back home to our own country,' explains Parasram Persaud, descendant of Indian indentured workers who were packed off to work in British Guyana in the early 1800s. 'My ancestor was from Bihar and he came to this land as a little boy,' says the 61-year-old who is a fifth-generation migrant worker and part of the large Indian diaspora in the South American country. 'But he never went back. They were all discouraged to go back because it saved the British a lot of trouble, not to mention money. First of all, getting new recruits would mean having to train them. And of course, repatriating us to our countries of origin would incur more expenses than if we were to settle here. So as part of the incentive to stay on, they promised us that the entire, unutilized cost of repatriation would be handed over to us. However, our families never did receive this entitlement and I am thinking of claiming it.' Persaud jokes, chuckling. So do the others—chuckle, that is—sitting and chatting at a shop in Georgetown, Guyana's capital city. Everyone knows it was a joke. It has been 200 years and the possibility of getting reimbursed had long since fizzled out. And now Guyana is their home.

'But we still pine for India,' says Jainarine Deonauth, a journalist and editor who is also the owner of the swanky garments store in a mall in the centre of town. It's a holiday and there are more friends dropping in to catch up than customers. Guyana is a small country with a population count, by the end of 2020, of around 800,000. What ensues is like the Bengali 'adda', the age-old custom of friends ferreting out time from their busy schedules to get together and converse over cups of tea or coffee.

'It's in our blood,' smiles Deonauth. 'Our roots go back to Bengal, after all.'

Like the ancestors of Parasram Persaud, Deonauth's family too arrived in British Guyana as plantation workers and settled. 'It was sometime in 1838 that they boarded a ship,' he says. 'Though there are not many records of those times, what we do know is from what has passed down to us through the generations by word of mouth.' Deonauth's ancestors were from a remote village in Bengal, who signed up or were compelled to sign up for the indentured system, possibly due to economic hardships. The indenture system targeted the needy masses, the memories of whose displacement could and did get lost in the oblivion of time. Their numbers remained virtually unaccounted for except as cold impersonal statistics. Close to two million (by some accounts three million or even more) people had been dislocated by the Indian indenture system. The mere rattling off of these numbers don't take into account the fact that each and every one of the figures which make up that total, was that of an individual who had dreams and aspirations to return home one day. To their parents, spouses, children and siblings.

Two hundred years after his ancestors were uprooted from Bengal, Deonauth has returned twice to India with an emotional visit to Bengal, where he had hoped to trace his long-lost ancestral home. 'But even if time permitted, which it did not, there was little to go by. There were no leads, no clues.' Deonauth has a dream. He wants, just once, to stand at the port, the dock in Calcutta, from where his ancient ancestors had left for the unknown two centuries ago and never returned. On their behalf.

'Did you know that these are referred to as Guyana port or Trinidad port? You don't? Don't they call it that in Bengal?' It is difficult to explain to Jainarine Deonauth, who proudly points out that most of the names of the Indian diaspora in Guyana are Bengali, that Bengal has all but forgotten the indentured Indians who were snatched away from them two centuries ago and made bonded labourers in a distant land.

The younger generation to which Deonauth belongs, has grown up hearing the various tales from those days at the turn of nineteenth century when the arduous sea journeys of their ancestors began. Deonath says,

> These were often tales of endless torture, when people died of exhaustion either on the ship or while working in the plantation fields. People died of seasickness on the ship or of tropical diseases like malaria, typhoid and other fevers when they arrived on land. There were stories of people who were shot dead for complaining about the miserable working conditions or for refusing to carry on working under exploitative circumstances.

These stories have a beginning, like the start of the journey of Deonauth's ancestors in Bengal but no ending because the plot got lost in the middle. 'Today, Guyana is our home and we love our lives here but it would be good to have closure.' He feels that Bengal and India could try to trace the roots of people of the diaspora. Part of the reason for the disinterest, feel people of the diaspora, is the fact that they were poor people. 'They came from the lower castes and lower classes,' he says.

One of the interesting facts about the Indian indenture system was that women too were recruited in large numbers. This provided incentives for the men to migrate because it was seen as a possibility that they could marry and settle down in their new place of employment. The logic was that if the labourers had their wives and families with them, they would be more likely to want to stay on beyond the five-year terms, which would benefit the employers as it would save on resettlement costs. Often, these women were single and got married to men who had migrated, and did not return. However, at other times, even married women, with children, were forced to leave families behind, driven by hunger and hardships. According to the descendants of these indentured Indians, they almost always hoped that they would one day return.

This is the heart-rending story of one such woman, as narrated exclusively for this book by her great-granddaughter Gangadai Persaud who lives in Guyana:

> My great-grandmother came from India with her 11-year-old son (Rangbahadur Singh) around 1838 and settled on a sugar plantation at Uitvlugt, West Demerara in Guyana. Unfortunately none of us can remember her name. It was so long ago. However we have heard her story many times. She had left her husband and other relatives in India to come to work in the then British Guiana (now Guyana). She was made to understand that British Guiana was a very rich country and the conditions of work would be very good and from her earnings she would be able to help her family back in India.
>
> However, after arriving here it was a completely different story. I was told that my great-grandmother had to work on the sugar plantation for a very small salary and the conditions of work were very harsh. She had to endure the struggle as she had a small son to take care of. Later on,

her son (who is my grandfather) got married. They all lived in 'logies', or what some may call mud houses, on the sugar plantations and worked very hard in the cane fields under colonial rulers to make ends meet.

My great-grandmother never went back to India. As difficult as it was, she endured and made Guyana her new home. My eldest aunt had told me when I was very small that my great-grandmother regretted that she came here and left her family back in India. She became very depressed as she had missed them very much. She subsequently died and left her son (my grandfather) to fend for himself.

At one time, he used to keep in contact with his relatives back in India, but the hard work in the cane fields and his own family commitments kept him very busy as the years went by and he lost contact with them.

The people who came on the ships had respect for each other, they all lived like family. They kept their traditions, such as going to temples, and so on.

As a child I remember all the kids from the logies would play together and tell stories about their relatives coming to Guyana on the ships from India.

I was born in a logie at Uitvlugt. Growing up in a logie was fun in those days. My eldest aunt told us stories about how my grandfather and his mother came to this country and worked hard to survive in their adopted country.

The living conditions were very poor, but they were determined to cope and make the best of what was available to them.

Some of the indentured labourers later bought their own plot of land and built houses and engaged in farming work, including cultivating rice, planting different types of vegetables, growing coconut, rearing cattle and producing greens in their kitchen gardens to survive.

Gangadai's great-grandmother was one of the hundreds of thousands of women who left an Indian village in the vain hope of coming back but never did. She herself is married to a man whose ancestors hailed from Bengal. They too had hoped to, but never got around to making the elusive return journey.

The British thus depleted Bengal of one of its treasured resources. Those that they had engaged as plantation labourers and sent off to work in their rural colonies in distant lands and gradually as urban factory workers, were those who were earlier mainly agricultural workers such as landless farmers, farmhands, sharecroppers and others from Bengal's villages.

Back in Bengal, the British continued to milk the rural economy for profit. The East India Company introduced draconian tax policies that squeezed revenue from the agricultural population even during draughts. This caused terrible famines to break out throughout the period of British rule and these wiped out millions of India's poor people. Historian Brian Murton[40] writes, 'Although all of India suffered to some extent in the early eighteenth century, without question the late eighteenth and nineteenth centuries were that country's time of famines.' According to Niall Ferguson, the number of people in Bengal who starved to death in a period of approximately 10 months was about a quarter to a third of its population.[41]

Scholars point out that there were different causes for the large numbers of famine deaths. However, historians generally agree that though the droughts were triggered by inadequate rainfall, which caused crops to fail, subsequent British administrative action (and inaction) aggravated them.

The deadliest, most flagrant violation of the rudimentary

---

[40]Brian Murton, 'Famines', *Cambridge World History of Food*, Cambridge University Press, 2000.
[41]Niall Ferguson, *Empire: The Rise and Demise of the British World Order and the Lessons for Global Power*, Basic Books, 2004.

rights of Bengal's poor was committed by the British Company when, instead of reaching relief to them, it was diverting food to its military bases. This, over and above the high rates of taxes it was charging the farmers. This is exactly what happened in the devastating famine of 1770 in Bengal.

According to Lawrence James, East India Company revenues had crashed and so had its stock prices due to the famine. This forced the company to obtain a loan from the Bank of England to fund its annual military budget of between 60,000 to 1 million pounds. And, in order make up the lost funds, collection of taxes was 'violently kept up to its former standard'. He poignantly remarked, 'The Company was widely regarded as a pack of bloodsuckers' and that 'the Whig leader, Lord Rockingham, called them guilty of "rapine and oppression" in Bengal.'[42]

The final famine of the British period took place in Bengal in 1943, four years before Independence. Shocking photographs of people, resembling skeletons, exist in different archives, including the online 'Wikimedia Commons' (Public Domain), for all to witness the horrors of those holocaustic days. In some, they stare vacantly towards the camera, as though in a pre-death trance. In others, they are already corpses, lying dead on pavements and roads.

Bengal's poor, thus killed during the British period, never got justice.

Of course, the poor of this land, including dalits (or oppressed) as the 'lower' castes and classes are called, were not new to injustices of various kinds. Injustice, in varying degrees, existed earlier too. 'Injustice' was perhaps never defined as such by those who suffered its indignities. It is even possible that they took such treatment as would today be defined 'unjust'

---

[42]Lawrence James, *Raj: The Making and Unmaking of British India*, St. Martin's Griffin, 2000.

as their lot, without ever questioning it. It is possible that they did not and could not distinguish between what is 'justice' and what 'injustice'.

There are ancient oral children's rhymes which speak of the tyranny of the wealthy against the weak (from the latter's perspective), which indicates that they could not have been completely blind to the idea of 'injustice' but a critical assessment of these would reveal that the idea of 'injustice' emerges from the simple narration of the realities of the masses rather than being pointed out as such. 'Injustice' is not brought up as a concept.

Consider, for instance, the evocative, pathos-ridden, heartrending song, a lullaby for children, from the point of view of a farmer, whose paddy crops were destroyed by predatory birds:

> *Khoka Ghumolo*
> *Para Jurolo*
> *Borgi Elo Deshey*
> *Bulbuli Tey*
> *Dhan Kheyeychey*
> *Khajna Debo Kishey?*

The undated limerick translates roughly into:

> Little lad has fallen asleep
> And silence has descended on the neighbourhood
> Borgis* have reached our land
> But the Bulbuli bird
> Has eaten up the crop
> How will I pay the taxes?

(*Borgis were the Maratha invaders who plundered western Bengal for an entire decade from 1741–51. Known for their mercilessness in collecting taxes from impoverished villagers, the term became a generic name for all cruel tax collectors of the time.)

The hapless farmer trying to put her naughty son to sleep so that her neighbours too can get shut-eye, doesn't cry about the inherent injustice in her having to dole out the rent even though she has lost the means to do so. It comes through from the mere narration of her melancholy tale.

Two centuries after the Borgis committed their humanitarian crimes, a poem by Rabindranath Tagore, indicated how not much had changed for peasants.

In his poem 'Dui Bigha Jomi'[43] (Two Acres of Land) Tagore has a farmer decry, without comment, the loss of his land to a rich landlord with:

> Shudhu bigha dui
> Chhilo more bhui
> Aar shobi gechey riney
> Babu kohilen
> Bujhechho, Upen
> E jomi loibo kine.

In English it translates to:

> (I) had only a couple of acres
> of land left,
> the rest were all lost
> in repayment of loans.
> (But) Babu said,
> 'Listen, Upen,
> I'm going to buy up these (the two acres) from you.'

The plight of the poor and the economic deprivation that they are and have always been subjected to, is a reality that the sufferers themselves have no doubt always been aware of. However, that

---

[43]Rabindranath Tagore, 'Dui Bigha Jomi', (one of the poems from the collection *Kotha* and *Kotha O Kahini*) Visva Bharati University, originally published in 1900.

this was wrong, that it was 'discrimination'—is something that they perhaps did not recognize or if they did, they had no way of articulating it, far less rectifying it.

And it must be noted that the indiscretions of the rich against the poor doesn't even always come out from the narration of their own realities by the poor themselves but from the writings of the upper-classes and castes. While it is unclear who authored the lullaby above, for instance, Tagore who penned the other poem was the quintessential representative of the Bengali upper-class and caste. The poor were dependent always on the magnanimity of the rich for the mere recognition and articulation of the injustice and indignities that they suffered.

And those, like Tagore, who recognized and articulated the injustices against them, whose heart bled and who could pen their empathetic pain, as though in blood, were few and far between.

For the most part, the poor were, from time immemorial, at the mercy of the feudal lords and zamindaars who practised their tyranny over them as their birth right, unchecked by anything other than their own sense of right and wrong. And their conscience was governed by centuries of religious, social, political and cultural conditioning.

In the times of the medieval kings and queens, a ruler was rarely prevented from doing what he or she wanted to do by anything other than this said conscience. Governance and styles of governance were determined by personalities and diktats. If a king or queen was kind and merciful, just and benevolent, it was a characteristic trait, not a precondition to be a ruler. And even the kindest, most merciful, benevolent and just of the rulers could be—and largely *were*—set in their ways and upheld, or at any rate inadvertently adhered to, the social, religious, political and economic traditions that prevailed.

For the downtrodden, acquiescence has been the only option for the most part, until such time as protest, dissent or rebellion, either from within or from without (and frequently both), challenged status quo. A glaring example is ancient acceptance of the inequalities inherent in the hierarchical caste system which determined an individual's rights and entitlements, not to mention economic and social standing on the basis of birth. The caste system continues to exist even though different people during different periods in history questioned it. The Jain spiritual saint, Mahavira, who taught the principles of equality, is widely believed to be amongst the earliest to advocate its abolition. Its most prominent critics of the modern era have been Mohandas Karamchand Gandhi (Mahatma Gandhi) and Bhimrao Ramji Ambedkar (Babasaheb Ambedkar), the scholar, economist and social reformer who penned India's Constitution.

The caste system is said to have existed in Bengal since the time that Hinduism entered the land between 1500 BCE and 1200 BCE. Its presence, thus traced back to the sixteenth century BCE, makes it the oldest, most dominant religion of Bengal since the ancient times. In the seventh century CE, King Shashanka, who is credited with founding the Bengali calendar, built the first Hindu kingdom, Gaur (also known as Gauda), which had its capital Karnasubarna (in modern-day Murshidabad) and was a separate political set-up.

There are mentions of Hindu kings and queens in ancient Bengali literature and Hindu religious rituals such as pujas of different deities. The Pali epic poems dating back to the fifth century CE chronicles the journeys of legendary royal prince, Vijay Singha, whose grandmother was a royal princess—the daughter of the king of Vanga (Bengal) and Queen Mayavati, originally from Kalinga (Odisha). Accounts of seafarers such as the merchant Chand Saudagar suggest Bengali Hindus were adventurous and they travelled to other lands in the Far East where they established kingdoms and their religions. While Sinhalese, the language of Sri Lanka is supposed to have been founded by the descendants of Vijaya Singha who chased out the local Yakkas to rule Sri Lanka, according to a section of historians, Singapore is a former kingdom of Vijay Singha, the Bengali king Vanga's great grandson.

Moreover, that Bengali, which belongs to the Indo-Aryan group of languages, is the predominant language of the land is indication that Hinduism, the religion of the Indo-Aryans, had the most influence over Bengal even though Buddhism, Jainism and later Islam established itself, followed in time by Christianity, Judaism and even to a much lesser extent Sikhism.

Historians have pointed out that Hinduism has transformed over the years with the ruling elite, including priests and kings, often introducing rules and regulations and codes of conduct according to the needs of governance and economic, social, political or other compulsions of the time. Indeed, the *Manusmriti*, the ancient Sanskrit text which lays down the codes of conduct for Hindus, including their duties, rights, virtues and laws, is said to be a later documentation, not part of the original four *Vedas* and the *Upanishads*.

In the *Indian Empire: Its People, History and Products*, William Wilson Hunter[44] points out that the language of the text suggests that it is dated later than the late Vedic texts such as the *Upanishads*, which are dated around 500 BCE. Though there exists debate about the chronology of the texts of the *Manusmriti*, according to a section of scholars it is between 200 BCE and 200 CE, at least 300–500 years after the *Upanishads*. Patrick Olivelle in *Manu's Code of Law*[45] published by Oxford University Press, points out that the mention of gold coins as a fine, suggests that the text may date to the second or third century CE.

---

[44]William Wilson Hunter, *Indian Empire: Its People, History and Products*, Nabu Press, 2012.
[45]Patrick Olivelle, *Manu's Code of Law: A Critical Edition and Translation of the Manava-Dharmasastra (South Asia Research)*, Oxford University Press, 2010.

Though the caste system is believed to have arrived with the Aryans themselves around 1500 BC, it too is understood to have undergone innumerable changes in structure and practice.

Anath Taran Ghoshal, Hindu scholar and temple priest explains, 'While the four Vedas are considered the original, sacred texts which delineate the principles of Hinduism, down the ages, practices didn't always adhere strictly to the tenets but adapted according to the times.'[46]

Proponents of Hindu principles point out that in its original form, the caste system was more a social structure which, rather than being just a religious tenet, was intended to keep order in society through equal distribution of labour. While Brahmins were given the task of conducting religious services and achieving expertise in various fields of knowledge, Kshatriyas were put in charge of governance, defence, military and waging and fighting wars. The Vaishyas, on the other hand, were to look after the running of the economy, trade and business and the Sudras were a large group who were to manage the 'ground', which included everything from farming and food production to keeping things clean—whether sweeping the streets or cremating the dead and disposing off the bodies of those who were not worthy of a proper ritualistic burning such as those who committed suicide. (Those who died by suicide were considered unholy in Hinduism and their bodies were thrown into the river so that their sins could be washed away; they were treated like animals whose carcasses did not deserve the holy flames of fire.) Essentially the Sudras formed the menial workforce of society.

The assignation of specific duties to specific groups of people and ordaining that each group stick to their own duties was justified with the argument that it was the only way to achieve excellence in society. The Hindu philosophers argued that

---

[46]Anath Taran Ghoshal in an interview to the author.

mastery over any subject and expertise in any skill could only be achieved if knowledge of these subjects and skills are passed down from generation to generation. A Brahmin, by passing on his knowledge to the next generations, would eventually create masters of particular streams of learning for instance, and Sudra labourers by passing on his skills to the next generations, would eventually create a master workforce.

So, the four major categories roughly corresponding to the roles of priests, kings, traders and labourers, which forms the caste system, were likened by the ancient Hindu thinkers and philosophers to the human body in which every part was equally important and the head (the Brahmins) and the feet (the Sudras) each had its place and significance. This is found in the *Rig Veda*, one of the four Vedas.

Thus justified, the original theorists of the caste system (assuming that they were social thinkers and not ruling policy devisers who formulated regulations which were governed by vested interests) however, did not take into account that in practice it would be exposed to the frailties of human nature—greed for power, need for domination and abuse of entitlement.

Which, unfortunately, is how it unfolded in history.

'Domination and subjugation of the "lower" castes by the "upper" castes has been the chief characteristic of the caste system throughout its existence,' says Maroona Murmu.[47] 'The abuse of power by the upper-castes has been its mainstay,' she adds.

Though the caste system, with its inherent inequality, was present prior to the days of the British, it was the British, with their penchant for charting everything in detail, who put permanent seals on it. The *Manusmriti* was first translated into English in 1776 by Sir William Jones and was used to formulate the Hindu

---

[47] Maroona Murmu, Assistant Professor of history at Kolkata's Jadavpur University, author and a scholar on the subject of caste.

Law by the British colonial government, according to Donald R. Davis Jr.[48]

'The British highlighted caste divisions and meticulously recorded the different categories in writing, thereby putting a permanent stamp on a pre-existing and exploitative system which was thus far only an unwritten practice,' Murmu says. She points out that it was the British which first tagged an entire indigenous tribe, namely the 'Thuggees' as 'a criminal tribe'. The Thuggees (discussed in a later chapter) were tribal folk living in jungle villages, whom the British accused of being robbers and murderers and subjected them to witch-hunts, followed by persecution and incarceration.

The dalits, the adivasis (literally, 'original and indigenous dwellers'), the scheduled castes (SC), the scheduled tribes (ST) and other backward castes (OBC), all became a part of the lower rung of the caste system, whose newly re-emphasized 'lowly' status became vulnerable to attacks and abuses by the 'upper', contemptuous classes.

'The British legalized the caste system and to this day we are governed by and are suffering the indignities of their divisive laws,' Murmu says.

Pointing out the distinctions between 'varna' and 'jati', the two key components that constitute the caste system, Murmu explains that the former is the division of society according to occupation and the latter is the categorization of groups of people according to various factors, including their anthropological, ethnic or social lineage. While there are only four varnas, there are hundreds of jatis. Murmu says that during the British period when written records of different jatis were being created, there was a propensity to claim superior lineage and often, this determined the eventual

---

[48]Donald R. Davis Jr., *The Spirit of the Hindu Law*, Cambridge University Press, 2013.

categorization. 'The ranking ultimately depended on convincing the British rather than any legitimate basis,' says Murmu.

She has a unique perspective on the issue of caste. Not only has she delved deeply into the study of its dynamics, authoring books on the subject but she herself belongs to a scheduled tribe, one of the dalit (oppressed) or 'lower' castes. More than her extensive research on the topic, it is her empirical experience of living life as an 'oppressed' individual in her own country and being considered a 'lower' ranking human being by her own religion that has shaped her understanding of the discriminatory nature of the caste system. She can enumerate a long list of abusive behaviour towards her from fellow countrymen and women who targeted her for no other reason than that they were contemptuous of her.

An incident that took place on 2 September 2020 would possibly go down in history as an example of how caste prejudices and caste discrimination continued to thrive unabated even as late as the early twenty-first century. Murmu was at the receiving end of a volley of scathing remarks about her caste on the social media platform, Facebook, in response to a comment she had posted on her wall. She had advocated postponement of examinations because of a Coronavirus pandemic that had erupted earlier in the year. The deadly disease was still spreading and she suggested that life was more important than an academic year. 'One year cannot be more precious than someone's entire life,' she had written. What ensued was a barrage of criticism, led by a third-year student of a reputed women's college and followed by hundreds of other social media users, estimated to be at least 1,900 in number. Citing Murmu's caste and her background as a member of a scheduled tribe, the abusers ridiculed her and rubbished her remarks. The hate messages questioned her educational qualifications, cast aspersions on her eligibility to teach at a prestigious university and dismissed her views as a reflection of the 'demerits' of caste-based reservations in education and other spheres. 'Incompetent and undeserving people get ahead by taking undue advantage of the system of caste reservation in education,' read one of the messages, 'while the deserving people get left behind.' Murmu, hurt and humiliated, eventually filed a police complaint and a case of harassment against her tormentors.

Murmu says that discrimination on the basis of caste is driven home early in life for a dalit. Recalling another incident when she was in the second standard (in a Christian school in Calcutta where the medium of instruction was English), she says, 'One day, one of my teachers asked me, in front of the entire class, whether I was a scheduled tribe. I was caught completely off-guard. I had no idea. My family was progressive and these issues were never discussed. When I told her I did not know, she said, surprised, 'You don't know your own caste?' She asked me to find out from my older brother, who was in the same school. I ran to his classroom and called him out urgently. His class was on, but sensing the immediacy he asked to be excused and stepped out. He informed me that we belong to a scheduled tribe.'

The episode has scarred Murmu for life. Academically meritorious, she completed her degrees from India's premiere institutes including Presidency University, Kolkata and Jawaharlal Nehru University, Delhi, before starting work as assistant professor at Jadavpur University. 'But in the case of dalits and adivasis, achievements are rarely attributed to merit and more to the system of "quota", she rues.

Bengal, especially, the capital city Kolkata, which is considered the 'cultural capital of the country' is often perceived to be cosmopolitan, liberal, progressive and secular and discrimination on the basis of caste is generally frowned upon. This perception is attributed to several factors including, historically, it being the locus of the Bengal Renaissance and the country's first progressive, liberal and secular organizations and movements, which rejected regressive thinking. Leaders of the Bengal Renaissance advocated social unity and inclusivity, which influenced popular thinking, and their ideas were expected to have percolated down the generations and created mindsets of equality.

Other factors which gave rise to the perception that Bengalis are progressive and not casteist is based on the fact that from 1977 to 2011 it was the seat of power of a secular communist government which claimed to have had no place for discrimination based on caste.

Left politicians point out that the emphasis on class rather than caste during the Left rule in Bengal played a key role in re-establishing the state as liberal and secular in more recent times. 'The commitment of the Left Front government in standing by the working classes regardless of caste or creed, both in the rural and urban areas, precluded the exploitation of caste divisions,' explains Mohammad Salim, senior Communist Party of India (Marxist) leader and Politburo member. Indeed, the socio-economic class that constituted the Left electorate comprised and contained within it the dalits, adivasis, scheduled castes, schedule tribes and other backward classes, as well as underprivileged minorities.

Yet, occurrences such as those narrated by Murmu expose the ugly reality of the existence of caste discrimination even amidst the so-called 'educated' youth and, as pointed out earlier, even as late as early twenty-first century. Murmu says, she has grown up facing these types of discrimination.

One of the commonest forms of discrimination dalits and adivasis encounter is the presumption that SCs, STs and OBCs are somehow less qualified than those who do fall in the general quota because they often get admitted to educational institutions or find employment in government sectors through reservations. This is corroborated in the unabashed admission of a Calcutta schoolteacher who says, 'I always check the surname of a doctor before seeking an appointment and avoid those from SC, ST or OBC backgrounds. To me, those who get entrance into medical institutions through reservations will always be suspect.' A Calcutta gynaecologist, who belongs to an adivasi tribe, observes that such insults, though common, 'still sting'. She said that she had studied just as hard for her medical examinations as her classmates and passed with high marks but has found it difficult to shake-off the 'quota' tag.

A key indicator of the prevalence of caste discrimination is in the area of matrimony. Marriages, especially arranged ones, still have a checklist of the brides' and grooms' compatibility quotient, and topmost is whether their castes match. Even 'love' marriages are not spared. 'Marrying into a so-called lower caste is considered taboo even today and can cause considerable consternation in the family,' says Ipsita Mitra, who, being from an elite caste and a Kshatriya family, found it difficult to convince her parents that she wanted to marry a man from another caste. 'My parents didn't speak to me for months, but they gradually accepted the marriage, realizing I was marrying a good person.'

A host of other discriminatory behaviour in society points to the existence of caste barriers. 'It is still a practice in many upper-caste households not to drink water handed to them by a dalit or adivasi, far less eat together,' says Anath Taran Ghoshal, the Hindu scholar and temple priest. 'One is expected to do penance by fasting if he or she does break the rule.' Ghoshal, however, insists that Brahmins have a responsibility to ensure that they remain 'humble' and do not hurt or humiliate other castes. 'A true Brahmin is he who is generous, kind, knowledgeable and wise. If he is "the head" he knows the true value of the "feet" on which everything stands. That is where the tradition of bowing down the head to touch the feet comes from.'

A section of political commentators points out that politics in Bengal is also not free from the influence of caste. 'While compared to states like Uttar Pradesh and Bihar, the predominance of caste politics may be somewhat less, mostly because the emphasis on class takes care to cater to the same constituency,' observes Biswanath Chakraborty, political scientist and psephologist, 'but to say that Bengal has completely steered clear of caste politics is incorrect.'

An example is the Matua sect, which, once considered an untouchable caste, scattered across various regions of the land, was organized into a large community of Sudras by their leader, the spiritualist Harichand Thakur, and has since been considered a powerful influence in swinging the dalit vote.

Interestingly, while during the British era the caste system virtually became a vehicle of discrimination, another set of foreigners from Europe appeared to provide the dalits an escape route. Deprived of equality and dignity by their own people, their own religion and their own land and pigeonholed into these divisive categories by the meticulously written records of the British rulers, the dalits and other lower castes and classes turned to a new way of life when it presented itself. It promised them better prospects in terms of education.

These Europeans presented before the poor dalit people of Bengal an alternate way of life, in which caste hierarchies did not have to exist. In fact, in this new way of life, they could aspire to not just equality but also education. In this new way of life, they could also aspire to a better quality of life, which often meant just basic subsistence, elusive to many of them, living in the peripheries in penury. Not surprisingly, the promise of this new life was immensely attractive to those who felt they could free themselves from the bondages of social and religious inequality.

This group was a religious people from Europe who came to Bengal around the same time that the merchants of the East India Company did and they were the Christian missionaries.

The first Christian missionaries arrived in Bengal in the sixteenth century with the Portuguese establishing the first church in 1599, in a riverside village called Bandel, in modern day Hooghly district. Indeed, it was the Portuguese who is said to have first used the Spanish word 'casta' which means 'breed', 'lineage' or 'race' to describe the social and religious structure of the people of Bengal and the English term is derived from it.

But it was not a cakewalk for the Christians to set up their religious practices. They faced opposition not just from established religions of the land—at that time, other than Hinduism, being the Mughal period, Islam too reigned—but also from others.

It was a time of invasions and attacks and the church in Bandel was burnt down just 33 years after it was constructed, in 1632, when the Moors—a highly militarized Muslim group of warriors originating from Africa who had already conquered parts of Europe including Spain—plundered the region.

But the Christian missionaries were resilient and persevered in the face of every odd. And so, the first church of Bengal was rebuilt in 1660 and still stands, serene and silent, on the banks of the Ganges, as a witness to the times 400 years ago and is considered one of the holiest places of pilgrimages for Bengali Christians.

It however took a little more than another century and a half for the Christian missionaries to really establish themselves.

And when they did, indeed, they offered the poor people of the land an alternate way of life. But that new life came with a price. That price was called 'conversion'.

VII

MIND THE MISSIONARY, HAIL THE HUMANIST

'Oh Cloud, who has drifted here from a faraway sky/Go back home, I can hear your heart cry.'

—Kazi Nazrul Islam[49]

On a cold day in November 1793, a ship sailing from England had brought a 32-year-old man named William Carey, his 38-year-old wife Dorothy and their four sons, aged 11, eight, three and four months, to Bengal. Carey was a British Christian preacher who, a year earlier, had written a thesis paper entitled, 'An Enquiry into the Obligations of Christians to Use Means for the Conversion of Heathens' which, as the title suggested, was an exposition on the necessity of Christians to spread the message of Christ with the intention of converting non-Christians to Christianity. Not everyone agreed with him and after a meeting of preachers when he asked a rhetorical question about whether or not there was the need for him and others to head out to other parts of the globe to convert its inhabitants and save their souls, he was told by a senior minister, John Colette Ryland, 'Young man, sit down. When God pleases to convert the

---
[49]From the Nazrulgeeti, 'Megh, jao re phirey'.

heathen, He will do it without your aid or mine.'[50]

However, Carey felt compelled to practice what he preached and in spite of being discouraged by many, decided to move to India with the mission of not just converting locals but simultaneously imparting education and knowledge in various fields to poor children in British colonies.

Though he had completely made up his mind to go to India by February 1793, his wife, who was nearly nine months pregnant, was not convinced.

She and Carey were very different. She was illiterate and could not even sign her name, having simply entered a 'cross' in the marriage registration book. Carey, on the other hand, was a scholar, scientist and linguist, who went on to translate the Bible into several languages. He wrote essays, journals and books and also taught. Eventually he founded the first college and university in India, which was in Bengal's Srirampore, where he spent 40 years of his life until his death.

He had met Dorothy when he was in his late teens. He and her brother-in-law worked together and Willam spent a lot of time in their home.

Dorothy, or Dolly as she was called affectionately, had initially decided against accompanying her husband to India because she felt that the change would adversely affect the health of her still unborn child as well as her other three children. She had already lost two daughters at childbirth and infancy and she was wary. Initially, they agreed that William and their eldest son Felix would go to India and depending on the situation there—the ease of finding accommodation, healthcare facilities (which would be essential in a tropical country like India, the diseases of which

---

[50]Clifford G. Howell, *The Advanced Guard of Missions*, Pacific Press Publishing, 1912. (The reference can also be found in an extract from the book, available at https://www.wholesomewords.org/missions/bcarey10.html. Accessed on 21 July 2021.)

they were neither used to nor immune to)—they would return within a year and take the rest of the family back to India.

But the day before Carey was supposed to set sail, in April 1793, he and another missionary friend, Dr John Thomas, who had already been practicing medical missionary work in Calcutta but was in England to raise funds, convinced her to change her mind. Thomas himself was returning to India with his wife and daughter and explained to Dorothy that life was not all that difficult there. She finally relented but on the condition that her sister Kitty would accompany her to India. She agreed and they hurriedly packed their bags, readied the children and set sail for a foreign country where they had never set foot before.

The hardships of the sea journey began almost from the word go. The East India Company had apparently sent word to the captain of the ship that it would not be allowed to dock at the Calcutta port if it carried the missionaries because their unauthorized travel would violate regulations of trade monopolies. The ship, which had still not moved out of the UK seas, unloaded the family at the Isle of Wight from where the Careys finally managed to find a Dutch ship which agreed to transport them to India. That was in June 1793.

Before that, Dorothy had given birth to another son, her fourth. She was physically exhausted and psychologically too, as she, supposedly, never completely recovered from the emotional damage she suffered from the loss of her two daughters at childbirth. While her husband clearly loved her dearly—he did not want to leave without her—he was too busy with his work as a minister to help her with the daily household chores. She was saddled with the responsibility of raising the children virtually on her own though Carey did provide intellectual inputs.

Finding their footing in the new land during the first year after their arrival in Calcutta proved to be a more arduous journey for the Careys than even the sea voyage was. It entailed looking for a place to live and a job that would pay enough to support the family of six. Being a Baptist Christian, Carey faced hostility from non-Baptist missionaries in Calcutta. The East India Company, which had opposed his coming to Bengal in the first place, also refused to allow him to stay in Calcutta.

The Careys found themselves having to live in the remotest regions of Bengal including in the Sundarbans.

In the villages bordering tiger-roaming jungles and crocodile-infested rivers, they were exposed to mosquito bites and contracted malaria at regular intervals. Forced to drink contaminated water, they suffered from bouts of dysentery.

After a series of moves from one rented house to another, with the money they had brought draining away, Carey and his family found themselves pushed out to the north-eastern suburbs of Medinipur where Danish Church colonies offered him refuge. One of Dr Thomas's friends who owned indigo factories in the vicinity offered Carey work as a manager and though it provided a semblance of financial security as well as a house to live in and food on the table, monetary hardships faced by the large family never completely disappeared. The health of the children, who found it difficult to acclimatize themselves to the vastly changed environment, had deteriorated. Within six years, their son Peter died of dysentery. This compounded by the other stresses, eventually led Dorothy to suffer a nervous breakdown which, according several historians, was so severe that it bordered on 'lunacy'.

According to records of contemporaries, Dorothy had fits of madness when she raved and ranted and often publicly cursed her husband, holding him responsible for her sufferings. She had also grown suspicious and would accuse him of having romantic affairs. A few months before her son died, her sister had left them to get married to an official of the East India Company and Dorothy had no one to turn to during moments of anguish.

Friends of William had advised him to put her in a mental asylum. But he, afraid that they would treat her badly, refused to do so and instead, during her frenzied fits, kept her locked up in a room in their house.

It is said that the mad wife confined to an attic in *Jane Eyre*, the classic 1847 novel by Charlotte Bronte, was inspired by Dorothy, as the Careys' story had become well-known even in faraway UK.

Dorothy died in 1807 and William made the following diary entry, 'Tuesday, Dec. 8, 1807. This evening Mrs Carey died of the fever under which she has languished some time. Her death was a very easy one; but there was no appearance of returning reason, nor any thing that could cast a dawn of hope or light on her state.'

The tragic story of William and Dorothy Carey has intrigued many historians, biographers and other writers. They have taken extreme and opposite stances as well as the entire gamut of nuanced ones in-between about how and why Carey continued to pursue his goal of establishing his faith, undeterred by his dysfunctional, virtually debilitating family life. Several of these took a sympathetic view of the tireless crusader of Christianity and vilified the woman who failed to be an equal and able companion to the great man. One biographer wrote of the 'unlettered' and 'unimaginative' peasant woman who 'possessed neither the nerve nor the strength for hardship.'

But—and thankfully—volumes have also been written on how Dorothy was a victim of her circumstances. These point out how she was virtually forced to uproot herself from familiar territory and thrown into an unknown land, where she was subjected to the endurance of extreme poverty, disease, death and uncertainty. She had found herself in an impossible situation, torn by love for and duty towards her husband, which is why she eventually followed him to India, and the misgivings she had about moving lock, stock and barrel to a foreign country and an alien culture from which she never returned.

A year after Dorothy's death in 1808, William married again. His second wife, Charlotte Rhumohr, was from the Danish mission and is said to have been his 'intellectual equal' unlike poor Dorothy. She and William were said to have been besotted with each other, exchanging letters of how much they missed each other when they were away from one another on work. However, 13 years after their marriage, Charlotte, who was the same age as William, too died. William married a third time—this time his bride was nearly 17 years younger than him and was more a nurse to him in his old age than a companion—but two years after the wedding, William died.

Carey's personal life becomes significant in the context of his enormous accomplishments in the public domain. How he managed to achieve what he did—he is credited with successfully establishing the missionary movement in Bengal and subsequently the rest of India—in spite of such debilitating domestic strife is a matter of great amazement. He may have been so focused on his mission that the troubles in his private life did not deter him from pursuing his goal. Or it is even likely that he immersed himself in his missionary work with almost superhuman spiritual gusto to escape his deeply troubled reality.

He started schools in the villages of Bengal to teach reading, writing, mathematics, science and accounting, over and above the principles of Christianity, to impoverished children. However, while the children of the poor were the main beneficiaries of the missionary schools, the lure of English education brought in students from the upper-classes too. Carey opened colleges and universities for theological and other studies. He established the first ever degree-awarding college in Bengal's Srirampur—Srirampur College—which became a model for future colleges, universities and other academic institutions. At the same time, he produced copious written works on subjects as varied as science and spirituality. A polyglot, he learnt several Indian languages, including Bengali, Sanskrit and Hindi and translated the Bible into these. Carey was a social reformer in other ways too. Appalled by the tradition of 'sati', he led a movement to have it banned. Indeed, he was amongst those European social thinkers whose contribution to the shaping of modern Bengali society cannot be overstated. The 'father of missionary activities' in India, as he came to be known, instituted the educational systems which eventually helped produce many of the intellectual minds that led Bengal and subsequently the rest of India into the modern age.

Converting people to Christianity did, however, remain the main goal of the missionaries and, in 1800, the first recorded baptism of a Hindu took place when the teachings of Jesus were imparted to Krishna Pal, a carpenter, who had gone to Carey's doctor friend John Thomas for fixing a broken arm. Pal was told that while physically he would be healed in no time, it was his spiritual mending which was a matter of concern. The Christian missionaries convinced him that the purging of sins and attaining salvation of the soul was as important as fixing dislocated joints, if not more, and that it could only be done if he embraced the Christian faith. Pal was moved by the selfless work of the missionaries and the equality that existed in their society, and readily gave up his caste. William Carey baptized him in the Ganges and from then on Pal devoted his time in helping the missionaries in their myriad endeavours.

When Pal died in 1822, at 58, he had accumulated a body of writings, including hymns dedicated to Christ that were translated from Bengali into English by Carey and other prominent missionaries of the time, namely Joshua Marshman and William Ward. 'The Shipwrecked Sinner Looking to Jesus', 'Oh, Thou My Soul, Forget No More' and 'Salvation by the Death of Jesus' were amongst his most acclaimed and these were published in British journals and sung during mass and at funerals.

Pal had dined with the foreigners publicly, which was a taboo for Hindus at that time. Others too followed in his footsteps and renounced their castes to embrace Christianity. Though initially there were fewer 'conversions' from the upper-castes than the lower castes, children from the upper-classes and castes, as stated earlier, too were sent to Christian missionary schools because of the superior quality of the education they offered.

Raja Ram Mohan Roy was one such pupil. He was a product of the times, an era which was becoming increasingly 'progressive'. There are uncanny similarities—and differences—between William Carey (17 August 1761–9 June 1834) and Raja Ram Mohan Roy (22 May 1772–23 September 1833). Both had unhappy marital lives. Both married three times. Both of their first and second wives died before them and the third wives of both outlived them. But while Carey was born in Paulerspury, England and died in Srirampur, India, Roy was born in Radhanagar, India and died in Bristol, England.

What make these coincidences in their personal lives remarkable is that in their public lives too, the two of them represented a commonality: both were pioneering social reformers of the late eighteenth and early nineteenth centuries, whose initiatives changed Bengal forever. Both founded iconic educational institutions including schools and colleges. Indeed, the similarities between Carey and Roy were seemingly endless. While Carey became known as the 'father of the missionary movements in India', Roy became known as the 'father of the Bengal Renaissance', the cultural, literary, social and religious movement that shook up the status quo in every sphere of life in Bengal. The most essential difference between Roy and Carey, however, was that Roy was amazingly broad-minded and liberal compared to Carey who was rather rigid in his insistence on the need for religious conversion. Having said that, Carey, it must be remembered, believed that he was doing his utmost best for the salvation of the souls of the people to whom he dedicated his life; enough for him to merit a comparison with one of Bengal's most iconic leaders, who Roy was.

Though Carey was 11 years older than Roy, their lives overlapped. And when Carey came to India in 1793 as a 32-year-old preacher, Roy was a 21-year-old student from an upper-class Bengali family, who was imbibing the changing cultural atmosphere around him.

Like most young adults, Roy was revolting against everything that his parents were trying to teach him. In Bengali or Indian culture, obedience to parents, teachers or the elderly in general was the norm. Hinduism especially, as evident from ancient literary traditions, advocated educational models, (known as gurukuls) in which the pupils or disciples would be required to unconditionally surrender themselves to the elders including parents, grandparents, aunts and uncles, not to mention teachers and instructors. But it must also be remembered that those were the days when adulthood was achieved at a very early age leaving little time for the kind of youthful rebelliousness that is associated with children, especially teenagers and young adults of the twentieth and twenty-first centuries.

Ram Mohan Roy's first marriage took place when he was just nine years old and he became a widower just a year later. Child marriage was prevalent in those days and often children as young as newborns were made to wed each other if their families decided on such a match. However, the bride was almost always younger than the groom and it was a matter of great shame for a girl's family not to be able to marry their daughters off. The inability of a family to marry off their girls was stigmatized because it was an indication of either the family's poverty—dowry, given as 'gift' to the groom's family was an integral part of marriages—or their daughter's lack of beauty. Even a girl as young as nine years of age could be considered to be a burden on their family and, such was the disgrace of having unmarried girls in the family that, if a match could not be found for a girl by the age of 12 or 13, she could even be forced to marry an old man on his deathbed. But her plight did not end there. When the aged man died, which he sometimes did even as the marriage ceremony was taking place, with the divine mantras still being chanted, the young bride would be expected to jump into the funeral pyre of the dead man and become a 'sati' or a 'pure wife'. In most cases, the man would have more than one wife as polygamy was not illegal in Hindu society in those days.

Though Raja Ram Mohan Roy was from an orthodox Hindu family, he was a representative of the changing cultures in Bengal in which the youth was influenced by the European values that had established themselves in the land for over two decades. From an early age, he innately questioned his family's dogmatic stances on religion, traditions and norms. And his own tragic personal experiences shaped the gender views which would see him take on and challenge prevalent practices that discriminated against women, like polygamy, dowry, sati, child marriage and the denial of property rights of daughters.

Born in a riverine village in Radhanagar, in Bengal's Hooghly District, his parents were pious—devotees of Lord Vishnu and Lord Shiva. The fact that they belonged to two different Hindu sects posed difficulties for young Roy over and above the mental conflicts that he was already subjected to because of the environment of clashing Indian/Bengali and European sensibilities in which he was growing up. His father, Ram Kanto Roy, being a Vaishnavite (follower of the philosophy that Lord Vishnu was the supreme creator of the universe and life) taught him that the principles of divinity were those which could only be manifested through worldly pursuits. Lord Vishnu and his wife or consort, Goddess Lakshmi, were to be worshipped for wealth and well-being and through the fulfilment of the duties of life—including marriage, childbearing, childrearing and work, etc.—the attainment of heaven was to be achieved. Historians have observed that these early teachings had prepared Roy to embark on the 'laukik' (earthly) and he set out to prepare himself for a career as a clerk (with the British East India Company) and subsequently, as a public officer (for the Company government) who could work hard and earn money.

On the other hand, his mother, Tarini Devi, was a Shaivite (follower of the philosophy that Lord Shiva was the creator of the universe and life) and she inculcated the principles of higher ideals and scholarly pursuits in her son, teaching him to believe in transcending the world and attaining the state, in the heavens above the Himalayan mountains, where dwelt Lord Shiva and his consort or wife Goddess Parvati. One of Roy's biographers, H.D. Sharma, points out that Roy was 'torn between the two parental ideals from early childhood' and 'vacillated the rest of his life, moving from one to the other and back.'[51]

It is likely that he was an extraordinary accomplisher who was able to straddle both. Just because his feet were firmly planted on the ground when it came to dealing with practical matters of public administration did not mean his head was in the clouds when it came to ruminating about the abstract.

In fact, Raja Ram Mohan Roy had a great gift. He synthesized the different ideals floating about in the atmosphere of the time to come up with entirely new concepts that have endured the test of time, spanning no less than two centuries, to become truths: religious truths.

And the ambit of his work ranged from rooting out social evils from the ground to planting theories about ultimate good—or God—in the minds and collective consciousness of Bengali society. He founded philosophies that discoursed on the nature

---

[51] H.D. Sharma, *Raja Ram Mohan Roy: The Renaissance Man*, Rupa & Co., 2002.

of the unknown and applied them to the practical world of the known.

In 1828, Roy founded the Brahmo Samaj, an alternate religion which propounded the idea that there was only one Supreme Being which, in Hinduism was Brahma, in Islam, Allah and in Christianity, God. 'There is only one God,' he had famously declared. 'None equals Him. He has no end. He is present in all living beings.'

He was 56 by this time and clearly, he had already traversed the ways of the world. Indeed, the Braho Samaj was a culmination of years of deliberation, debate and discussion amongst the thinkers of the time. Roy and his contemporaries had earlier formed themselves into a group, called Brahmo Sabha (Sabha meaning congregation) which regularly met and exchanged ideas and views. It comprised the day's progressive people—intellectuals, journalists, scholars, writers, artists and scientists.

Their minds and consciousness were ignited by the crosscurrents of cultural changes charging through Bengal. Theirs was the first fusion generation. They grew up in Bengali households but their government was British. The lessons they learnt at home were challenged by the teachings that were imparted to them at the schools they attended. The values they inculcated were traditional but the thoughts they imbibed were laced with modernity.

The Bengali youth of this period was caught between two worlds. They imbibed and respected their own traditions and yet they admired and aspired to the culture of the Europeans. They despised the malaise that invaded their own society—especially caste and gender discriminations prevalent in their religious practices—but they also equally resented the subjugation of their people by the foreign invaders. They eschewed the worship of hundreds of gods and goddesses but they also rejected the domination of hundreds of their own men and women by outsiders. They embraced the European values of reason over superstition but they also held steadfastly onto the idea that reason and religion were not mutually exclusive just as much as superstition and spirituality were not one and the same thing.

The Brahmo Sabhaites argued, and eventually concluded, that every religion was a different path to one destination. Every culture in the world had some good and some bad. The society that embraced the good and eschewed the bad would become the exemplary civilization. The Brahmo Sabhaites argued that if the East was emulated for its spiritual knowledge and the West for its practical know-how, it would lead to progress not just in the material world but eventually in the divine sphere. Indeed, Brahmo Samaj was the 'ideal' religious and social treatise.

Raja Ram Mohan Roy was not an agnostic or atheist as some orthodox Hindus of the day called him because of his strong opposition to a host of religious practices of the day. He belonged to a family of orthodox Brahmins but other than his parents' deep faith in religion, he himself clearly believed in the idea of a source, or Source, from where life sprung.

Indeed, religion at that time in Bengal determined social life and it was ingrained in the individuals who lived in those times. And so no social theory could or would be devoid of its influence.

But Brahmoism, as it gradually came to be called, was as much an exposition about the nature of the divine as it was about society and conduct in all its aspects, political, economic, cultural, etc.

Like Hinduism, or really all religions across the world which determine ways of life and conduct, Brahmoism too laid down a path which could be followed by those who embraced it.

Only, this path was not forced on the people as the one road to the ultimate destination, whatever that may be. It did not advocate restrictive norms which tied people to duties assigned by their caste. Nor did it aim to convert people.

At the highest level it was about a divine acceptance of all religions. But it also had a practical dimension as it established the concepts of peace, tolerance and in essence, equality. It shook up Hindu society and the ideas of caste hierarchy. It also contradicted Christian ideas of conversion and the notion that salvation could only be attained by an individual if he or she surrendered to a Christian God.

Though they had earlier worked together and fought against orthodox Hindu practices such as dowry, polygamy, child marriage and sati, Raja Ram Mohan Roy and William Carey eventually fell out because of their differences. While Carey was critical of social injustices in Hindu society, he did not share Roy's views about the needlessness of Christian conversion. Roy was not convinced that Christianity was the only path to salvation. Carey was.

Roy's opinions were shaped, as stated earlier, as much by his family's teachings (with his father and mother imparting different philosophies) as by the lessons he was learning during formal training from European instructors. But his own life experiences were perhaps his greatest influencers.

Roy, as mentioned earlier, was married at nine and his wife died within a year. To be called a 'widower' or its Bengali equivalent, at the tender age of 10, must have been psychologically damaging. Though the social stigma of being a 'widower' was much less severe in that era, than that of being a widow, judging by Ram Mohan's tireless struggle to have the practice of child marriage abolished later in his life, he was deeply disturbed by his companion's death. The depth of his passion for doing away with the practice indicates that it did not originate in a vacuum.

There are those who are dumbfounded spectators in the midst of the outpouring of grief, distress and sorrow around them. There are those who cry, howl heart-wrenchingly or weep, often not comprehending the depth, the immensity of death or the magnitude of its meaning. There are those who silently acquiesce, as only children can, intuitively acknowledging that it is pointless to do anything but accept inevitability.

Here is an account from an author who lost his mother when he was two years old and was subsequently raised by his paternal grandmother. Born in 1929 in Giridih, now in Jharkhand, in a wealthy Bengali zamindaar family, he recalls the cold winter of 1931, when, he thought, she lit up briefly like the last flicker of a dying flame.

He recalled his feelings thus:

> I have sketchy recollections of her as always lying down. Later I learnt she had contracted tuberculosis and was on her deathbed. I remember feeling sad. One day she came out into the verandah to sit in the sun. I can't remember her face but she was like a shadow. In my fading memory the landscape of the grey courtyard of the old house with its cement-coloured stairs was like a sepia-toned canvas fraying at the edges. It was before the time when photographs were common and if the recollections are determined by any outside influence, it could be descriptions of her from my father and grandmother and other relatives, though that was rare. And so, this must be a very individual memory unclouded by any other external factor. I recall feeling ecstatic that she was up and have vivid memories of crying out in delight, *'Ma, bhalo, Ma? Ma, bhalo, Ma?'* (Ma, good, Ma? Ma, good, Ma?).

He didn't remember the exact moment of her death. The adults must have shielded him from witnessing the preparations of taking her to the burning pyre.

That was nearly 100 years ago. Well, 88 years ago.

From those who as children lost their closest, one can still try to catch a glimpse into what went through their tender minds when faced with death.

In *Pather Panchali* (*The Song of the Road*), Satyajit Ray's 1955 cinematic adaptation of Bibhuti Bhushan Bandyopadhyay's 1929 novel of the same name, the little boy Apu, who has just lost his beloved sister Durga to a fever, doesn't cry. He looks stunned as he instinctively rushes to where she used to store her secret girly belongings. He fishes out an item that he knew she had lifted from a neighbour and had hidden it, and runs out of the door of their hut before chucking it into the pond.

When Apu's wife died—as depicted in Ray's sequel, *Apur Sansar* (*The World of Apu*)—he was so heartbroken that he only found solace in spirituality. But when Apu married he was no longer a child.

When Ram Mohan Roy's wife died, he was. And, if one may evoke the aphorism 'fact is stranger than fiction', he was not a character in a novel or the protagonist of a film but a person who lived and faced death.

How did he, as a mere child, confront his harsh reality? How did he, as a chit of a boy, deal with mortality?

Were he and his wife close? Were they dear to each other? Were they friends? Did they play together? The implications of conjugal life may not have been completely understood by either him or his young bride at that time. But children were expected by society to consummate marriages.

Ram Mohan Roy must have questioned society's cruel imposition of such an enormous responsibility on his young bride. And he must have questioned society's callous imposition of such an enormous tragedy on his young mind. It scarred him for life.

Roy was married off again at age 10 and he had two sons with his second wife. He continued to be haunted by his unbridled hatred for social injustices, especially its treatment of girls and women. Other than child marriage, the practices of polygamy, dowry and most importantly, of the barbaric burning alive of girls and women at the funeral pyres of their husbands, horrified and repelled his sensibilities. He was driven by a compulsion to exorcise these social evils. Eventually he was able to do so.

Though his father was an orthodox Hindu Brahmin, they were also wealthy landlords who could afford to and as was the trend in upper-classes at that time, did spend money on the education of their sons. Moreover, both of his parents wanted him to pursue academics and for that, they were even willing to let him leave home. While travel on account of trade was by then common in Bengal, it was mostly the merchants or business classes which engaged in it. The upper-class, especially upper-caste Bengalis, still had reservations about foreign tours because they were usually sticklers for following Hindu religious customs such as consuming pure food untouched by lower castes and not eating beef and other foods deemed unclean, and felt that during journeys abroad these could be compromised. But aversions to sending their sons out to foreign countries, especially to Britain, gradually began to dissipate when English education became an aspiration for these families. The British East India Company was ruling Bengal and getting a job with the Company was considered a lucrative option by most Bengali babu classes. While traditionally the womenfolk, especially the mothers, still hated the idea of parting with their dear sons, even if for a short duration, they too reluctantly let go. Roy's mother too was protective and possessive though she too eventually allowed him to leave home. But that was only up to Patna, in Bihar. He went there to study Persian, Urdu and Arabic in a madrassa.

Roy had received his primary schooling in Bengali and studied Sanskrit in his village. Though English education, as mentioned earlier, was in demand for employment with the Company, the influence of the Mughal Period had still not completely waned. Islamic languages were the language of the courts at the centre in Delhi and learning these languages was considered important. After receiving training in Patna, during which he not only mastered the languages but read literature and scriptures including the *Holy Quran*, he began to write journals and articles in these. He subsequently went to Kashi in Benaras (Varanasi), to study more advanced Sanskrit after he completed reading the ancient Hindu scriptures including the *Vedas* and *Upanishads*.

Roy learnt English when he was 22 years old. But he was quick to pick it up and wrote, read and spoke fluently in no time, gaining so much command over the language that he soon became a scholar of English literature. Being a voracious reader who was hungry for knowledge, he soon went through the works of philosophers, especially Aristotle and Euclid, in their English translations.

Ram Mohan Roy's erudition was unmatched even for the times, which gradually came to be known as the era of Bengal Renaissance, during which tremendous churning was taking place in terms of intellectual progress, growth in education in the sciences, mathematics, literature and the arts.

In fact, it was Raja Ram Mohan Roy himself, who is credited with making all the churning possible with his indefatigable pursuit of social change, the key components of which were advancements in education and the upholding of rights of people, especially gender rights of women.

His zeal to redress wrongs and create a just society, combined with his intellect, was a potent mix that eventually resulted in him gaining the respect of his British employers and, as a result, influence, power and wealth. But for Roy, these were not attributes that were to be used for his personal goals. He used his influence not just to fight for social reforms but to ensure that lasting, legal policy changes were effected so that these changes could be made permanent. It was because of his relentless lobbying that the East India Company Governing Council eventually banned the practice of 'suttee' or sati. Roy travelled to England in 1829 as a representative of the then Mughal king. In fact, it was the

Mughal king who had conferred the title of 'Raja' on Roy. In England, Roy was given a warm welcome by King William IV. However, he fell severely ill after contracting a fever while visiting friends in Bristol, where he eventually died.

VIII

GENESIS AND THE GENERATIONS: THEY COME AND THEY GO

'Why hang'st thou lonely on yon withered bough?/ Unstrung forever, must thou there remain;/ Thy music once was sweet—who hears it now?/ Why doth the breeze sigh over thee in vain?'

—Henry Derozio[52]

Henry lay dying on a Calcutta bed though he was only 22. Cholera made no distinction between old and young. It was the fatal disease of the century, having, reportedly, originated in Bengal in 1831 and then crossed the seas and travelled the roads into Europe and other parts of the world.

Even in faraway London, cholera, which was initially believed to be an airborne disease, claimed over 50,000 lives. Though at first, people living in congested areas—slums, which grew as a result of rapid industrialization, with their squalid unhygienic conditions—contracted the killer bacteria, it soon spread to the upper middle-class houses. The fear of the deadly disease reaching their own doorsteps eventually prompted parliamentarians of England to wrack their brains to try to devise a solution.

---

[52]From Derozio's poem 'The Harp of India'.

A gentleman named Edwin Chadwick first introduced the idea that getting rid of the sewerages, which had cropped up unplanned around the city, by flushing these out and channelling the waste water into the Thames River would bring an end to the epidemic. However, since London's central river was also the main source of drinking water for its population, the problem exacerbated. Incidents of cholera doubled and even tripled, leading another environmental expert, Dr John Snow, to conclude that cholera was not airborne at all, but waterborne.

But long before the fight to discover a cure for cholera had even begun, poor Henry of Calcutta had fallen into its deathly grip. As life gradually ebbed out of him, did he glance outside, following the last rays of the Calcutta sunlight filtering in through chinks in the windows and wonder why fate had dealt such a cruel blow to him? At the time of his death, would he have harboured hatred for those who did not let him speak his truth? Those who tried to throttle his voice when he was alive? Or had he slipped too deeply into unconsciousness to recall or even care? We will never know. One thing is for sure, however, and that is, that Henry Louis Vivian Derozio would not have known that one day he would be celebrated for all those things he was condemned for in his lifetime and all those things he had thought he had left unfinished.

Each individual who has ever walked the face of the earth has unwittingly played some kind of a role in shaping the future. But there are those who, often unwittingly, achieve extraordinary success in catalyzing change. They may not consider it 'success' even but they nevertheless create paths where there were none. They divert the course of the river. They turn tides. They bring about sea changes. And what they do leaves footprints in the flow of time. These changes are so significant that they shake up status quo forever and alter the course of human history.

Henry Louis Vivian Derozio was such an entity.

He belonged among that late eighteenth and early nineteenth-century breed of individuals who were born with iconoclastic ideas, questioning minds and the innate propensity to want to turn traditions—especially those they considered 'oppressive'—on their head, inside out and upside down.

Shaking up society to the core, they tried to throw out outdated notions of caste and class. They chased away, years of gender discrimination and cruel and barbaric rituals pertaining to the treatment of women in society, especially in marriage such as the prevalent practice of 'sati' mentioned earlier. They could not comprehend, far less accept, the injustice underlying a social structure in which multitudes lived deprived of basic subsistence while others wallowed in plenitude. Therefore, they advocated and tried to bring about equality.

Even in the face of what looked like insurmountable obstacles, these social thinkers, by the courage of their conviction, were able to successfully usher in reforms in almost every field, from religion to education. Because of them laws were formed—laws that impacted every aspect of life, whether social, political or economic. And whatever hurdles these individuals confronted and whatever fate their efforts met, eventually, almost invariably, their endeavour resulted in an overhaul of systems. If not immediately, definitely eventually.

Indeed, of these 'thought leaders' as they have since come to be known, Henry Louis Vivian Derozio's name figures most prominently. The poetry he wrote from a very early age revealed his deep sensitivity to the predicaments of the common people, especially the poor, and his deep love for his land, whose boundless beauty inspired him.

He was barely 14 when he wrote his poem, the 'Fakeer of Jangheera'. These lines from that poem reveal what has been considered his precocity and genius:

> Mungheera's rocks are hoar and steep
> And Ganges' wave is broad and deep
> And round that island rock the wave
> Obsequious comes its feet to lave.

Though academically brilliant, he had dropped out of school, David Drummond's Dharmatala Academy in Calcutta, to work in his father's business. Afterwards, he went to Bhagalpore (now Bhagalpur) in Bihar where the indigo plantations were growing as a trade. There, he was so taken in by the breathtaking scenery of the Ganges that he penned down the above lines.

Another poem, 'To India, My Native Land' reflects his deep patriotism:

> My country! In the days of glory past
> A beauteous halo circled round thy brow
> And worshipped as deity thou wast
> Where is that glory, where is that reverence now?
> Thy eagle pinion is chained down at last
> And grovelling in the lowly dust art thou
> Thy minstrel hath no wreath to weave for thee
> Save the sad story of thy misery.

If Raja Ram Mohan Roy was considered the father of the Bengal Renaissance, Derozio is credited with injecting into the movement the ammunition that would keep it fired. An entire generation of Bengali intellectual youth were inspired and influenced by his ideas and his teachings, which eventually paved the way for unprecedented changes in Bengali and subsequently Indian society.

Born nearly three and a half decades after Raja Ram Mohan Roy, on 18 April 1809 in Calcutta, Derozio was half-European and half-Indian. His father was Portuguese and his mother, Bengali.

It must be pointed out here that at that time, the phrase that was used commonly to describe people of mixed (that is part-European and part-Indian/Asian) parentage was 'Eurasian' and the phrase 'Anglo-Indian' applied to Eurasians who were of British and Indian descent and also to people of British origin who had made India their residence. This latter category included mainly the British officials of the East India Company, soldiers of the British naval and armed forces, Christian missionaries from Britain and others. The Oxford English Dictionary, in fact, defines as 'Anglo-Indian' three categories of people and they include those of 'mixed British and Indian parentage, of Indian descent but born or living in Britain or of English descent or birth but living or having lived in India'. Today the phrase 'Anglo-Indians' refers most specifically to the first category or the people who descended from both British and Indian ancestry.

In *Christmas in Calcutta: Anglo-Indian Stories and Essays*,[53] the author points out certain common characteristics of Anglo-Indians. They speak English as their mother tongue, are Christians and they are descended from both European and Indian ancestry.

Eurasians and Anglo-Indians came into existence and evolved over the three or four centuries since the European—British, Dutch, French and Portuguese—merchants started trading and settling in India. There was a disproportionately smaller number of European women in India compared to the large numbers of men. They, therefore, started to marry local women.

Historian Michael Herbert Fisher in *Counterflows to Colonialism: Indian Travellers and Settlers in Britain 1600-1857*[54] and 'Excluding and Including "Natives of India": Early Nineteenth-Century British-Indian Race Relations in Britain'[55], documents the

---

[53] Robyn Andrews, *Christmas in Calcutta: Anglo-Indian Stories and Essays*, Sage Publications, 2013.
[54] Michael Herbert Fisher, *Counterflows to Colonialism: Indian Travellers and Settlers in Britain 1600-1857*, Permanent Black, 2005.
[55] Michael Herbert Fisher, 'Excluding and Including "Natives of India": Early-

period of the British East India Company rule in India and the early days of interracial marriages and unions between British men and Indian women, throwing light on how the unique ethnic group of Eurasians, known as the Anglo-Indians, gradually came to be. He points out that during the British East India Company rule in India in the late eighteenth and early nineteenth centuries, it was not at all uncommon for British officers and soldiers to marry local women and have Eurasian children 'owing to a lack of British women in India'. According to him, the Company, though not without some initial apprehensions, endorsed a policy of local marriages for its soldiers. In 1688, the board of directors in London had written, in an advisory to its Council at Fort St. George (Chennai, then Madras):

> Induce by all means you can invent our souldiers (sic) to marry with Native women, because it will be impossible to get ordinary young women, as we have before directed, to pay their own passages although Gentlewomen sufficient do offer themselves.

The Company's officials were concerned that if its employees and soldiers were not married it would lead to 'wickedness'. It was thought that married men with family ties would be more likely to be better behaved than bachelors.

The historian points out, however, that though not uncommon,

> In practice only a small minority of British residents married whilst in India and the poorer they were the less likely were they to marry. It seems that in Bengal between 1757 and 1800 only one in four British covenanted civil servants, one in eight civilian residents and one in 10 army officers married

---

Nineteenth-Century British-Indian Race Relations in Britain.' *Comparative Studies of South Asia, Africa and the Middle East*. DOI: 10.1215/1089201x-2007-007, 2007.

there. Amongst military and other ranks the proportion was between one in 15 and one in 45.

According to the historian, the population growth also resulted from unwed unions. It is noted,

> Many children were born to unofficial partnerships: 54% of the children baptized at St. John's, Calcutta between 1767 and 1782 were Anglo-Indian and illegitimate. British women of good social standing were scarce; in 1785 surgeon John Stewart wrote to his brother from Cawnpore (modern day Kanpur): 'Many of the women here are mere adventuresses from Milliners shops on Ludgate Hill and some even from Covent Garden and Old Drury (well-known areas of prostitution in late 18th century London). They possess neither sentiment nor education, and are so intoxicated by their sudden elevation, that a sensible man can only regard them with indignation and outrage.

Though the burgeoning of the Eurasian community became a social reality, interestingly, the progenies of mixed marriages and unions faced various social stigmas from both the Indians and the British. As children they often found their roots questioned and as adults, they found it difficult to get employment.

While the Hindus, especially of the upper-castes, shunned them as 'impure', the Europeans, especially the upper-classes, considered them 'hybrids'. They considered them to be 'neither here nor there' as an Anglo-Indian descendent jokingly describes how her ancestors were perceived during that period. Nor was the stigmatization and ostracism limited to mere social unacceptability.

Even as late as 1813, Eurasians were not included in the laws, rules and regulations that the British had set up for itself, namely, the act called Regulation VIII of 1813. At the same time, these Eurasians were denied any categorization as far as Hindu castes was concerned. The existing Muslim laws loosely governed them but these were not formalized. The result was that the Eurasians lived in Bengal and other parts of India almost without any kind of legal or social status.

It goes without saying that their economic conditions too reflected this social and legal neglect and the community was relegated to the peripheries, often living in derelict slums and squatters.

And yet, because most of the Eurasians, thanks to their European heritage, did attend Christian schools and had access to excellent academic education, they were highly knowledgeable and qualified. Many scholars and educators of that period were from the Eurasian community. They were sought after by educational institutions to impart teachings in the fields of religion, philosophy, mathematics and the sciences, not to mention the languages, including of course, English.

Gradually, realizing their own worth and increasingly questioning the treatment that was meted out to them in spite of their importance, if not indispensability in society, the Eurasians took to rectifying the injustices.

In the 1820s, a few members of Calcutta's Eurasian community got together to form what they called the 'East Indian Committee' the chief aim of which was to fight for the rights of their people. They penned down a series of suggestions on how to improve their lot and published a series of pamphlets. One of the earliest such documents was an 1821 pamphlet entitled 'Thoughts on How to Better the Conditions of Indo-Britons' by a writer who used the name 'Practical Reformer'.[56] It urged Eurasians to overcome their own sense of restrictions and advocated that they join mainstream activities such as trade.

---

[56]James Reginald Maher, *These Are the Anglo Indians*, Simon Wallenberg Press, 2007; originally published in 1962 by Swallo Press.

However, a later pamphlet entitled, 'An Appeal on Behalf of Indo-Britons'[57] created more impact in changing societal attitudes towards Eurasians. It was one of the most important treatises of the time by the Eurasian committee that fought to have the laws amended in order to include the community in its ambit. A petition demanding that the Eurasians' grievances be addressed was signed and a gentleman by the name of John William Ricketts took up the responsibility of bringing the matter to the notice of the British Parliament. He travelled to England for the purpose and did what was considered, if not quite the unthinkable, but at least the very difficult and that was that he thoroughly convinced them. Word that his mission was met with resounding success had travelled to India and by the time he reached Calcutta via Madras he had become a hero of sorts. In both Madras and Calcutta, he was greeted with thunderous applause by people who had queued up at the ports to catch a glimpse of their saviour. In Calcutta, the celebration continued and a report of his journey and the mission was read out at a public gathering held at no less a venue than the city's Town Hall, reserved for important meetings and conferences.

For the Eurasian community, this was only the beginning of a set of important achievements which would transform their lives because further victories awaited them. In 1833, the British Parliament passed a law which forbade discrimination against Eurasians seeking government jobs. Forced to implement it the very next year, in April 1834, the government began to employ Eurasians in Indian government jobs.

Though these were lasting changes for the benefit of the Eurasians, their glory days did not last long. Within only a couple of decades, a question mark began to hang on the very survival of the community, the growth of which depended largely on

---

[57]Ibid.

the phenomenon of inter-racial marriages. Of course, marriages took place within the closed community of Eurasians too and the generations produced through these unions also carried the community forward but what essentially kept the rather newly-emerged anthropological race from shrinking or getting stunted and eventually dying out was the reinforcement from outside the community (that is, the regular occurrence of interracial marriages between Europeans and Indians, which had been taking place over the past two to three centuries).

But by mid to late 1880s, with the arrival in India of more and more European women, marriages between European men and Indian women grew rarer and rarer.

As for what led increasing numbers of European women to move to India—it was only a matter of time that they would do so after the men had tried and tested the waters (and the land for that matter) for nearly three centuries. The experiences of those like the missionary William Carey and his unfortunate wife further prepared the ground for families in Europe and gave them an idea as to what to expect and how to prepare for life in an unknown foreign land.

Indeed, the William Carey episode highlighted a problematic social situation facing the European families of those times who had men set sail for the East in search of livelihoods. For three centuries, it must have been a cause for considerable dilemma. Perhaps in the earlier days it was not even within the realms of possibility for women to accompany their men, whether sailors, soldiers, traders or teachers. With time, as it started to seem more likely that they too could undertake the sea journeys and make the faraway lands their homes, it perhaps became a point of discussion, debate and dilemma as, again, the William Carey case showcases.

At any rate, the Eurasian community dwindled gradually and eventually a set of laws that discouraged interracial marriages was implemented, especially after a major rebellion by Indians, the Rebellion of 1857 (which will be discussed in later chapters). The anti-miscegenation regulations were a big blow to the Eurasian community. It was an artificial legal barrier introduced by the British that effectively curbed the natural flow of an anthropological development.

By this time Bengal, and specifically Calcutta, had grown into a thriving cosmopolitan region and city with a number of different minority communities and ethnic groups existing simultaneously and more or less harmoniously, even though they lived mostly in their ghettos. Other than the Europeans and Eurasians including the Anglo-Indians, there existed other communities of people who had migrated from western Asian and eastern European countries, including the Afghans, Armenians, Greeks, Iraqis, Jews and Persians. Burmese, Chinese, Indonesians, Japanese, Koreans and other far eastern peoples too had settled in the land over periods of time. Ethnic groups from different parts of the country also had arrived in the region over centuries, their migration compelled by various reasons, and they included other than eastern regional neighbours namely Biharis and Odias, Gujaratis, Marwaris, Rajasthanis, Kashmiris and others.

'Our ancestors were brought to India from China by the British to work in tea plantations here in the early days of tea cultivation,' says George Leone, a businessman, whose family had settled in Calcutta three centuries ago and where they own restaurants and tannery businesses. 'Large numbers of people were displaced by the forced migration but gradually, that is, for the new generations who were born in India, this is our country and Bengal is our home.'

Indeed, Bengal remains, perhaps due to its geo-political circumstances and the fact that it has supported waves of arrivals for centuries, one of the most cosmopolitan and inclusive regions in the world today. It has absorbed and assimilated into its vast, generous landscape, even if at times, in the peripheries, each one of the migrant communities that arrived in it, allowing them space and opportunity to carve out a niche for themselves.

Calcutta is the only Indian city with a separate neighbourhood for the people who migrated to India from China. Though it is called Chinatown, it is not just a residential area for the Chinese community but a vibrant commercial centre thronged by entrepreneurs, large restaurants, small eateries and a host of businesses, big and small, particularly those manufacturing or dealing in leather shoes, bags and other items. Monica Liu, whose ancestors fled political persecution in China to arrive in Calcutta and who today is a resident of Calcutta's Chinatown, where she owns restaurants, says that people in Kolkata have a 'high level' of tolerance for the members of every community. 'We look different from the majority Bengalis because of our ancestry but we are never made to feel different,' she says.

Chinatown is considered as integral to Calcutta's multi-cultural and cosmopolitan landscape as any other part of it. Its unique 'Calcutta-Chinese' cuisine has made it one of the 'must-do-before-I-die' destinations for visiting tourists. While the old Chinatown, located in central Kolkata, is famous for its early-morning roadside eateries that sell scrumptious and inexpensive breakfasts of chicken and fish pie, dumplings and desserts, the new Chinatown on the city's eastern periphery is home to the more modern and bigger restaurants.

The Anglo-Indian community of Calcutta too is as integral to the city today as any other community, if not more, given that this city, this country, is virtually the birthplace of their race. Anglo-Indians have earned a distinctive place in world history with their contributions to various fields including education, literature, politics and entertainment. They complete Calcutta with their social clubs, their unique culture and, not to mention, their special cuisine. The 'Bow Barracks', an old neighbourhood from the British era, located in central Calcutta, not very far from the locus of the East India Company's ancient business district, still houses the greatest number of Anglo-Indian homes. Like most communities, the Anglo-Indians too lived according to their socio-economic statuses and the Bow Barracks give glimpses into the distinctions which existed even then between rich and poor.

Henry's father, Francis Derozio, was from a privileged background and held a rather well-paying job. He was considered a 'progressive' descendent of an orthodox religious family who did not just marry out of his community but tried to modernize his life in other ways. He, for instance, changed the family name from the more Christian 'De Rozario' to Derozio. He tried to instil values of cultural integration into his son, young Henry.

While most Eurasians preferred to identify with and uphold their European backgrounds—not simply because it was that of the rulers but because of the idea of 'white supremacy', which had begun to be inculcated into the 'native subjects' by the colonizers—since a young age Henry showed signs of identifying more with his Indian side. His mother tutored him in Bengali and it was from her that he imbibed the love and respect for the rich heritage of the land. He empathized with the growing patriotism of his countrymen against the British.

It was a mark perhaps of Henry Derozio's greatness that he refused to take the easy route out of the social stigma of being a 'subject' in a colonized country. He could have cozied up, as most in his community preferred to do, with the 'ruling' class by highlighting that part of their biological backgrounds which enabled them to do so. Indeed, with the growing acceptability and recognition of Eurasians they started to be counted as amongst the 'Anglo-Indians' who, as mentioned earlier, had thus far referred to the British or Europeans who lived in India. But Henry, no doubt, was so deeply sensitive to the pain of discrimination—while other or most Eurasians were in a hurry to embrace their white backgrounds—he may have internalized it and owned it. Critically questioning *why*, in the first place, Indians and Eurasians—because of their Indianness—be 'inferiorized' (if one can coin such a term to describe how the British rulers instilled a sense of inferiority in their subjects), he may have wanted to subvert the stigma by laying claim to it.

And yet, while it is largely accepted that he proudly declared his own Indianness, when it came to the orthodoxies of the country's established religions, namely Hinduism and Islam, he went hammer and tongs in trying to rid these of all that was oppressive in them.

Two points must be made here.

First, it must be noted that 'all that was oppressive' is a subjective idea, one which is open to interpretation. It is not that Derozio and other thought leaders had a written list of 'all that was oppressive' in the country's religions which they went about rectifying. On the contrary, the practices that they rebelled against were established conventions. From the point of view of common sense, a practice such as sati, which came into existence after hundreds and thousands of years of evolutionary progress, ought to have been considered not just oppressive but brutal and cruel in any civilized society, the fact is that it was not considered to be so. Even as late as the 1800s, not everyone believed that the practice of sati was brutal or cruel, leave alone oppressive. 'Like most superstitious beliefs that were passed down from generation to generation, it was considered a pious, devoted woman and wife's duty, an act which would earn her place in heaven,' said a historian.[58]

The brutality and cruelty of such practices as sati, however, was evident to those like Derozio. Though they would have perhaps innately questioned these practices, what no doubt triggered their critical thinking was the European model of society that they were exposed to. Juxtaposed against a system in which seemingly reason

---

[58]Anath Taran Ghoshal, priest and scholar on the subject of Hinduism, in an interview to the author.

ruled and in which caste discrimination did not exist (though class distinction was just as prevalent) and in which gender equality was more the rule than the exception, the superstitious religious rituals and beliefs, rigidly skewed against women and lower castes of the eastern faiths stood out like sore thumbs.

It must be pointed out here that that is not to overlook the fact that Europe itself had only just recently come out of the darkness of religious superstition and blind orthodoxy as also violent forms of gender discriminations against women.

Throughout the Dark Ages or the Medieval Period, as the years spanning the thousand years between the fifth and the fifteenth century CE is known, 'errant', 'disobedient' women (read independent and creative) were hunted down and burnt at the stake as 'witches'. Other barbaric practices too were common, including forms of 'punishment' which included hanging of convicts publicly to branding criminals and dragging them through streets. Often these cruel acts were cheered on by the society of that time as a form of entertainment.

This was also a time of Christian religious dogma and superstitions, manifest in various prevalent practices of the Catholic Church that advocated 'oppressive' and sometimes 'corrupt' (again, in hindsight and from the point of view of those who fought against such prevalent practices during that time) rules and regulations. One such prevalent practice was the 'purchasing' of the right to heaven and a less severe punishment for one's sins, known as 'indulgences' which was a system introduced in the Catholic Church and in which people paid money in return for a certificate.

In Europe, the Dark Ages ended with the beginning of the era of Enlightenment. It was called the European or Italian Renaissance or simply, Renaissance, having originated in Italy. This was a time of education and emancipation; a time when brutal, barbaric religious rituals were replaced with reason and rigorous intellectual debate and discussion to determine truth over blind faith.

Of course, it had still, by no means, become an ideal society. Patriarchy, it goes without saying, continued to exist in varying degrees. But when compared to practices such as the burning alive of widows, European society post the dark ages came out looking much the more civilized one by the time it had arrived in India.

The other point to be noted is that Derozio's questioning of the oppressive practices of the religions of India actually is not incongruous with his preference to identify with his Indianness. On the contrary, his endeavour to rectify what he considered was wrong in his society, including his religion, was an indication of his deep commitment to his country and his intense love for his Indianness.

He felt that Indian youth should be educated in order for them to liberate themselves from the shackles of servitude. The irony was that this education was based on the very principles—rationality, scientific thought—of the western world against whose imperialism and oppression it was to be used as a tool. But the greater irony was that the society, for whose empowerment he sought to impart such education to its youth, turned against him.

Derozio was fired from his job as a teacher in Calcutta's Hindu College for advocating unorthodox views which, according to the Hindu-dominated governing committee, had the capacity to 'corrupt' the minds of the Bengali youth and bring about 'destruction' in the moral values of society. He was held responsible for 25 students of prominent Hindu families withdrawing from the institution.

But in the intervening four years—between May 1826 when he was appointed as an instructor in English and history at the Hindu College, and April 1831, when he was expelled, he had managed to command a considerable following comprising his students and other youngsters who were taken in by his revolutionary ideas. They became known as Derozians. Later, they came to be called the Young Bengals.

Indeed, Derozio's technique of teaching, in which he interacted with students in class, encouraging them to speak up, was such a contrast from the traditional—in which the teacher lectured and the student listened, rarely getting a chance to interject, far less raise questions—that it became an instant sensation. Other than advocating exchanges of ideas and participation in discussions and debates in the classroom, he also taught them to think freely and question existing social, cultural and religious norms. Two years after he joined, he helped his students form a literary and debating club called the Academic Association, followed by the Society for the Acquisition of General Knowledge which aimed at acquiring knowledge in different fields and disseminating information.

Derozio's life was cut short but his influence lived on for long. In fact, the reforms that were eventually brought forth in different areas of society have been attributed to the iconoclastic ideas he introduced through his teachings. His progressive thoughts formed the backbone of the social, political and religious movement of that time that became known as the Bengal Renaissance or the Bengali Renaissance. Very much like the western world's European Renaissance, which chased away the proverbial darkness of the Middle Ages with enlightenment, replacing ignorance with education, superstition with reason and retrogressive ideas with progressive ones, the eastern world's Bengali Renaissance was the precursor of the Modern Age of India. New ideas found expression in different literary forms. Poets, diarists, journalists and other writers emerged, authoring numerous books and journals, fiction and non-fiction, in topics as wide-ranging as the sciences and philosophy. Just as literature flourished, so did the arts, including dance and music. It was a time of great cultural churning. It was the transitional time between the past and the present.

Did Derozio, in that delirious duration of transitional time, between life and death, even realize that?

IX

SHINING THE LIGHT ON LOVE AND LEARNING

'If you want peace, do not find fault with others, find your own faults and eradicate them.'

—Ma Sarada

The nineteenth century, or more specifically nineteenth century Bengal, was a bridge in time between the medieval and the modern, the past and the present. The era witnessed massive reforms in many areas of life in Bengal including in the cultural, economic, political, scientific, social and religious spheres that came to be known as the period of the Bengali Renaissance (also, the Bengal Renaissance).

When one reads of periods that experienced vast changes in history, one perhaps doesn't always grasp the sheer magnitude of the upheaval that it would have wreaked on the lives and minds of people going through such unprecedented revolutionary experiences. There would be people dying, leaving the world, having hardly experienced the new ways of life.

There would be people born right into the changes and growing up not knowing any other way of life. And then there would be the vast majority of people undergoing the changes, witnessing them. But other than these categories of people who lived through revolutionary changes in their time, there was another group of people who were directly responsible for making the changes happen.

They were the catalysts without whose thoughts, deeds, actions and words these changes would just not have taken place. They made it possible. They sometimes knew that they were creating the atmosphere that was conducive for turning social norms upside down and inside out. Sometimes, they did not.

That is, the changes came about without conscious effort. Often through the natural expression of their innate propensities, which were often even divine.

The first name to figure prominently in this context is that of Lord Ramakrishna Deb, the spiritual visionary, who transformed religious conventions of the day simply by imparting knowledge of his own empirical experiences with divinity to the disciples who flocked to him. Born, Gadahar Chattopadhyay, on 18 February 1836 into an impoverished but pious Brahmin family in the Bengal village of Kamarhati, he received no formal education and his teachings emanated from the depths of the wisdom he gained during his meditative trances.

He became known as, or is often referred to as, the 'founder' of the Ramakrishna 'Order' but it would be more appropriate to say that he (and his teachings) was the inspiration behind the founding of the Ramakrishna Order. Not only because it was not him but Narendra Datta or Swami Vivekananda, his closest disciple, who formally initiated the Order in 1897, 11 years after Ramakrishna's death, but also because Ramakrishna dwelt so deeply and almost so perpetually in the realms of consciousness that were beyond what constitutes 'the worldly', with all its associations of 'practical', that the idea of him 'founding' something, anything, especially something so organized as an 'order' seems to be an alien concept. An oxymoron even. The idea of a 'founder' of an 'order' conjures up images of a meticulously orderly mind which would engage in the mundane if need be:

the setting down of rules and regulations pertaining to day-to-day conduct; the writing of accounts; the maintaining of registers and all those other administrative activities associated with the founding of an 'order' even that of a spiritual philosophy.

Perhaps religious organizations and their activities, whether philanthropic, charitable or other, have become more associated with their worldly, day-to-day administrative functions than the spiritual philosophies that they are based on. Even as far as 'divine activities' (as opposed to the 'worldly activities') are concerned, the external manifestations of worship are more evident than the higher, transcendental ideals of religious institutions. That of course, one could argue, is but stating the obvious.

One could ask, incredulous, 'How can the inner thoughts of the pursuers of the divine be witnessed as clearly as their external, worldly activities like philanthropy or charity, for instance?' Yogis', monks' and ascetics', consciousness of the realms beyond the material world during meditative states are not as clearly visible to the observer as their worldly activities, like the distribution of blankets to the destitute.

But going back to the subject of the formation of the Order which gradually became the Ramakrishna Mission, if Ramakrishna himself was too transcended a soul to have had the requisite worldliness to 'found a religious order', his beloved pupil, the yogi Swami Vivekananda was the representative of the 'perfect harmony' between transcendental divinity and practical worldliness. He straddled the entire spectrum of the levels of consciousness. Though he renounced the life traditionally chalked out by society for human existence, including marriage and other worldly pursuits, devoting himself entirely to meditation and contemplation of the ultimate truth, guided by his spiritual guru, Ramakrishna, he nevertheless 'returned' as it were, to the physical plane of existence if only to lay down a philosophy that would guide humanity.

Ramakrishna's connection with the worldly realm was limited, though there are endearing and amusing glimpses of his sudden awareness of and unusual interest in the extremely mundane. Once, in the middle of one of his philosophical discussions with his devotees, he stopped and chided one of them who had just moments earlier, got up and sent off a beggar with only a couple of paisas. 'Couldn't you part with a few more paisas?' Ramakrishna asked him. 'Must you be so miserly?' Of course, this reprimanding too stemmed from the spiritual mind with the philanthropic heart being an off-shoot of it. The point to be noted here is Ramakrishna's surprising observation of the little details of daily life. He explained the inexplicable—namely the notion of God—in simple language that could be understood by the masses, using anecdotes and parables that they could identify with. When one of his devotees, a householder who had not embraced an ascetic's life, asked whether it was possible for people like him to also attain God, Ramakrishna used an example that a domesticated individual could understand easily. 'Live in this world like a "maid servant",' he had told him. 'She works in your house and looks after your child, but her mind goes back to her own home and her own child.' In other words, the physical world is transient and not one's real home. One's existence here is temporary so one must practice detachment. And the mind should dwell in the permanent, which is God.

Ramakrishna's existence, the 50 years that he lived, was spent largely in transcended states of consciousness and ecstasy when his body, as one devotee had once described, 'Was like a deserted house in which the owner no longer lived.' The seeming lifelessness could be taken for death, except that the trances were punctuated with cries of delirious joy and utterings of deep, philosophical thoughts. Devotees believed that he had merged with Brahma or God and indeed, when Ramakrishna returned from his reveries, he did narrate having had visions of what could be constituted as Brahma or God. His devotees, in fact, considered him to be an incarnation of Brahma or God.

Even as a child, little Gadadhar went into states of ecstasy. These were sometimes triggered by visits to places of worship cutting across religions. Sometimes these were brought on by distant sounds of chanting of mantras or the spiritual songs of different faiths. Sometimes these were set off even by ordinary life and nature, for instance, the sight of birds, especially white cranes, flying in the sky just before a storm broke. Ramakrishna was devout from an early age and joyful moments and beautiful sceneries evoked in him feelings of oneness with God. He often experienced ecstasy even while playing outdoors. The picturesque surroundings of his hamlet in riverine Hooghly District bringing on a trance every now and then. Whether it was raindrops falling on the crystal waters of a lotus pond, creating silver ripples. Or gusts of wind swishing through vast expanses of golden paddy fields, creating yellow waves. Or soft sunlight glistening on the lush green leaves of trees after a fresh monsoon shower. Fused with the natural joyousness of a child at play, these evoked in young Gadadhar a state of happiness so extreme, he literally left the body. The fits were initially mistaken to be epileptic seizures. His mother, Chandramoni Devi, even feared that her son was suffering from a mental illness. But at other times, he was not just like any other normal child, his loving personality endeared him to his family, relatives, neighbours and other villagers. According to biographers, local doctors of the time, who conducted intelligence and other tests for psychological disorders available at their disposal, declared him sound. This comforted his mother, who was reassured that it was more likely that he was a child with extraordinary spiritual gifts. Before his birth both she and her husband had experienced spiritual signs. She had dreamt that none other than Lord Vishnu, an avatar of Brahma, had turned into a great white light and merged into her womb.

Gadadhar was sent to the free village school but he found

no interest in bookish studies and at the age of 12 dropped out completely. However, he was intrigued by the stories of the great epics, the Ramayana, the Mahabharata and the Puranas, which were orally narrated to him by his mother and religious wanderers who often passed through the village and took shelter at various temples and shrines. Though poor, Gadadhar's family often opened their doors to travelling holy men, as per traditions in pious Brahmin families of the time. From them, Gadadhar managed to learn reading and writing and languages like Sanskrit.

The suspicions of 'insanity', however, resurfaced intermittently throughout the life of Gadadhar. Especially when he was given charge as the chief 'pujari' or priest in Calcutta later in years. Gadadhar's father, Khudiram Chattopadhyay, died when Gadadhar was just seven years old. As per the tradition of the time, the eldest male member of the family—in their case Gadadhar's elder brother Ramkumar—became the head of the household. But not long after, poverty drove him in search of work to the city of Calcutta. At that time, Rani Rashmoni, the philanthropic, deeply spiritual queen of Janbazaar in the outskirts of Calcutta, had a temple built for the Goddess Kali in the banks of the Ganges River in Dakshineshwar, nearly 50 kilometres from Calcutta. Since she belonged to the lower, 'shudra' caste, she found it difficult to find a Brahmin priest for the worship. Rashmoni's son-in-law, Mathur Babu, whom she entrusted with the responsibility of helping her in matters of running her household and helping her with her philanthropic work and looking after her subjects, happened to meet Ramkumar on his arrival in Calcutta. When he offered him the work, Ramkumar gladly took it up. Ramkumar also established a school to teach Sanskrit.

Soon, Gadadhar too followed. After Ramkumar left for Calcutta, Gadadhar was entrusted with the responsibility of worshipping the deity at their home in the village but he was needed in Dakshineshwar to help out his elder brother. He and his nephew, Hriday, left for Dakshineshwar. The year was 1855. The 19-year-old Gadadhar was given the job of decorating the Goddess. A year later, Ramkumar died. His premature death drove Gadadhar to extreme grief but he had dreams and visions that instructed him to takeover matters of worship. Indeed, Rani Rashmoni made him chief priest. And that was the beginning of Ramakrishna's desperate quest to get a vision of the Mother Kali, not just as a deity made of stone but as a real entity, with whom he could talk and get answers from. He wanted proof that there was a God, a Goddess. He started talking to her, asking, begging and finally demanding that she reveal herself to him. He wept, he pleaded, he scolded and he shouted at her day and night. In order to entice her to come to him and show herself, he danced in front of the idol of Mother Kali. He slunk into depression when days, weeks and months passed without 'darshan' or any visions. He was on the verge of committing suicide, when, as he later revealed, he finally saw her—a radiant light, she was the most beautiful thing he had ever seen.

For the next 30 years, Ramakrishna embarked on an unprecedented spiritual journey when he immersed himself in the pursuit of the Divine through every major religion of the time—including Christianity, Islam and different forms of Hinduism. Instructed by spiritual gurus in each of the faiths, he followed the rituals strictly and, in the end, concluded that there is one God, who is called by different names (Brahma, Allah, God) in different religions. And that all religions were merely paths to the same goal of reaching God. He further concluded that the aim of human existence is to realize God. He explained the meaning of life with a metaphor from the Hindu theological concept of 'dwaitabad' or 'dualism' (though, again, in his case, it was self-realized, not just learnt from the scriptures). 'Dualism' argues that we are separated from God in order to know Him/Her. We live in order to experience the love and sweetness of God. Dualism says,

'You (God) are sugar...I love to eat sugar. Therefore, I don't want to become sugar.' In 'advaitabad' or 'non-dualism', the ultimate and ideal state of human existence is to merge with God. In this, individuals are like globules of sugar, as it were, which ought to dissolve into sugar syrup. Though 'dualism' too recognizes that the ultimate state of being is to eventually dissolve into God, it nevertheless advocates the idea that separation allows us to experience God's greatness and glory while we live.

Back in his village, Ramakrishna's mother was so alarmed hearing these stories of her son's 'madness' that she decided to arrange his marriage in the hope that conjugal bliss would cure him of his 'psychological problems'. Ramakrishna himself apparently told her who his bride would be and, according to most accounts, he had neither ever met her earlier nor knew of her. Yet he named a little girl of five, called Saradamani Mukhopadhyay, who lived in another Bengal village called Joyram Bati. Ramakrishna was 23 but the 17-year age difference between husband and wife was not considered unusual in those days. After their marriage, Sarada continued to stay at her own home for some time and later joined her husband at the Dakshineshwar Temple. She was a devoted wife, whom Ramakrishna worshipped (quite literally, as the embodiment of Mother Kali). Their marriage was never consummated and he is believed to have once asked her if she was fine with the idea of being only a spiritual consort as he did not want to be dragged down to lower levels of existence, which the need for physical intimacy was a reflection of. In fact, it is said that while learning Tantric principles, the only ritual he refused to take part in was those at the initial stages, involving sexual activity. Vivekananda and several other disciples of Ramakrishna too took vows of celibacy. Sarada herself was deeply spiritual and she continued to teach her husband's spiritual philosophy after his death. She became known as Ma Sarada and was a mother to all of Ramakrishna's disciples. Ramakrishna's path-breaking, empirically-acquired spiritual realizations paved the way for extraordinary shifts in the way religion, especially Hinduism, would be perceived and practiced. Ramakrishna, while reinforcing the traditional idea of deity-worship, was also shaking up, right to the core, other orthodoxies of Hinduism. He broke caste barriers and in order to crush any insidious pride he may have nurtured about being a Brahmin, the highest religious caste in Hinduism, he did what was unthinkable at the time. He ate with people of lower castes. To completely free himself from the illusion of 'ego' Ramakrishna used to insist on going into the houses of sweepers and clean their washrooms. His innate iconoclasm was evident since his childhood, in fact. While his father had been an extremely orthodox Brahmin, who was well-respected throughout his village and neighbouring areas for his strict adherences to Hindu scriptures and the austere regulations laid out for Brahmins, Gadadhar questioned the basis of certain rules. At the time of his 'poitey' or 'sacred thread ceremony' (a formal religious ritual which initiates a Brahmin boy into adulthood and involves bestowing him with a sacred white thread which he is required to wear throughout life), he insisted that Dhani Kamarini, a lower-caste woman and the midwife who had delivered him, be his 'bhiksha mata'. Bhiksha Mata is a Godmother-like figure who is supposed to be the first to give alms to the boy for the period of his penance during the holy initiation. Traditionally, it was an honour reserved strictly for Brahmin women. In his adult life, only for a brief period did Gadadhar try to practice the strict codes of conduct for Brahmins and that was just after he moved to Dakshineshwar. Since the Kali Temple was built by Queen Rashmoni, who was from the non-Brahmin Kaivatya caste, he had expressed reservations about eating in the premises. His brother Ramkumar, however, reasoned with him, explaining to him that in the holy shrine of Mother Kali, there were no distinctions. Subsequently, Ramakrishna abandoned all his feelings of differentiation of caste, dismissing the Brahmin's sense of superiority as an attachment or 'maya' that binds one to the illusory world. During his Christianity and Islamic phases, he supposedly consumed meat that was not considered edible for Hindus, especially Hindu Brahmins.

Ramakrishna's extraordinary spiritual philosophy started to draw the attention of large sections of people from different walks of life. His teachings and revelations about the nature of God, life and religion did not just have mass appeal; even the intellectual elite of Bengal were mesmerized by his revolutionary takes on traditional theological concepts.

During this time, Bengal was already in the grips of the Reawakening or the Renaissance, when old orders were being broken down and replaced with new systems. The religious and social reforms brought in by Raja Ram Mohan Roy and the changes that were effected in educational and cultural spheres by thought leaders like Henry Derozio, had been taking place.

As far as religious reforms are concerned, the most significant one of the time, which ushered in key changes, was of course, the formation of the Brahmo religion by Raja Ram Mohan Roy as discussed earlier. Debendranath Tagore, born on 15 May 1817, in the influential and industrialist Tagore family of Bengal, was a young man when the religious reforms reached their peak. Debendranath's father, Dwarakanath Tagore, was a friend of Raja Ram Mohan Roy. Debendranath had attended many sessions of the Brahmo Samaj and was influenced by the ideas, rationale and logic. The Brahmos believed in a monotheistic God, who is called by different names in different religions and who was the unseen Creator of all of existence. Brahmos rejected the practice of Hinduism's idol-worship which, they argued, was polytheistic, not defining any one source. Brahmoism further questioned the hierarchical caste system. Large sections of Bengal's intellectual and educated class adopted it as their religion.

There was some overlap between the Brahmo tenets and the

philosophy of Ramakrishna and many, like the former Brahmo social reformer, Keshab Chandra Sen, became enamoured of the teachings of the saintly Ramakrishna. The 50 years that Ramakrishna lived—most of which, as stated earlier, was spent immersed in 'tapasya' or austere meditation—coincided with the changes and churning that was going on all around.

Though the Bengal Renaissance has been likened to the European (read: Italian) Renaissance, it has also been observed by historians that unlike the latter, the former was directly a result of colonization. Romesh Chunder Dutt writes:

> The conquest of Bengal by the English was not only a political revolution, but ushered in a greater revolution in thoughts and ideas, in religion and society... From the stories of gods and goddesses, kings and queens, princes and princesses, we have learnt to descend to the humble walks of life, to sympathize with the common citizen or even common peasant... Every revolution is attended with vigour, and the present one is no exception to the rule. Nowhere in the annals of Bengali literature are so many or so bright names found crowded together in the limited space of one century as those of Ram Mohan Roy, Akshay Kumar Dutt, Ishwar Chandra Vidyasagar, Ishwar Chandra Gupta, Michael Madhusudan Dutt, Hem Chandra Banerjee, Bankim Chandra Chatterjee and Dina Bandhu Mitra. Within the three quarters of the present century, prose, blank verse, historical fiction and drama have been introduced for the first time in the Bengali literature.[59]

It was one of the few 'progressive' outcomes of an entirely

---

[59] Romesh Chunder Dutt, *The Literature of Bengal: Being an Attempt to Trace the Progress of the National Mind in its Various Aspects as Reflected in the Nation's Literature from the Earliest Times to the Present Day*, BiblioLife, 2009 (originally published in 1895).

oppressive historical event that colonization was. It was the proverbial silver lining around a dark cloud. British culture—including its casteless religion, its ideas on gender and social equality and its emphasis on educational reforms which advocated inclusiveness of the classes—influenced Bengali thought. The intellectual youth, in particular, was intrigued by the possibility of a society which would exist without religious hierarchy and without gender discrimination.

In effect, this period was a fusion between eastern and western ideals and indeed, the overriding thought in the minds of the Bengali intellectuals during the Bengali Renaissance was the idea that the East and the West could learn from each other and give rise to an ideal society.

Vivekananda, who took Ramakrishna's spiritual philosophy to America and Europe explained that the right balance of eastern spirituality and western materialism was the only way forward in the evolution of world society.

The Bengali Renaissance was really a glimpse of such a society. Not just in the sphere of religion and social reformation, it was a time of immense progress in the fields of science and medicine (with the scientific discoveries and innovations of such geniuses as Jagadish Chandra Bose, Prafulla Chandra Ray and Mahendra Lal Sircar) as well as in the areas of literature and the arts (with the poetry of Derozio and Michael Madhusudan Dutta and the prose of Bankim Chandra Chattopadhyay and Sarat Chandra Chattopadhyay), not to mention in the field of education with reformists of the stature of Ishwar Chandra Bidyasagar, bringing in a new era of thinking and writing.

This was also a time of great advances in the sphere of women's education and emancipation in Bengal. And here the contribution of a number of European thinkers and social and religious reformers stand out. Among them was Margaret Elizabeth Noble, better known as Sister Nivedita.

Born on 28 October 1867 in Dungannon, a town in Northern Ireland's Tyrone County, Margaret had met Swami Vivekananda in November 1895, when he was in London for a period of three months, during his tour of Europe and America. The daughter of a pastor who doted on her, Margaret had been taught since childhood that serving others was the true goal of life and the only pursuit that would lead to the realization of God. Her father died when he was only 34 years old, leaving Margaret, her mother and her two younger siblings, a brother and a sister, heartbroken. Before his death, he had told his wife that Margaret was meant for a higher life and that if she were to choose to embrace a path different from an ordinary life, she should be encouraged to do so. Margaret was pious, devoted to philanthropy, studious and accomplished and she took up teaching work at the young age of 17. She, however, gradually became disillusioned with the regimented and institutionalized systems both in the spheres of education and religion in her country and she started her own school with the goal of making learning a freer and livelier experience. Her independent mind and free-spirited approach attracted many, including a young engineer from Wales. Margaret and the young man got engaged to be married but within a year, her fiancé died of a rare disease. The second tragedy in so short a time and at such young an age left Margaret devastated and further pushed her into the pursuit of God and the search for Truth about the meanings of life and death. She was well-versed in the Christian religious doctrines since childhood but had begun, by this time, to feel that she did not find the answers to all the questions that she had had, and she started to read and study the natural sciences as well as the texts of other religions for which she developed great reverence.

In the 12 books that she has authored, which have been compiled in a five-volume series called *The Complete Works of Sister Nivedita*, she has written about her longing for knowledge of the mysteries of creation during this phase of her life. Talking about her waning interest in Christianity and growing attraction towards Buddhism as well as towards the natural sciences (later she was to devote herself entirely to Hinduism, namely the Vedanta philosophy of Ramakrishna and Vivekananda), she had said:

> During the seven years of wavering, it occurred to me that in the study of natural science I should surely find the Truth I was seeking. So I began ardently to study how this world was created and all things in it and I discovered that in the laws of Nature at least there was consistency, but it made the doctrines of the Christian religion seem all the more inconsistent. Just then I happened to get a 'Life of Buddha' and in it I found that here also was a child who lived ever so many centuries before the Child Christ, but whose sacrifices were no less self-abnegating than those of the other. This dear child Gautama took a strong hold on me and for the next three years I plunged into the study of the religion of Buddha, and became more and more convinced that the salvation he preached was decidedly more consistent with the Truth than the preaching of the Christian religion.[60]

It was during this time that she attended a lecture on Vedanta philosophy by Swami Vivekananda at the house of an aristocrat in London, 'on a cold November afternoon', in the words of Lizelle Reymond.[61] Margaret was deeply touched by the religious discourses of the eastern monk. He did not just delve into the deeper spirituality of Hindu thought but also discussed an ideal

---

[60] Sister Nivedita, *The Complete Works of Sister Nivedita*, Advaita Ashrama, 1967.
[61] Lizelle Reymond, *The Dedicated: A Biography of Sister Nivedita*, BEE Books, 2017.

society which could be formed if Eastern spirituality and Western materialism could combine. He also spoke vociferously about his desire to see his country freed from colonial rule.

Thus began Margaret's journey into Hinduism. Margaret described her first impressions of Swami Vivekananda thus: 'A majestic personage, clad in a saffron gown and wearing a red waistband, sat there on the floor, cross-legged. As he spoke to the company, he recited Sanskrit verses in his deep, sonorous voice.'[62] Swami Vivekananda delivered several lectures throughout the duration of his stay in London and Margaret attended these. She discovered that the void that had driven her to delve into different religions and the sciences had begun to fill. Three years later, in 1898 she left for India and took initiation from Swami Vivekananda. He gave her the name 'Nivedita' which means 'the one who is dedicated to God'.

Nivedita shuddered to think what her life would be like had he never stepped out of India or if he did not arrive in Europe. And she wrote about knowing, when she met Swami Vivekananda, that she had been waiting for him all her life. She had written:

> Suppose he had not come to London that time! Life would have been a headless dream, for I always knew that I was waiting for something. I always said that a call would come. And it did. But if I had known more of life, I doubt whether, when the time came, I should certainly have recognized it. Fortunately, I knew little and was spared that torture... Always I had this burning voice within, but nothing to utter. How often and often I sat down, pen in hand, to speak, and there was no speech! And now there is no end to it! As surely I am fitted to my world, so surely is my world in need of me, waiting—ready. The arrow has found its place

---
[62]Sister Nivedita, *The Complete Works of Sister Nivedita*, Advaita Ashrama, 1967.

in the bow. But if he had not come! If he had meditated, on the Himalayan peaks! ... I, for one, had never been here.[63]

She further wrote about the impact Swami Vivekananda had on her and other seekers of truth. She had written:

> To not a few of us, the words of Swami Vivekananda came as living water to men perishing of thirst. Many of us had been conscious for years past of that growing uncertainty and despair with regard to Religion, which has beset the intellectual life of Europe for half a century. Belief in the dogmas of Christianity had become impossible to us, and we had no means, such as we now hold, by which to separate the doctrinal shell from the kernel of reality in our faith. To these the Vedanta has given intellectual confirmation and philosophical expression of their own mistrusted intuitions.[64]

Margaret was eager to join Vivekananda in his mission of spreading the ideals of Vedanta philosophy and was intrigued by his ideas on ameliorating the misery of his countrymen and women cruelly yoked to the burden of colonization.

Vivekananda too knew when he met Margaret in London that he needed someone like her, passionate, dedicated and devoted to the service of people, not to mention accomplished and educated, to lead his mission of bringing education and emancipation to the girls and women in India. In the book *Human Values and Education*, there is mention of how 'Swami Vivekananda was deeply pained by the wretchedness and misery of the people of India under the British rule and his opinion was that education was the panacea for all evils plaguing the

---
[63]Ibid.
[64]Ibid.

contemporary Indian society.'[65]

Vivekananda wrote to Margaret. The letter stated, 'Let me tell you frankly that I am now convinced that you have a great future in the work for India. What was wanted was not a man but a woman, a real lioness, to work for the Indians, women especially.'[66]

Margaret's biographer Lizelle Reymond wrote that responding to Swami Vivekananda's call Margaret travelled to India, leaving behind her friends and family, including her mother. The ship Mombasa, in which she travelled to Calcutta, reached on 28 January 1898. Less than a month later, on 22 February, she visited Dakshineshwar Temple, where Ramakrishna had attained his vision of the Goddess Kali. Another month later, on 25 March, which Margaret had described as 'the holiest, most unforgettable day' of her life, Swami Vivekananda, her guru, dedicated her to God and to the service of India. On 11 March 1898, in a public gathering at the Star Theatre, then one of the city's most popular theatres, he introduced Nivedita to the people of Calcutta. In his speech, he said, 'England has sent us another gift in Miss Margaret Noble.' In this meeting, Margaret expressed her desire to serve India and its people. On 17 March, she met Sarada Devi, who greeted Margaret affectionately as 'khooki' or little girl. These details are found in *Nivedita of India*, by Swami Sarvabhutananda, then secretary of the Ramakrishna Mission Institute of Culture, Calcutta.[67]

Historians have noted how passionate Nivedita was about setting up a school for girls and in order to raise money for it she toured Europe and America. These references are found in

---

[65]Aruna Goel and S.L. Goel, *Human Values and Education*, Deep & Deep Publications, 2005.
[66]Swami Vivekananda, *The Complete Works of Swami Vivekananda*, Advaita Ashrama, 2016. (The original letter was dated 29 July 1897.)
[67]Swami Sarvabhutananda, *Nivedita of India*, The Ramakrishna Mission Institute of Culture, 2002.

Western Women and Imperialism: Complicity and Resistance[68] and in *The Encyclopedia of Women Social Reformers*.[69]

Swami Vivekananda was extremely enthusiastic and he organized a meeting at the house of a devotee of Ramakrishna named Balaram Bose, where many others were called in order to discuss the issue with Sister Nivedita. Nivedita apparently appealed to all those present to send their daughters to the school. However, she did not get much response. In *Nivedita of India*, the anecdote is described in charming detail.

> During her speech, Vivekananda entered the room and took a seat behind everyone. Nivedita did not notice it. But, when Nivedita appealed to collect girl students for the school, she suddenly discovered Vivekananda in the room pushing others and prompting, 'Ye, get up, get up! It's not good enough to just become girls' fathers. All of you must cooperate in the matter of their education as per national ideals. Stand up and commit. Reply to her appeal. Say, "We all agree. We shall send our girls to you."' But no one stood up to support Nivedita's proposal. Finally, Vivekananda forced Haramohan (a fellow devotee of Ramakrishna who was present) to agree to the proposal and on behalf of Haramohan, Vivekananda promised to send his girls to the school.

A newspaper article titled 'Restoration Bid for Sister Nivedita's House Faces Hurdle'[70] states that, 'On November 13, 1898, on the day of Kali Puja, at 16 Bose Para Lane in the Bagbazar area of Calcutta, she started the school.' It is mentioned in *Nivedita of India* that 'the school was inaugurated by Sarada Devi, in the

---

[68] Nupur Chaudhuri, *Western Women and Imperialism: Complicity and Resistance*, Indiana University Press, 1992.
[69] Helen Rappaport, *The Encyclopedia of Women Social Reformers*, ABC-CLIO, 2001.
[70] Ankita Chaudhury, 'Restoration Bid for Sister Nivedita's House Faces Hurdle.' *The Times of India*, 24 July 2011. Accessed on 5 October 2012.

presence of Swami Vivekananda and some of the other disciples of Ramakrishna. Sarada Devi blessed and prayed for the school saying, "I pray that the blessings of the Divine Mother may be upon the school and the girls; and the girls trained from the school may become ideal girls.'" The biography throws light on Nivedita's tireless efforts, often battling stiff resistance, in reaching the goal of education and emancipation of girls.

> Nivedita went from home to home in educating girls, many of whom were in pitiable condition owing to the socio-economic condition of early 20th century India. In many cases, she encountered refusal from the male members of the girl's family. Nivedita had widows and adult women among her students. She taught sewing, elementary rules of hygiene, nursing, etc., apart from regular courses.[71]

After Swami Vivekananda's death on 4 July 1902, at just 39 years of age, Nivedita, heartbroken, nevertheless continued on with his mission, diving deeper into the movement for India's freedom until her death on 11 October 1911 at the age of 43.

The era of women's education and emancipation, of which Sister Nivedita was a guiding star, had other luminaries who shone bright. They included such names as Annie Besant, the British educationist and philanthropist, who championed the cause of women's rights and was one of the founders of the Banaras Hindu University. Like Nivedita, who though nearly 20 years younger than Annie Besant, had become her friend, she did not just fight for equality for girls and women but eventually joined the movement for India's Independence. In Bengal, not surprisingly, this was to become an age which saw increasing numbers of girls and women emerge from the shadows to storm the bastions

---

[71]Swami Sarvabhutananda, *Nivedita of India*, The Ramakrishna Mission Institute of Culture, 2002.

previously dominated only by men. The story of Kadambini Basu (later Ganguly, after she was married to Dwarakanath Ganguly), who battled male resistance to become one of the first two female doctors in India, and really the entire British Empire, is well known. She was also the first Indian and South Asian female physician to have earned a doctor's degree in western medicine, graduating from a South Asian university.

American historian, David Kopf, writing about Kadambini says:

> Ganguli's wife, Kadambini, was appropriately enough the most accomplished and liberated Brahmo woman of her time. From all accounts, their relationship was most unusual in being founded on mutual love, sensitivity and intelligence... Mrs. Ganguli's case was hardly typical even among the more emancipated Brahmo and Christian women in contemporary Bengali society. Her ability to rise above circumstances and to realize her potential as a human being made her a prize attraction to Sadharan Brahmos dedicated ideologically to the liberation of Bengal's women.[72]

In an article 'The Life and Works of Kadambini Ganguly, the First Modern Indian Woman Physician', research scholars describe the terrible attacks she encountered from the envious and malicious male detractors and how she battled them. It states:

> She joined the medical college (of Calcutta University) despite strong criticism from the conservative society opposing women's liberation. In 1886 she was awarded GBMC and became the first woman physician with a Western medical degree in all of South Asia. In 1893 she travelled to Edinburg and qualified as LRCP (Edinburg), LRCS (Glasgow) and GFPS (Dublin). She returned to India to practice medicine

---

[72]David Kohath, *Brahmo Samaj and the Shaping of the Modern Indian Mind*, Princeton University Press, 2015 (originally published in 1979).

and also actively campaigned for women's rights in the conservative society that resisted change. She was indirectly called a 'whore' in a journal but unfazed Kadambini took it to the court and successfully won the libel with a jail sentence of six months for the editor.[73]

A well-researched article entitled, 'Dwarakanath Ganguly, A Forgotten Hero', attributes much of Kadambini's success to her husband and his unstinted support of her, including dragging to court and winning the case against the vicious editor of a journal who had cast aspersions on her character. It observes:

> When the editor of a popular periodical *Bangabasi* referred to her as a courtesan in his article it is said that a furious Dwarakanath confronted him and (in a not very subtle manner) made him swallow the piece of paper where the comment was printed. He also took legal action as a result of which the editor was sentenced to six months' imprisonment and fined one hundred rupees. Dwarakanath who had also been campaigning to ensure accommodation and enrolment of female students in Calcutta Medical College legally threatened the authorities after which they allowed Kadambini to study.[74]

The errant editor, according to Wikipedia quoting sources, was Mahesh Pal.

The success story of Kadambini Basu Ganguly (18 July 1861 to 3 October 1923) inspired and continues to inspire generations of girls and women.

---

[73]Amrith R. Rao, Omer Karim, Hanif G. Motiwala, 'The Life and Works of Kadambini Ganguly, the First Modern Indian Woman Physician', *Journal of Urology*, Volume 177, 4 Nov, Supplement, 21 May 2007, pp 354–355.

[74]Amit Das, Biswajit Roy, 'Dwarakanath Ganguly: A Forgotten Hero', *The Indian Messenger Online*, April 2018, http://im.thesadharanbrahmosamaj.org/2018/04/03/dwarakanath-ganguly-a-forgotten-hero/. Accessed on 21 July 2021.

X

AN OCEAN OF KNOWLEDGE AND A SEA OF CHANGE

'The welfare of the world is not possible unless the condition of women is improved. A bird cannot fly on only one wing.'

—Swami Vivekananda

Ishwar Chandra Bandyopadhyay was walking down the street, along a quiet Bengali residential neighbourhood, when he heard the heart-rending wails of a woman emanating from a house. On enquiring from people who had gathered outside, he learnt that the woman's husband had died and she was as much grief-stricken for losing him as she was about the fact that he had left her with no money for survival. 'Vidyasagar' as Ishwar Chandra came to be known (the epithet, meaning ocean of knowledge, was conferred on him because of his vast scholarship), asked what the name of the deceased man was. After learning his name from the bystanders, he went over to the house from which the woman's wails were emanating and standing at the doorsteps, started to holler the name of the deceased man. 'Hey there, so and so,' he is understood to have shouted, in Bengali, several times, followed by, 'You home?' Inside, the weeping stopped abruptly. The bewildered widow came out and told him that he had passed on. To which Vidyasagar reportedly replied, 'Oh, that's a shame.

I had borrowed some money from him. A large sum actually. I had come to return it to him and to find out if I could give it back little by little. Say, a certain amount every month. Would that be okay with you?'

Vidyasagar's generosity was legendary as was his compassion for the needy and the downtrodden. One of the key figures of the Bengal Renaissance, he was responsible for engineering a number of path-breaking educational and social reforms, including the legalization of remarriage of Hindu widows. He was deeply troubled by the unequal treatment of men and women in Hindu households. Girls, barely into their teens, were often married off to much older men—even to those on their deathbeds—supposedly to save the honour of the family because it was considered a matter of great shame to have unmarried daughters beyond a certain age (usually late childhood) living in her parents' home. There were exceptions, of course, but this was in general the practice of the day. In fact, the deep-rooted anguish often associated with the birth of girl children, especially in underprivileged or illiterate Indian households even today, can perhaps be traced back to this insensitive religious custom. The burden of having to marry them off or face social ostracism, made daughters unwanted. Raised as someone who would have to be given away and therefore not one's own in their own biological families, they were often treated with far less caring (and sometimes even with contempt) than their male siblings. In their in-laws' house, they were, of course, anyway the outsider. If widowed, they were doomed to lead lives of extreme austerity. They were forbidden to wear colourful clothes, jewellery or make-up, which for married women of the time comprised a series of rituals including smearing sindoor in the front parting of the hair and painting the soles of the feet with a red liquid, Alta. Not only were the widows denied the pleasure of decking up in these cosmetics but the only acceptable attire for them was plain, white cotton cloth. Widows had to shave their heads and eat vegetarian food. This was considered a way to both prevent attracting the attention of men, as well as to keep their own libidos down. It was unthinkable for widows to remarry. Men, on the other hand, could not just marry again and again if their wives died, but they could be wedded to more than one woman at a time. Vidyasagar was determined to end such discriminatory practices. He was one of the chief petitioners to the Legislative Council for legalizing widow remarriage and he lobbied relentlessly for banning the marriage of children too.

Though he was otherwise held in high esteem in Hindu society as an academic, linguist (he modernized and simplified the Bengali language), translator, writer and philanthropist, he faced scathing criticism from Hindu orthodoxy for the social and religious reforms that he advocated, impacting their social and religious status quo. The proposed draft for the constitution of a 'Widow Remarriage Act' was challenged with a counter petition from the Hindu society known as Dharma Sabha and it contained more than four times the number of signatories than in the original proposal. However, Vidyasagar is understood to have put pressure on the then Governor-General of India, Charles Canning, who had taken charge on 28 February 1856, eventually convincing him to intervene and have the bill passed. On 26 July 1856, The Hindu Widows' Remarriage Act, 1856, came into existence and was effective not just in Bengal but in every other British East India Company jurisdiction throughout India. It was the second most significant social reform legislation after the abolition of sati pratha, when on 4 December 1829, after the tireless crusading of Raja Ram Mohan Roy, the 'Bengal Sati Regulation' was passed by the then Governor-General of India, Lord William Bentinck.

People who were inclined towards rigid religious orthodoxies of the time perceived these acts by British rulers (of readily succumbing to the pressure of liberal and progressive thinkers like Vidyasagar and endorsing legislation proposed by them that outlawed regressive local customs) as designs to subvert, weaken and undermine the dominant religion of the land with the express purpose of conversion (to Christianity, the religion of the British). But while there is no denying that throughout British rule religious conversion or the attempt to spread British culture, language and habits were realities, the fact remains that the eagerness with which Bentinck or Canning responded to the demands for and their presiding over the passing of these path-breaking and much-required legislations have earned them a hallowed place in Bengal's history.

Governers-General of the British instituted in India, before Bentinck, rarely supported progressive legislature in favour of the native people, far less take initiatives for social reforms, perhaps for fear of reprisals for interfering in the religious customs or social traditions of the land. Or they simply could not care less. Perhaps they felt that their primary job was to look after the concerns of the British and not about the welfare of the people of India. Instead of delivering able governance, governors-general throughout East India Company rule, by and large concentrated chiefly on their imperial duties of consolidating power with the express purpose of generating profit. The extent to which they would go, in terms of looking after the concerns of the local people, was limited to the regular written reports that they were mandated to submit to the British government in London detailing the goings-on in Bengal and other parts of India where they ruled. For instance, soon after assuming power as the first governor-general of Bengal in 1773, Warren Hastings sent only a cursory brief to the government in the United Kingdom detailing the possible causes of a terrible famine in Bengal four years earlier, in 1769, which fixed responsibility on the East India Company and its 'violent' land-tax policy. However, he did not bother to go beyond and take punitive action against the perpetrators in order to deliver justice to the people of India. On the contrary, it soon emerged, that he believed in exercising absolute control over the natives of the land to the point that he was eventually tried, in the UK, for his excesses in India, with the noble Irish Parliamentarian, Edmund Burke, supporting his impeachment. Burke had famously said, 'The only thing necessary for the triumph of evil is for the good men to do nothing'.

In India, those appointed governors-general, usually did nothing. That is, they did nothing to rein in the evil unleashed upon the natives by the lascivious officials of the British East India Company. But then, it could be argued, that neither were they, most of them at least, 'good men'.

British rulers like Bentinck and Canning were clearly exceptions. Unlike their predecessors, they did not shirk responsibility as administrators and Raja Ram Mohan Roy and Ishwar Chandra Vidyasagar could extract from them the progressive legislation they wanted. Sure, it is entirely possible that these British governors were driven by vested interest, as alleged by their detractors who saw, in their readiness to ratify progressive legislature, ulterior motives. However, there is no denying that they took the correct decision, even going to the extent of courting controversy, by doing their bit to push through these legislations which rattled dominant religious communities. Those who argued that they were driven solely by compulsions of imperialism and that their real motives were to replace existing religious and social traditions with those of the colonizers, could be negating the possibility of a humane side to these rulers. It is not unlikely that they were governed by the same sense of compassion and justice that drove iconic crusaders like Raja Ram Mohan Roy and Ishwar Chandra Vidyasagar to call for reforms.

Perhaps they were equally horrified by the inherent barbarity of religious practices of the day, like sati pratha. Perhaps they were psychologically disturbed by the cruelty of customs that deprived girls and women the right to live life and the right to a modicum of freedom (whatever little that was allowed to the female gender in those days). Detractors could again argue that for Raja Ram Mohan Roy and Ishwar Chandra Vidyasagar, the beneficiaries of the cause they championed were their own people. The multitudes of the girls and women of Bengal who were kept down and were crushed under the weight of inhuman, insane patriarchy in the name of religion were those from amongst whom emerged their own beloved mothers, sisters, wives and daughters. Indeed, thought leaders who revolted against gender oppression were themselves, deeply sensitive to the plight of girls and women of this land. And they necessarily displayed characteristics which were indicative of their innate respect and reverence for girls and women. Their keenness to crusade on their behalf stemmed from genuine concern rather than rhetoric.

Vidyasagar's empathy for women is traced back to the early days of his childhood. Born on 26 September 1820 in an orthodox Brahmin family in a Bengal suburb, at the age of nine he was sent to Calcutta where his father Thakurdas Bandyopadhyay worked. They lived in the house of a friend named Bhagavat Charan, whose large family took good care of the little boy, encouraging him, brilliant as he was, in his studies. Vidyasagar was, however, closest to Bhagavat Charan's youngest daughter, Raimoni, who was the biggest influence in his life. Her kindness and affection for him kindled in him the highest of regard for women. Vidyasagar's devotion to his mother too was reflective of this and it bordered on worship. The story goes that, once, while he was working at Calcutta's Fort William College (as head of the department of Sanskrit), his mother sent word from their village in Birsingha, now in West Bengal's Medinipur district, that the date of his brother's marriage had been fixed and that he was expected to be present. Vidyasagar's application for leave was turned down. When he threatened to resign, his British boss relented though he said that he failed to understand the tearing urgency of a young man to honour the simple request of his mother. However, getting leave was not the most difficult task as Vidyasagar was to soon discover. It was the month of July and the rainy season was upon them. On his way home, he was delayed by a terrible thunderstorm and a torrential downpour. To make matters worse, he had to cross a huge river, the Damodar, which was known for its deadly undercurrents during the monsoon. The sole ferry was anchored on the other bank of the river, bobbing up and down on the wild waves. Not another soul was in sight. It was getting late and Vidyasagar worried that the wedding would have started and there would be no point in landing up late. He jumped into the swirling waters and swam across. Though he missed the main ceremony, his mother was ecstatic to see him.

Though Vidyasagar had to surmount a great deal of societal opposition for the causes he espoused, he nevertheless also found support from influential people of the time, including, Mathur Mohan Biswas or Mathur Babu, the son-in-law of Rani Rashmoni, who had established the Dakshineshwar Temple after Ma Kali appeared to her in a dream and instructed her to do so. Gadadhar Chattopadhyay or Lord Ramakrishna (the nomenclature, by some accounts, was made by Mathur Babu) as earlier pointed out, was appointed its chief priest. Vidyasagar had met Ramakrishna too and without renouncing the world, became a devotee. The idea that women ought to be revered as the embodiment of their mothers, even the divine Mother Kali, was part of the philosophical discourse of Ramakrishna and the concept of sati or burning alive the woman at the pyre of her husband was completely unacceptable and contrary to the idea. Ma Kali represents Shakti or female power whose identity is independent, not subservient to male energy, represented by Her consort Lord Shiva, who, in order to emphasize this, lies at her feet in mythological representations.

In fact, Bentinck, while formulating the law which banned sati pratha, had observed that Hinduism itself did not insist upon or even advocate the practice. He had written, 'It is nowhere enjoined by the religion of the Hindus as an imperative duty; on the contrary, a life of purity and retirement on the part of the widow is more especially and preferably inculcated.' Bentinck had further pointed out that the large majority of Hindus themselves abhor the custom. He had written, 'And by a vast majority of that people (Hindus) throughout India the practice is not kept up, nor observed. In some extensive districts it does not exist. In those in which it has been most frequent it is notorious that in many instances acts of atrocity have been perpetrated which is shocking to the Hindus themselves and in their eyes unlawful and wicked.'

Bentinck's painstaking efforts, as evident from these written records, to establish that sati pratha was not integral to the practice of Hinduism, is indicative that he himself was deeply disturbed by this brutal custom. He had described his personal opinion on sati pratha, thus: 'The practice of suttee (sic), or of burning or burying alive the widows of Hindus is revolting to the feelings of human nature.'[75]

Therefore, those who took the narrow view that being a British officer associated with the notoriously mercenary and imperialistic East India Company, Bentinck acted solely from vested or imperialistic interests did injustice to the possibility that he too, like Raja Ram Mohan Roy or Ishwar Chandra Vidyasagar, may have been driven by humanity, compassion and a sense of justice and equality.

And the important point to note here is that whatever the

---

[75]Lord William Bentinck, *Bengal Sati Regulation XVII Act 1829*, Government of India Legislative Department (1897) and Calcutta: Superintend of Government Printing, p. 81, retrieved on 6 September 2011.

case may be or whatever the real reasons were for ushering in progressive legislation, if indeed the real motive of the British East India Company officials was to challenge the land's existing religious orthodoxy with a view to establish their own, it is interesting and telling perhaps that it should be done by creating laws which were clearly geared towards the upliftment of the women of the land and the upholding of their rights. It is ironic that what offends the sensibilities of one half of a religious community should benefit the other as though they were mutually exclusive.

Perhaps they have always been. Religions the world over have formulated regulations and rituals that vary according to gender and the privileges are, in most cases, tipped in favour of the males. Listing these would be an exercise in the obvious. And so, women, in religious and political conflicts, have been used—wooed with sops, as it were—by rival groups to get to the enemy.

At any rate, as he pronounced the ban on the practice of sati pratha in Bengal and in all jurisdictions under the East India Company rule throughout India, Bentinck declared, 'The practice of 'suttee' or burning or burying alive the widows of Hindus, is hereby declared illegal and punishable by the criminal courts.'[76]

Bentinck, during his tenure as Governor-General of India from 1828 to 1835, had presided over a number of other important legislations, which were milestones as far as social, religious or educational reforms are concerned. He introduced numerous educational reforms including making English the official language of higher education. Though female infanticide was formally banned much later, with the Female Infanticide Prevention Act, 1870, when Richard Bourke of Mayo was Governor-General of India, in Bengal, Bentinck declared female infanticide outlawed. He also criminalized the practice of human sacrifice, which existed in various parts of the land.

---

[76]Ibid.

Interestingly, however, both Bentinck and Canning have earned as much wrath of the Indian people as they did their respect. Canning was the British administrator during the first Indian rebellion against British rule. And Bentinck initiated a series of legal measures which criminalized an indigenous rural tribe of supposed bandits, the 'thuggees', generating controversy. This criticism, however, is more recent. Earlier, for nearly a century and a half, the actions he took against the thuggees was considered an important step towards curbing what was said to have been a dreaded social menace of the time, which was thought to have existed in the land for nearly six centuries.

Meaning loosely 'the act of deception' or 'the condition of concealment' in Sanskrit, thuggees were said to be a community of organized criminals, who looted, robbed and killed road and river travellers by tricking them into believing they were fellow pilgrims or passengers. The typical method said to have been employed by thuggees was to surreptitiously infiltrate groups of travellers in gangs, camouflaged as fellow travellers on long journeys. They would then proceed to win the trust of the travellers with fake helpfulness, friendly gestures and even disarming charm. Once they gained their confidence, they would isolate individuals, using different pretexts, distract them by various means and then strike. Usually, one of the thuggees would creep up from behind and strangulate the victim with a noose made of handkerchiefs or other cloth, as his accomplices engaged him in conversation or otherwise kept him distracted.

The earliest reference to thuggees is said to be in a fourteenth century document, *History of Firoz Shah*, written by Ziauddin Barani, sometime around 1356. He wrote that around the year 1290, nearly 1,000 thuggees who operated around Delhi were captured by the army of Sultan Jalal-ud-din-Khalji but instead of killing them, he had them exiled to the nether regions of the land from where they spread to various parts. Reference to this is found in historian Martine van Woerkens's *The Strangled Traveller: Colonial Imaginings and the Thugs of India*.[77] Sir H.M. Eliot is quoted from *History of India as Told by Its Own Historians* thus:

> In the reign of that sultan (about 1290), some Thugs were taken in Delhi, and a man belonging to that fraternity was the means of about a thousand being captured. But not one of these did the sultan have killed. He gave orders for them to be put into boats and to be conveyed into the lower country, to the neighbourhood of Lakhnauti, where they were to be set free. The Thugs would thus have to dwell about Lakhnauti and would not trouble the neighbourhood of Delhi anymore.[78]

Lakhanauti, also known as Gour or Gouda, was a region in ancient Bengal, which now falls in the state's Malda district, 362 kilometres from Calcutta.

There is discrepancy about whether their religion was Hindu or Muslim, with suggestions that both faiths intermingled as the band grew over the years. Thuggees supposedly passed down their expertise from generation to generation, with the children learning the ropes from their elders. Other accounts suggest that there were various types of recruitments and included inducting into the clan, children of murdered travellers. Thuggees were said to have never killed children or women because they, both the Hindu and the Muslim parts of the sect, worshipped the goddesses, especially Mother Kali.

The Bengal thuggees, after spreading out from Lakhanauti, were supposedly situated in the remote regions—deltas and jungles of the Sundarbans, where tigers roamed the land and

---

[77] Martine van Woerkens, *The Strangled Traveller: Colonial Imaginings and the Thugs of India*, University of Chicago Press, 2002.
[78] H.M. Eliot, John Dowson, *History of India as Told by Its Own Historians*, Low Price Publications, 2008.

crocodiles haunted the rivers, and they were difficult to track down. Bentinck reportedly waged a war on thuggees and even set up a separate governmental department to carry out the witch-hunt across the land. The head of this department, called The Thuggee and Dacoity Department, was William Henry Sleeman. He used a series of techniques, including intelligence-gathering and offering rewards to informers, to reportedly nab thousands of thuggees and crackdown on their trade, which was eventually eradicated. Incidentally the word 'thug' with its current meaning of a criminal or violent person, entered the English language around this time and its etymology is traced to the thuggees. However, the thuggees were not common criminals and differed from other road robbers in that they operated as a cult with specific and traditional ritualistic determinants on how they should rob and kill.

Paintings dating back to the late eighteenth and early nineteenth centuries depict the purported horrific methods employed by these thugs. They often disfigured and mutilated their victims after killing them in order to avoid being identified by British police. The logic being that eye witnesses would have seen them with the murdered individual before the crime. Also, after looting and killing them, they often supposedly even gouged out their eyes, and then dumped their bodies in wells or ditches.

A watercolour painting done by an anonymous Indian artist, for instance, shows what is supposed to represent a hapless individual being strangulated by a robber, while two of the latter's companions and accomplices hold down his feet and hands respectively as he is stretched out, face down on the ground. A pencil sketch by either the same artist or another, whose name is not known, purports to depict three travellers, just having been strangulated, being disfigured as their eyes are carved out of their sockets, with their dead heads dangling over the edges of a well, in which they would be dumped after being further mutilated.

A series of legal acts known as the 'Thuggees and Dacoity Suppression Acts, 1836 to 1848', were enacted by the British. It culminated in the rounding up of hundreds and thousands of tribal and other rural, jungle or delta folk, who were subsequently handed out the most stringent punishments, post cursory trials, which included at the least, imprisonment, and at the most, hanging.

V.B. Ganesan, in his review of Kim A. Wagner's book, *Thuggee: Banditry and the British in Early Nineteenth-Century India*, writes, 'Between 1826 and 1835, a total of 1562 thugs were tried; 382 sentenced to death, 909 to transportation, 77 to imprisonment for life. In 1839, Sleeman declared that "thugee" as an organized association had been effectively destroyed and even though some instances occasionally popped up over time, the thuggee campaign was over.'[79]

In recent times, questions have been raised about the very existence of thuggees, not to mention the supposed threat they posed during British Indian rule, with a section of world scholars dismissing the entire idea as an imperial invention. Historian Woerkens is amongst those to have raised doubts as has Wagner.

In 'The Deconstructed Stranglers: A Reassessment of Thuggee', Wagner writes,

> Maunsell, a lieutenant in the 23rd Native Infantry of the Bengal Army set out on horseback in October 1812...on a visit of inspection...accompanied by two sepoy orderlies and a horse carrying his belongings and equipment. All three were armed. Maunsell with sword and holster pistols, the sepoys with the Brown Bess muskets and bayonets.[80]

---

[79]V.B. Ganesan, 'Review of *Thuggee: Banditry and the British in Early Nineteenth-Century India*', *The Hindu*, 22 September 2014.
[80]Kim A. Wagner, 'The Deconstructed Stranglers: A Reassessment of Thuggee', *Modern Asian Studies*, University of Cambridge, 2004.

Wagner writes that on the second day of the journey the three had camped near a village, 'in one of the wayside groves known as "choultries" in common use then by travellers, with a well, a few lime trees, a little grass and a shrine.' In delightful detail, Wagner continues to describe the scene as he visualized it:

> After the hot and dusty ride, the horses tethered, the tents pitched in the shade out of the late afternoon's blaze, the green paroquets chattering and the small monkeys shrieking in the branches. Maunsell, according to custom, would have pulled off his hot red broadcloth uniform with relief and splashed in buckets of cool well water in the enclosure behind his tent. In imagined security, he probably stretched out on the camp bed in the hot night and slept soundly after his long day in the sun.

But when the three did not reach their destination even three days later, 'A troop of cavalry was ordered out to search the road,' writes Wagner. 'In a wayside grove, they found among the ashes of a recent fire, charred, regimental buttons and badges that were identified as those of Maunsell and the sepoys. They were assumed to have been murdered but their bodies were not found.' Wagner conjectures,

> Had exceptional qualities and influential friends had brought Maunsell's name before the eyes of the great in India, the outcome would have been different, because the evidence would have been sifted more thoroughly, the suspects questioned more severely and the truth might have come to light. Instead, a punitive force attacked and destroyed the villages nearby, seizing at random any inhabitants thought likely to have taken part in the murder and handing them over to the Indian local authorities for trial. And in the East India register of 1812 Maunsell was

reported to have died in action against banditti on 22 October.

The idea that the 'the thuggee threat' was a British concoction, cooked up to validate its rule in India and its crackdown on its people has found support amongst historians in Bengal too. Maroona Murmu, assistant professor of history at Calcutta's Jadavpur University, says, 'The entire exercise was to track people down in the remotest regions and put tags on them. It was a way to brand the lower castes and classes and criminalize their way of life.'

Indeed, the British had gone to the extent of criminalizing entire tribes and communities through a series of legislation collectively called the Criminal Tribes Act (CTA). In Bengal, the Sabar, also called Shabar or Saroa, belonging to the larger ethnic, indigenous and aboriginal group, the adivasis, was thus designated. Branded as 'habitual offenders' these forest dwellers, who were concentrated in the present-day Jangalmahal region, comprising the West Midnapore, Bankura and Purulia districts, were not adept at agriculture and lived off forest produce. 'Our mineral-rich land has been deemed lucrative for centuries and the British wanted to snatch it from us,' says a local leader of a political party in a village in West Midnapore. 'And that's why they confined us by calling us criminals.' He says that their people's traditional use of 'weapons' of defence such as bows and arrows, knives and axes were cited as indicators that they were 'violent tribes'. He says, 'The innocent people of our land were picked up by police when dacoits and common criminals created trouble.'

The possibility that different bandit gangs could have existed in the country is not that unlikely. Even today, dacoits carry out organized road robbery, waylaying highway travellers along the long stretches of highroads that cut through various jungles. Whether the jungles of Chambal in the state of Madhya

Pradesh, which was once notorious for its bandits or the forests of Jangalmahal, in the district of Jhargram in West Bengal, less than 200 kilometres from the state capital of Kolkata, where many a night traveller, driving past, have been looted. The modus operandi included trapping travellers by sprinkling the road, come evening, with sharp objects such as nails and pieces of glass so that tyres get punctured, forcing vehicles driving through to screech to a halt in the middle of night, in the middle of the jungle. The other common system has been to block the highway with felled logs. The travellers are then surrounded by the bandits, robbed and often, even killed.

However, the British had grossly exaggerated the threat and generalized the phenomenon without proper understanding of the diverse groups, tribes and communities which existed in the land. Because of their ignorance, innocuous forest dwellers and villagers were branded bandits.

And if violent action emanated from these remote regions whether in the form of robbery or killing of outsiders, says the local leader of the political party in those days, 'It was because of poverty or defence (respectively).'

So, if the tag of 'habitual offenders' was applied to these indigenous communities and tribes whose way of life and livelihood were erroneously considered inherently 'violent' and 'hostile' towards outsiders from the point of view of 'civilization' as the British or sub-continental mainstream knew it, it was a travesty of justice. If the violence of peripheral people, who are hostile towards outsiders, spilled over into mainstream civilization it was because mainstream civilization intruded into and invaded their turf and territory, much like the highroads that cut through pristine forests.

Be that as it may, the crushing and suppressing of the menace (if indeed it was that) of thuggees is supposed to have brought relief to civilized society in general and travellers in particular and was deemed another progressive legislation.

But the scepticism of contemporary scholarship about the actual threat posed by and even the very existence of 'thuggees' has opened up fresh debate about and a reassessment of the motives and actions of the British rulers.

Ishwar Chandra Vidyasagar, it goes without saying, was a staunch critic of the British. There are anecdotes galore about his witty repartees to the colonizers who were notorious for spewing insults at the locals. An article entitled, 'The Vidyasagar Legacy: What He Stood for and What He Was Against', points out the following:

> Once Ishwar Chandra Vidyasagar was travelling by train in a compartment with some Englishmen. He sat between two of them. One man asked, 'Who is this donkey?' The other asked, 'Who is this pig?' A third Englishman asked, 'Who are you?' Ishwar Chandra coolly replied, 'I am a human being sitting between a donkey and a pig.' The two Englishmen felt ashamed of themselves. They felt even more ashamed when they saw a large crowd of people waiting with garlands to receive Ishwar Chandra when he got down from the train.[81]

But he had the unique ability to make the British do his bidding. In 1856, just before the British administration in India was to crackdown on a massive revolt against itself by the people of India, Vidyasagar, who was then 37-years-old, extracted from it the first in a series of revolutionary laws that changed the future of education and gender and caste equations in the country forever. And then he proceeded to go and live in a region called Karmatar, which has been called a 'sleepy hamlet' 20 kilometres from the district headquarters of Jamtara, now in Jharkhand, amongst the

---

[81] Kanika Katyal, 'The Vidyasagar Legacy: What He Stood for and What He Was Against', *Newsclick*, https://www.newsclick.in/vidyasagar-legacy-what-he-stood-and-what-he-was-against. Accessed on 9 July 2021.

adivasi people of the Santhal Parganas. Yes, the same people who were declared 'criminal' by the British administration. Vidyasagar died there on 29 July 1891 at 71. On 26 September 2019, the two hundredth birth anniversary of Vidyasagar, the Government of Jharkhand renamed Karmatand Block of Jamtara District as Ishwar Chandra Vidyasagar Block.

XI

FADING MEMORIES, FEARLESS MARTYRS

'For the freedom of my country, I want to die. The thought of the gallows does not frighten me. I want to be born again so that I can return and fight for my country.'

—Khudiram Bose

The date was 29 March 1857. The place was the military cantonment of the British East India Company army in Barrackpore, a suburban town 31 kilometres from Calcutta. The time of the day was afternoon. A 30-year-old 'sepoy' or foot soldier by the name of Mangal Pandey, belonging to the Company 34th Bengal 'native infantry' burst into this setting and started, what later came to be known in history, as the incident that triggered India's First War of Independence. The sequence of events that took place on that fateful day at that godforsaken venue has been pieced together by historians at different times. The accounts of Christopher Hibbert[82], Saul David[83], Rudrangshu Mukherjee and Kim A. Wagner provide poignant details of what would have transpired.

---

[82]Christopher Hibbert, *The Great Mutiny: India 1857*, Penguin, 1980.
[83]Saul David, *The Indian Mutiny*, Viking, 2002.

'The sepoy lines in Barrackpore were quiet during the afternoon of 29 March in 1857,' writes Mukherjee. 'Most of the sepoys were lounging around, and the white officers were in their bungalows enjoying their siesta before preparing to go out with their families to attend evensong.' Nobody anticipated that the serenity was about to be disrupted and history about to be made.

> In the afternoon, a sepoy of the 34th Native Infantry, wearing his regimental jacket but in a dhoti instead of the regulation trousers appeared before the quarter-guard. It was obvious that he was greatly agitated. He had with him a loaded musket and his talwar (sword). He belonged to the 5th Company and his name was Mangal Pandey.[84]

Wagner's account[85] too points out that an excited Pandey paced up and down the ground in front of the guardroom near the parade ground, armed with a loaded musket. The sepoy was also heard threatening to shoot any European that he sighted and apparently hollered for his colleagues in the native infantry to come out of their barracks and join him in his rebellion against the British bosses of the East India Company army. According to David, he was reportedly shouting, 'Come out—the Europeans are here.' And, 'You sent me out here, why don't you follow me?' At this time, word was rushed to the Adjutant of the unit, Lieutenant Baugh, to get to the parade ground and he apparently 'immediately armed himself and galloped on his horse to the lines.' Seeing him approach, Pandey trained his gun on Baugh and fired. But he missed. Instead, the bullet struck the horse and both the British man and his beast fell to the ground. However, the man quickly recovered, snapped out one of his pistols and fired

---

[84]Rudrangshu Mukherjee, *Mangal Pandey: Brave Martyr or Accidental Hero?* Penguin, 2005.
[85]Kim A. Wagner, *The Great Fear of 1857: Rumours, Conspiracies and the Making of the Indian Uprising*, Peter Lang Limited, 2010.

at Pandey. He too missed. Pandey then lunged at him with his sword and slashed Baugh on the shoulder and neck. Baugh fell to the ground, bleeding but did not die. Pandey would possibly have finished him off but as he was about to reload his musket, another sepoy by the name of Shaikh Paltu held him back. By this time, a British Sergeant-Major named Hewson had reached the parade ground and ordered an Indian officer in command of the unit, Jemadar Ishwari Prasad to detain Pandey. But Prasad reportedly claimed that his officers had all gone to get help and therefore it was not possible for him to arrest Pandey. In the meantime, Baugh had gotten up, possibly dusted himself and charged towards the field shouting, according to Hibbert, 'Where is he? Where is he?' Hewson, who was in the field, fighting with Pandey, gestured to Baugh to back off, alerting him to the fact that Pandey was pointing his gun in his direction. 'Ride to the right, Sir, for your life. The sepoy will fire at you,' he had reportedly shouted, according to Hibbert. And Pandey did fire. Baugh fell to the ground again, but he survived the attack this time too. Hewson who had tried to intervene was knocked down when Pandey hit him from the back with the butt of his musket. Both Englishmen were sprawled out on the ground, groaning in pain. By then other sepoys had come out of their barracks hearing the commotion and they watched mutely. However, when Shaikh Paltu, who was having a hard time holding Pandey down, asked them for help for himself and the two Englishmen, they sniggered at him. A few of them went up and struck the officers prostrated on the ground, as though to unleash on them all their pent-up anger. And they started throwing sticks and stones and shoes and slippers at Shaikh Paltu, whom they considered a traitor as he seemed to be the only one not taking part in the mutiny. They demanded that he release Pandey but Shaikh Paltu held on steadfastly. His grip was loosening because he too had been by then injured in the scuffle with Pandey but he and the two

Englishmen were saved by the arrival at the spot of a commanding officer General Hearsey and his two sons, who rode into the scene on their trotting horses. Seeing them, Shaikh Paltu and the two Englishmen, relieved, managed to pick themselves up and backed off in different directions. Hearsey ordered the sepoys to fall in line and when they initially refused, he declared that he will shoot dead the first guard who disobeyed. They finally followed his order and led him to Pandey. Hearsey seized Pandey. Pandey, noticing that he had been done in, tried to kill himself. He reportedly pressed the muzzle of his musket to his chest and discharged it by pulling the trigger with his foot. The bullet pierced him. He fell to the ground, bleeding. His regimental jacket caught fire. But he did not die. He was revived and within a week of his recovery he was court-martialled. During the trial, when he was asked whether he was under the influence of any substance on the day of the incident, Pandey reportedly confessed to having consumed bhang, a country liquor and opium, according to David. According to Hibbert, he told the court that he had mutinied on his own accord and that no other person had played any part in encouraging him.

Indeed, the testimony that followed an enquiry is understood to have recorded that Pandey, 'unsettled by unrest amongst the sepoys and intoxicated by the narcotic "bhang" had seized weapons and run to the quarter-guard building upon learning that a detachment of British soldiers was disembarking from a steamer near the cantonment.' Pandey was sentenced to death by hanging and he was executed on 8 April. Three sepoys also testified against the Jemadar Ishwari Prasad, informing the court that he had prevented them from arresting Pandey. Prasad too was sentenced to death and hanged on 21 April.

Though there are discrepant views on whether Mangal Pandey did act alone on his own accord as he declared during his court martial or whether he stated that in order to protect his fellow sepoys, there is general consensus that grievances had been building up and the sepoys were disgruntled. The mutiny, whether it was a planned one, which Mangal Pandey led and the others supported, or was a spur of the moment action which others joined in, even if only as mere spectators, it was the bursting forth of all the grievances and disgruntlements that had been bottling up inside them.

Their chief grievance, the immediate trigger for the revolt, was said to have been a religious issue. The Company army was using bullets which came in cartridges that were lined with paper lubricated with the tallow of cows and pigs. The soldiers were supposedly required to tear open the cartridges with their teeth and this was objectionable to both Hindu and Muslim soldiers. While cows are considered holy in Hinduism and its meat not eaten, the meat of pigs is inauspicious in Islam. Several accounts have also claimed that the soldiers acted on suspicion rather than actual knowledge that lard from animal gut was used, but the important point to note is that for the Indian sepoys, as well as for a large section of the civilians amongst the people of India, the rule of the British East India Company and its institutions, including its army, with its ruthless treatment of the native soldiers had begun to become intolerable. The use of beef and pork oil, whether a mere suspicion or a fact, was just the final nail in the coffin of a long list of grave grievances.

Indeed, Barrackpore had once earlier erupted into a mutinous revolt by Indian infantrymen against their British commanders. That was in the year 1824. The cantonment was established in 1765, making it the oldest military station of the British East India Company in the subcontinent and over the years the Indian infantrymen had grown accustomed to the high-handedness and ill-treatment by the Europeans. Their disgruntlements had been building up. That year, reportedly three battalions of infantrymen were ordered to march to Chittagong (now in Bangladesh) all the way from Barrackpore which was a distance of 559.7 kilometres. From the seaport there they were to board ships and sail to Yangon, in Burma (now called Myanmar). They were not provided with transport and were expected to cover the entire route completely on foot. Led by a soldier named Binda Tiwari, the soldiers put their feet down. Quite literally. They demanded, among other things, bullock carts to carry their weaponry, more advanced battle gear and a doubling of their salaries. Moreover, they did not want to journey by sea. They called the Bay of Bengal, 'kaala paani' or black water. But other than the dangers of the dark depths of the swirling sea, they had another set of reasons to refuse the sea journey. And that reason was that it would entail being cooped up in the enclosed space of a ship and intermingling with other castes. They therefore laid down the condition that they would only go if they were allowed to travel by land. Here it must be mentioned that the British East India Company's army unit in Bengal comprised chiefly of men from Hindu upper-caste families who were brought in from the western and northern parts of the country, namely the Bhumihars of modern-day Bihar and Uttar Pradesh and the Rajputs of modern-day Rajasthan and some parts of what is now Pakistan. The recruitment into the army of lower or even upper-caste men from the Bengal region was avoided because the British reportedly regarded them with suspicion ever since the days of the Battle of Plassey when they fought against the British East India Company. This practice (rather policy) continued for a century (1757–1857).

Throughout this time, that is, the 100 years that preceded the mutiny, the British, not wanting to antagonize their soldiers, allowed them to observe their religious rituals and upper-caste men took their meals in separate enclosures from those of the lower castes. Indeed, they were exempted from taking part in different military activities which would impinge on their religious rights. This included sea travel because as mentioned earlier, it entailed having to be confined within the closed spaces of ships and other sea vessels which would mean having to eat and live in close proximity with other castes.

But perhaps, 10 decades had emboldened the British East India Company and made its officials (who were by then, 100 years later, a completely new generation), complacent and arrogant. These officials denied the soldiers the earlier privileges and provisions. The first rebellion launched by the soldiers and led by Tiwari, was on 1 November 1824, when they took control of the Barrackpore cantonment. The next day, two battalions of European enforcements along with other military officials were sent to tackle the mutineers, who were promised that their demands would be met or at least looked into, provided they surrendered completely and unconditionally. But they refused and after negotiations failed, the Europeans fired indiscriminately, killing over 200 native soldiers. Tiwari survived and was arrested along with 11 others. After a cursory trial, he was hanged and his body, limbs chained, was hung from the branch of a tree, where it was left to rot for days.

The British East India Company's brutality in dealing with dissenters became notorious. They viewed the natives with contempt and, judging by their utter lack of qualms about shooting dead hundreds of their own sepoys and other employees for standing up for their rights, they did not value the lives of Indians. The colonized masses were useful as cheap labour as long as they obeyed their command and they became entirely dispensable if they displayed any awareness of their human and well, religious rights. According basic birth rights to the natives or practicing rudimentary humane treatment was completely done away with as the rulers gradually gained absolute power. Those who dared to oppose the British tyrants were dealt with mercilessly.

Though the first dissent was the 1824 mutiny and there have been sporadic claims by historians that Binda Tiwari and not

Mangal Pandey deserves the honour and title of being India's first martyr, perhaps the fact that the 1857 mutiny spawned a series of other revolts across the land, especially in north and west India, has contributed to the second rebellion being considered the beginning of the phase of nationalistic revolution. Known variously as the First War of Independence, the Indian Insurrection, the Indian Mutiny, the Sepoy Mutiny, the Great Rebellion and the Rebellion of 1857, the dissent was brutally crushed. But however cruel the punishment that was handed out to the rebels, it could not deter subsequent rebellions from erupting.

Indeed, far from dissuading subsequent dissent, it is said that Mangal Pandey himself had been inspired by stories of Binda Tiwari that circulated in Barrackpore and was emboldened by the actions of his brave predecessor. As a matter of fact, even in 1824, in spite of the harsh punishment that was meted out to Binda Tiwari, a punishment which was meant to be a deterrent as far as the British was concerned, his fellow sepoys constructed a temple in honour of their hero, barely six months after his death. They were obviously not afraid of the consequences of flouting the orders of their British employers which mandated that Binda Tiwari be treated as a traitor rather than a martyr. The punishment for dissent got more and more ruthless in the days after the 1857 Barrackpore revolt.

One of the most barbaric forms of punishment during this time included executing convicted dissenters by tying them to the opening of cannons and firing through their torsos so that their bodies would completely disintegrate in the blast. George Carter Stent, who served in the British East India Company army at the time of the rebellion of 1857 and 1858, described this 'blowing from a gun' method of execution thus:

> The prisoner is generally tied to a gun with the upper part of the small of his back resting against the muzzle. When

the gun is fired his head is seen to go straight up into the air some forty or fifty feet; the arms fly off right and left, high up in the air, and fall at, perhaps, a hundred yards distance; the legs drop to the ground beneath the muzzle of the gun; and the body is literally blown away altogether, not a vestige being seen.[86]

Though the British did not invent this draconian form of execution, which existed since the Mughal Era, it became one of most widely employed methods of punishment by the East India Company. Because the body, having evaporated and the head and limbs scattered over a wide area, could not be properly cremated or buried, this form of death was deemed by both Hindus and Muslims as irreligious, one which would deprive the victim of heaven. It was therefore a dreaded form of punishment which was used by the British East India Company as a tool of deterrence.

So, in effect, to try to crush a rebellion, the eruption of which could, at least in part, be attributed to growing British insensitivity to religious sentiments of the native people, the foreigners used as a weapon of deterrence the very same religious sentimentality. Of course, the inherent barbarity of these forms of execution was less associated with their purported design as deterrents and more with the brutish thirst, blood thirst as it were, for revenge on those who dared to question the East India Company. Other forms of punishment, with death by hanging being the most common, too were in practice.

Other than these official forms of punishment, during the Rebellion of 1857, torture and atrocities of the most diabolical kind became rampant. In fact, the Rebellion of 1857 is replete with horror stories of unimaginable forms of violence, physical and psychological, inflicted by each warring side on the other. Not just Indian soldiers and civilians but, during the period of 1857

---

[86]Peter Havholm, *Politics and Awe in Rudyard Kipling's Fiction*, Routledge, 2008.

and 1858, British East India Company soldiers too were butchered and there are reports of dastardly attacks and atrocities even on European civilians, especially the families of the Company's officials and soldiers. One of the most brutal incidents reported was in Kanpur (then 'Cawnpur'), now in the state of Uttar Pradesh, when the men members of the families of Company officials and soldiers, fleeing to safety by boat, were killed off and the women and children taken prisoner and holed up in a house called 'Bibighar'. They were reportedly eventually massacred there. Rape and other forms of sexual violence were carried out by both sides and retributive violence was so brutal and so barbaric, the uprisings of 1857 and '58 have gone down in history as having recorded some of the most gruesome techniques of torture.

Historian and editor Rudrangshu Mukherjee mentions several of these, including, 'searing with hot irons...dipping in wells and rivers till the victim is half suffocated...sequencing the testicles... putting pepper and red chillies in the eyes or introducing them into the private parts of men and women...prevention of sleep... nipping the flesh with pincers...suspension from the branches of a tree...imprisonment in a room used for storing lime.'[87]

The Cawnpur event and allegations that the women and children were subjected to rape before being massacred, when reported in newspapers in London, is said to have turned that part of public opinion in Britain, which had earlier supported Indians' fight for independence, against the mutineers. So much so that the diabolical and barbaric nature of the violence that was inflicted on the natives of India, whether they were soldiers or common civilians failed to generate the kind of condemnation that would have perhaps put a stop to the brutality. The voice of reason and more importantly, that of humanity, that would cry

---

[87]Rudrangshu Mukherjee, *Spectre of Violence: The 1857 Kanpur Massacres*, Penguin, 1998.

out in anguish against the cruelty inflicted on anyone irrespective of race or religion, had gone mostly missing.

And yet glimmers of light which transcends petty divides have shone serendipitously through, emerging out of the darkness of mutual hatred to reveal inner depths of human compassion. William Dalrymple records the observations of a 19-year-old British army officer, Edward Vibart, whose family was wiped out in the Cawnpur massacre. One of the most touching examples of this kind of sympathy for fellow human beings, even enemies, the account of the young man first describes the event in which his parents, two younger brothers and two sisters were killed and then expresses pity for those killed in retaliation. In his words:

> The orders went out to shoot every soul…it was literally murder…I have seen many bloody and awful sights lately but such a one as I witnessed yesterday I pray I never see again. The women were all spared but their screams on seeing their husbands and sons butchered were most painful. Heaven knows I feel no pity, but when some old grey bearded man is brought and shot before your very eyes, hard must be that man's heart I think who can look on with indifference.[88]

The Rebellion itself lasted for 17 months. Though it was sparked off by the mutiny in Bengal's Barrackpore of 29 March 1857, the subsequent revolts of 1857 '58 took place mainly in the northern and western parts of the country. One month after Mangal Pandey's hanging, when 85 sepoys, of a garrison of 90 in the cantonment town of Meerut in Uttar Pradesh, refused to comply with the orders of their British superiors to use their teeth to tear off cartridges, which they suspected of being oiled with animal tallow, they were court-martialled and sentenced to prison. Their

---

[88] William Dalrymple, *The Last Mughal: The Fall of a Dynasty, Delhi 1857*, Penguin, 2006.

jail terms were as high as 10 years. They were publicly stripped off their uniforms, chained, paraded and dragged off. Apparently, as they were being hauled off, they taunted their fellow sepoys (including the five who did not participate in the initial refusal), who were watching. The accused soldiers called their colleagues cowards and ridiculed them for being mute spectators and not coming to their rescue. The next day, on 10 May, which was a Sunday, there were murmurs that Indian sepoys were planning to break into jail and set their colleagues free. The British soldiers and officers stationed in Meerut did not take much notice. By afternoon, however, the market area of the garrison town had already erupted into a civilian rebellion with angry protests against the jailing of Indian sepoys. British soldiers who had gone to the bazaar were attacked and killed. Sepoys stormed into the prisons to rescue their colleagues and went on a rampage. Quarters of British officers and soldiers were set on fire, and on that day four men, eight women and eight children from the European side were killed. At night, the sepoys marched off to Delhi, where they forced the last Mughal emperor, Bahadur Shah, to accept leadership of the mutineers, which he did reluctantly. The 80-year-old king, though a cultural icon of the times, known for his fondness for the arts, music and literature, was keenly aware of the diminishing military strength of the Mughal Empire and of the enormous power that had been gained by the British East India Company army. Under the leadership of the previous Governor-General of India, James Andrew Braun-Ramsay Dalhousie, who had been on an aggressive expansion drive, most of the once mighty Mughal Empire had fallen into British hands. Bahadur Shah's inkling of his own weakness proved right because in the end the Rebellion was crushed, his sons were executed and he was banished to live in exile in a foreign country.

However, for some time, throughout 1857 '58, the chance that the British East India Company could be finally defeated, loomed large. Its army was kept engaged in one battle after the other, beset as it was by a series of continuous uprisings. Province after province joined in, in the war to drive the British out of the subcontinent. These included northern and western Indian provinces and kingdoms such as Jhansi, Kanpur and Lucknow. The local kings, queens, princes and other rulers of the regions were compelled to take action against the British East India Company in order to protect their turf against aggressions and annexations. In Jhansi, for instance, Queen Lakshmi Bai, had first tried to reason with the British, which had imposed on her land an arbitrary and entirely absurd law it had devised titled the 'Doctrine of Lapse'. This law enabled the East India Company to takeover kingdoms and provinces in which rulers were not succeeded by a biological heir. The queen's own son had died when he was only three months old and she and her husband had adopted a boy. After the king's death, the queen was informed by the British that the Company would acquire her kingdom because it did not recognize the adopted child as heir. Queen Lakshmi Bai had appealed for an exemption to the local British administrator, who it is said, was so impressed by her intelligence and beauty that he agreed to take up her case. On his advice she hired a British lawyer to argue on her behalf in the court of the Governor-General. But the Governor-General refused. She was asked to vacate her premises. The queen is understood to have proclaimed famously, *'Main meri Jhansi nahin doongi'* (I will not give up my Jhansi). When Lakshmi Bai's palace was seized by British forces, she escaped by jumping off the high walls of her fortress on a horse, with her son tied to her back. Though she and her son survived, the horse later died. The queen joined forces with another ruler, Tantia Ramachandra Pandurang Tope, but in a battle with British forces, she was killed. In spite of the persistence of uprisings against the British in the nearly two-year-long war for independence from East India Company rule, eventually the native forces were defeated.

The significance of the role played by Bengal in India's First War of Independence was immense. Not only did the first in the series of uprisings emanate from the region but it was the Bengal unit of the British East India Company's native army, with its mainly upper-caste men (who refused to bow down to orders that interfered with their religious practices), that led the way, even in the subsequent revolts. Though these were concentrated in the country's north and northwest, the eastern region, which comprised Bengal, Bihar and Orissa too recorded its share of rebellions. Indian sepoys mutinied in the important port of Chittagong or Chattogram (now in Bangladesh) in September of 1857 and seized the treasury, keeping it in their control for days. Subsequently, on 18 November, three companies of the 34th Bengal Infantry Regiment stormed the Chittagong Jail and freed all the prisoners. 357 kilometres away, in the capital city of Calcutta, more uprisings threatened to dislodge the British East India Company army. 591 kilometres from Calcutta, in the hilly forests of Jalpaiguri, now north Bengal, sepoys launched a simultaneous attack on the British army. 152 kilometres from Calcutta, in Murshidabad's Lalbagh area, more mutinies followed. And 315 kilometres from Calcutta, in the town of Dhaka (now the capital city of Bangladesh) more sepoys had gone on a rampage. Distances did not deter the spread of the rebellion, which erupted in far flung places, possibly encouraged by news of other revolts in other parts, or simply because it was time.

Bengal had other reasons to revolt, besides the East India Company's offensive policies that disregarded religious sentiments. The people of this land suffered tremendously as a result of its misrule. The treaties signed after the Battle of Plassey in 1757 and the Battle of Buxur in 1764 gave the British East India Company unconditional rights over taxation. Rapacious officers of the trading company tried to maximize profit by levying exorbitant land revenues and in so doing their cruelty cannot be overstated. To reiterate the kind of torment they subjected the people of Bengal to, even during droughts, when agricultural output was minimal, poor farmers were expected to pay up tariff at stiff rates, decided arbitrarily by the East India Company. The most horrific example of that was perhaps the famine of 1770 when a severe shortage of rain that year resulted in failed crops. Instead of providing relief to the people by way of easing taxes, the East India Company raised its tariffs, by some accounts, as much as 50 per cent compared to the earlier 10 per cent, on agricultural produce and ruthlessly insisted on collection.

What ensued was utter disarray in the lives of people, especially in the rural areas, who were pushed headlong into poverty. Droughts, as a natural phenomenon, were common but previously rulers exempted the peasants, who were affected, from paying taxes, which, at between 18 to 20 per cent approximately, were in any case much lower than that charged by the British East India Company. Famines, death due to starvation or other food crises were averted by most of the earlier regimes not just through tax exemption but with aid and even infrastructural facilities such as irrigation. But the British East India Company, in order to fulfil its profit targets and make up for the loss of revenue due to the famine, hiked up the rates. In what has come to be considered one of the worst famines in history, approximately 10 million people in Indian villages died of starvation that year.

One of the chief engineers of the policies which led to this horror was Robert Clive, whom historian William Dalrymple, while documenting this period, calls an 'unstoppable sociopath'. To the further devastation of Bengal, most of the revenue from land tax collected by the East India Company, was channelized outside the country. This revenue from land tax, of course, was not the only wealth which flowed out of Bengal. The East India Company's profits from trade as well as its officers' personal gains too found its way out of the land.

Throughout British rule, other famines followed and though these were caused by a combination of factors, the main reason was the greed of the East India Company officials in the earlier period and the tyrannical policies of the British Crown rule subsequently. The shortage of grains, which preceded famines, for instance, was exacerbated by the East India Company's decision to takeover large swathes of fertile farmland for the cultivation of poppy and indigo, which was considered lucrative. And the cause of the famine of 1943 has been attributed to the policies of the then British government led by Prime Minister Winston Churchill, who infamously diverted agricultural produce from India to fatten supply lines of British armies fighting in World War II. The deprivation of India's people, who died in millions due to starvation and disease, of the food grown by them is a crime of genocide no less horrific than some of the worst in human history. Interestingly, however, other than the rare voice of censure Churchill has not faced adequate international condemnation.

Thus, Bengal was plundered and its people rendered impoverished. But it was not just that it was systematically depleted of its riches, enormous wealth and its treasures by the British East India Company. The crime committed by the British East India Company against Bengal was so much more than that. The famine of 1770 wiped out nearly one-thirds of the population of the region and no one was punished for this. The British culpability lies in the fact that it looted and robbed the very land that poured out its bounty to it. It raped and killed the very people that nurtured it.

By the time the first mutiny broke out in Bengal's Barrackpore, the people of this land had had enough.

XII

OF BREADS AND BISCUITS, TEA AND TOAST

> *'The king of ghosts has gifted a boon/Eat as much as you like from midnight to noon.'*
>
> —Satyajit Ray[89]

The British government in the United Kingdom too had had enough. Though for different reasons. It was becoming increasingly inconvenient for Great Britain to allow the East India Company to function independently in India. Corrupt officials of the trading outfit in the subcontinent did not properly divulge information about the extent of the profit they earned, deemed to be much higher than the revenue that they did disclose. The British government was fed up of repeated reports of losses (as unscrupulous officers pocketed the huge profits) and irked that instead of earning from it, it was constantly required to pay for the upkeep of the merchant company. The East India Company took numerous loans from back home to sustain itself on foreign shores. To make matters worse, its policies like the 'Doctrine of

---

[89]From the humorous song, 'Bhooter Raja Dilo Bor' written and composed by Satyajit Ray for the film *Goopy Gyne, Bagha Byne*, based on his grandfather and writer Upendra Kishore Roychowdhury's story.

Lapse' turned local rulers in India against the British, triggering mutinies and battles. The British government held the East India Company's excesses responsible for the soldiers' mutiny and did not appreciate the fact that it had to send in reinforcements in order to buttress soldier strength of the East India Company's army. It was getting just too expensive for Britain which, therefore, decided that it was better to rule the Indian subcontinent directly than indirectly through the East India Company.

Therefore, post the defeat of the native rulers and soldiers in India's First War of Independence, in 1858, Great Britain dissolved the East India Company and transferred power to the British Crown. Twenty years later, in 1878, Britain reinforced its power over the land, when it declared Britain's Queen Victoria, empress of India. This period, beginning 1858 and known alternatively as the British Rule, Crown Rule or British Raj, as opposed to Company rule, continued for just under 90 years after the countrywide movement for Independence culminated in negotiating its end in 1947. But these nine decades were some of the most eventful, significantly altering the course of the history of Bengal and the whole of India.

Here it is important to note that while the British government in England expressed anguish over the conduct of the East India Company in India, especially as regards its treatment of the natives of the land, Britain's own ostensible concern had more to do with taking control rather than considerations of justice or equality for the people of foreign lands. It must be remembered that Britain had, by then, already established itself as an imperial power which had no qualms about annexing land and people the world over. This was done chiefly to fund the industrial revolution which had begun to take place in Britain more than a century earlier. The new colonies were the loci from where the vast raw materials that were required would be procured. Cotton and silk for the growing textile industries; tea and spices, exports and imports of exotic condiments, edibles and beverages, poppy, indigo, etc.

Not that within the British Parliament or in the government of the British Raj in India, there were no advocates of justice and equality. There were remarkable exceptions who may not have questioned the ethics of Britain's right to conquer and rule foreign lands but certainly reflected on, and were critical of, its imperialistic arrogance. They included Alan Octavian Hume, who was one of the few Britons to have been associated with the formation of the Indian National Congress in 1885. He had famously observed that, 'a studied and invariable disregard if not actual contempt for the opinions and feelings of our subjects, is... the leading characteristic of our government.'[90]

The new British government in India however did take pains to distance itself from the kinds of policies practiced by the East India Company. In order to purportedly rectify the defects of the earlier East India Company government, on 2 August the Parliament of the United Kingdom passed a law entitled the 'Government of India Act, 1858,' which was originally named, 'An Act for the Better Government of India'. Furthermore, in order to try to instil in the people of India a sense of reassurance that the new regime would be significantly different from and better than that of the British East India Company in terms of its policies, a proclamation by Queen Victoria, which followed the Government of India Act, 1858, was issued, decreeing that it would look after the interests of the local people just as much as it did its own subjects in Great Britain. Addressed to the 'Princes, Chiefs and People of India' it stated, 'We hold ourselves bound to the natives of our Indian territories by the same obligation of duty which bind us to all our other subjects.'[91]

---

[90]Jona Aravind Dohrmann, 'The Congress Party as the Creator, Preserver and Destroyer of the Indian State?' *Indien-Politik, Wirtschaft, Gesellschaft*, 2005.
[91]The Government of India Act, 1858 *Proclamation Issued by Queen Victoria, 1 November, 1858* original text of which is available online at https://www.bl.uk/

In practice, however, Great Britain did not live up to this promise. Equality was a far cry and Indians, in their own land, were treated as subordinates to their British colonizers. The British rulers, in varying degrees, were, at best condescending and patronizing or disdainful and contemptuous and at worst exploitative and oppressive.

Initially there was no Indian representation in the government of the British Raj. Later, attempts were made at inclusiveness. In 1892, a law, titled, 'The Indian Councils Act, 1892', was passed allowing a limited number of Indians—39 at the time—from the educated and upper-classes, to be appointed to the legislative councils and their roles were strictly advisory. The structure was rigid, with the Viceroy heading the central imperial legislative council and governors (11 in number at the time) leading the provincial legislative councils. Another reform in 1909 resulted in an amendment to the existing law and the 'Indian Councils Act, 1909,' was created to entitle Indians, again from the local elites, to be elected to the different legislative bodies—numbering 135 at the time. But they were to represent only select electorate groups and their constituencies were limited to these. These included groups of people of different castes and religions. This was the start of the politics of division according to castes and religions. Other than the 'Provincial and Central Legislative Councils', power-decentralization policies saw the creation of 'District Boards' and 'Municipal Corporations'.

Other administrative and legislative bodies too gradually accepted limited numbers of Indians. They were appointed or elected depending on the type of governmental organization. But whether central or provincial or whether appointed or elected, the roles of Indians were primarily those of deputies. The very

---

collection-items/proclamation-by-the-queen-in-council-to-the-princes-chiefs-and-people-of-india#. Accessed on 21 July 2021.

structure of these systems discriminated against Indians, not allowing them to supersede their British bosses.

However, that Indians would not be hired in the topmost positions was hardly surprising when one considers the real reasons for them being included in these British institutions in the first place. Different reasons necessitated the taking of these measures of course. One of the key reasons was to keep them appeased so as to prevent eruptions of violence such as the uprisings of 1857 and 1858. Another important reason for introducing local appointees and elected representative was to tap into their understanding of local issues. They were, after all, more knowledgeable than their British colleagues on ground matters.

It was not difficult to see through this and gradually Indians within the governing institutions began to voice their discontentment with British discriminatory practices. Indeed, they grew to represent the Opposition within the government and pressed for greater degrees of autonomy and finally demanded the right to self-government. Eventually, it led to the call for complete freedom and the formation of the Nationalist Movement, which in turn culminated in India's Independence in 1947.

Clearly, though the Uprising of 1857 and 1858 had been suppressed, the spirit of rebellion against the foreign rulers continued to simmer and finally erupted in flames.

Bengal remained central to the action. Of the three 'Presidencies' or demarcated territories under British control (Bengal, Bombay and Madras) even during the East India Company rule, Bengal was the seat of administration. Calcutta was the capital city and continued to be, well into the reign of the British Crown until 1919, when the capital was shifted to New Delhi.

British influence on Bengal and particularly Calcutta, therefore, cannot be overstated. The 'colonial hangover' as the phenomenon, describing the continuing legacy, is called, is still reflected not just in the country's software, so to speak, (its systems of governance including the executive, judiciary and legislative, for instance) that the British left behind, but also in the remaining hardware—the administrative buildings with their typically colonial architecture, the infrastructure that the colonizers imported and established into the soil of the land in order to carry out their functions. These stand testimonies to the influence that the colonizers exerted, as much as the country's culture, cuisine, language and lifestyle did. And, again, perhaps nowhere is this colonial influence more glaringly visible than in Bengal, especially Calcutta.

The Howrah Bridge, a bridge over the Hooghly river which connects Howrah to Calcutta, and which has become an iconic symbol of the city of Calcutta for its durability and strength, as well as its majestic appearance, was first proposed in 1862, during the British Raj, when the Bengal government requested George Turnbull, chief engineer of the East India Railway Company to construct a link between the important trading ports of Howrah and the capital city of Calcutta. A sort of metaphor for Bengal itself, for its ability to withstand untold pressures, Howrah Bridge has spawned entire works of art, having become, over the years, a central theme in poetry, prose, photography and popular motion pictures. In 1958, exactly 100 years after the British Raj was established, a movie was named after the Howrah Bridge, directed by renowned Hindi filmmaker Shakti Samanta, which is said to have been the most successful film of that year. Starring Madhubala and Ashok Kumar, two of the most celebrated actors of the time, the film is set in the city of Calcutta.

In fact, much of Bengal's infrastructure, till today, is traced back to the days of the British Raj or even earlier, to the time of the East India Company rule. Dalhousie initiated many major infrastructural projects, including bridges, canals, roads and of course, the railways. Another area that witnessed rapid technological development was in communications, and postal departments saw the installation of telegraphic systems. The improvement in transport and communications was necessitated, again, by the industrial revolution and the collection of raw material from various corners of the country.

It is important to note here, however, that in the case of Bengal and the rest of the country, the cost of these infrastructural and other technological advancements was borne by the multitudes of Indian taxpayers and not by private individuals or corporations that funded developments in Britain. Historians Burton Stein and David Arnold, writing about this, pointed to the injustice which landed India's peasants and farmers in economic distress. They write:

> Unlike Britain itself, where the market risks for infrastructural development was borne by private investors, in India, it was the taxpayers—primarily farmers and farm-labourers—who endured the risks, which in the end amounted to fifty million pounds. In spite of these costs, very little skilled employment was created for Indians. By 1920, with a history of sixty years of its construction, only 10 per cent of the 'superior posts' in the railways were held by Indians.[92]

Indeed, and unfortunately, it is not easy to identify any other motive behind the vast progress, development and improvement that is attributed to British rule, whether Company or Crown, other than its own self-serving interests. Except for, as earlier mentioned, such acts as the abolition of sati pratha and child marriage (though ulterior motives were ascribed to these too, as we have discussed earlier), the British rarely ruled India with concern or compassion for its subjects. On the contrary, and this is a recurrent observation, the British engaged in flagrant exploitation of Indians.

---

[92]Burton Stein, David Arnold, *History of India*, Wiley Blackwell, 2011.

Having said that, these advancements in communications, infrastructure and technology, though for Britain's own benefits rather than for the upliftment of India's masses, ushered in unprecedented changes in the country.

Like its infrastructure, Bengal's colonial past haunts its architecture too. Virtually every street corner, especially in the older parts of Calcutta, is testimony to its legacy.

And of these said street corners, there is one block which stands out more than the others. That block is Dalhousie Square or BBD Bagh. It stands out not just for the sheer number of colonial buildings that it houses in close proximity but for the history that it is steeped in.

The block is a vast patch of land, stretching from the clusters of imposing structures which served as the government offices of the reign of both the Company and the British Raj, all the way down to the river Hooghly. Indeed, not very far from the river port of Sutanuti, where Job Charnock had landed in 1690, this was the very location of the British East India Company's first factory fortresses, Fort William. It was here that in 1756, a year before he himself was defeated and killed in the Battle of Plassey, that the then nawab or ruler of Bengal had arrived with his army from his palace in Murshidabad and engaged the British in a battle, which he won. It was here that the infamous 'black hole' incident (in which 146 prisoners of war were said to have been crammed into a 14 by 18-foot dungeon, where 123 of them died of suffocation) took place. Today, ruins of the cell in which the horrific incident is said to have occurred still stands, its walls torn down, as a silent testimony to the ghastly days, two and a half centuries ago, when battles for the control of Calcutta, Bengal and India was the daily routine.

Today, this vast patch of land is the central business and office district of Calcutta, housing the Writers' Building, which has been the Bengal state secretariat since India's independence (until recently when the new regime shifted the secretariat to Howrah); the Assembly House, the seat of the state's legislative assembly; the General Post Office; the Calcutta High Court and Government House or Raj Bhavan, among others.

Usually referred to by its colonial name, Dalhousie Square (after the East India Company Governor-General, Lord Dalhousie), it was renamed Benoy Badal Dinesh Bagh (BBD Bagh) after the three martyrs of the Indian Freedom Struggle, Benoy Basu, Badal Gupta and Dinesh Gupta. The story of the ends of their lives too is deeply rooted in the soil of this ancient, eventful and vast patch of land in Calcutta. It was 8 December of the year 1930, when the Indian Freedom Movement was at its peak. The three young men, who belonged to the Bengal Volunteers, a secret revolutionary group, barged into the Writers' Building carrying loaded revolvers. They were not intercepted at the entrance because they were camouflaged as workers at the British offices and were dressed in European clothes. Their mission was to kill Colonel N.S. Simpson, inspector general of police, who was notorious for his cruelty and brutality in dealing with Indian political prisoners, especially freedom fighters. The three freedom fighters were successful and shot the cruel cop dead. Subsequently, a gun battle ensued inside the long and labyrinthine corridors of the government building. Soon they found themselves overpowered by police. Unwilling to be caught, they attempted to take their own lives. Only Badal, who immediately consumed poison (potassium cyanide) died on the spot. The others shot themselves but survived. Benoy was taken to hospital where he died five days later and Dinesh was arrested and hanged. Sporadically structures have come up around the Writers' Building, including a statue in front of it of Benoy, Badal and Dinesh, depicting the martyrs marching to the battle ahead, with the group leader, Benoy, leading the charge.

Designed by Thomas Lyon in 1777, the 150-metre-long Writers' Building stretches out almost the entire horizontal length of the lake, Lal Dighi, in front it. Architecturally, it is typical of the early British colonial designs which were introduced to the new settlements. Initially, the colonizers would use the neoclassical or gothic revival or baroque styles for their constructions but gradually over the years, they integrated the imported, so to speak, with the indigenous, including those influenced by Hinduism, Islam, Buddhism and other local religions and cultures. This became known as the Indo-Saracenic style of architecture.

Very often the type of building—whether institutional, governmental, official or residential, etc.—determined the architectural style which was to be adopted. The Writers' Building was constructed for the purpose of providing accommodation to the junior clerks, called 'writers' of the East India Company. Greco-Roman in style, it was fitted with a massive pediment on which stands the statue of Minerva, the Roman Goddess of Wisdom, the counterpart of the Greek Goddess Athena. More sculptures of Greek and Roman gods and goddesses were installed, with the expansive terrace being dotted with these. Another feature of this form of architecture was the installation of verandahs and porticos. A 128-feet long verandah, lined with Ionic columns, each of them 32-feet-high was added to the first and second floors of the Writers' Building in 1821. Over the years, other extensions were constructed to what has come to represent a magnificent mansion, with two new blocks being installed between 1889 and 1906. These blocks could only be accessed via the twisted iron staircases that were added to it, and which are still in use. Other features that have remained unchanged over the years is the red surface of the exposed bricks which cover the entire outer wall of the building.

As far as residential houses of British officers were concerned, a variety of styles evolved, merging the indigenous with the imported. While the Writers' Building was three floors high—in fact, the first three-story building in Calcutta—most of the domestic homes were one or two-story houses, usually surrounded by front lawns or kitchen gardens. Even today, in Calcutta and the surrounding countryside of Bengal, one can serendipitously come across an old colonial-era bungalow or two and even chance upon mansions, reflective of the Indo-Saracenic style.

During this period, Bengal, particularly Calcutta, was influenced in many other ways by British life and to this day the state and city continue to nurse these colonial hangovers. Among these are the two 'Cs', its cuisine and its club culture; the alliterative, Calcutta colonial cuisine and club culture, so to speak.

Elitist clubs of colonial Bengal, which were instituted as spaces where the cream of British society living in or visiting Calcutta could socialize, were set up in prime locales. These were notorious for their discriminatory treatment towards the locals. 'Dogs and Indians not allowed'—or instructions to that effect, hammering home the point that the colonized natives were equal in status to lowly creatures as far as the white colonists are concerned—is a message that was conveyed through signboards which commonly hung from doors to the entrances.

The Bengal Club, which was established in 1827, during the reign of the British East India Company, continued to disallow Indians to seek membership well into the middle of the twentieth century. It was not until 1959, that is 12 years after Independence, that non-whites could finally apply.

Historians have pointed to the irony that the premises had originally belonged to an Indian, the renowned writer, Kali Prasanna Sinha. But then, wasn't the entire imperial experience an exercise in irony? Considering that the colonizers deprived the very Indians to whom the land that they had annexed rightfully belonged, of the privileges which it accorded itself in every which way possible, it is hardly surprising that the British would usurp entitlements when it came to club culture.

But what is even more ironic is that in independent India, the elitism that caused considerable consternation in Indians during the British East India Company and British Crown rules was allowed to continue and still continues to thrive more than 70 years after the British departed.

Though protests, demonstrations and strong private and public criticism has sporadically challenged these clubs' British-era elitism, there has not been adequate enough of a movement against the practice of continued exclusivity for it to have been eradicated completely. Indeed, there exists a kind of tacit indulgence in allowing discriminatory treatment to continue in the name of preserving heritage and tradition. Literature on colonial club culture, by and large, has failed to express anger over the sheer violation of human and national dignity that these clubs perpetuated by taking almost condoning tones—usually laced with indulgent humour—while describing the exclusivity of elitist clubs of the British era. This is perhaps necessitated by the compulsions of the writers of such literature, who, by virtue of belonging to the 'right class' (read: Anglicized, educated, economically and socially upper-class Indians) became the inheritors of the legacy, replacing the departing colonizers.

Innumerable, post-Independence instances have pointed to the fact that though the British are long gone, they have left behind their dubious legacy of discrimination. Extant, elitist, colonial clubs throughout India have unabashedly forced colonial exclusivity down the throats of the country's citizens by, for instance, barring them entry for being attired in what was ostensibly 'inappropriate' clothing but was actually an insistence on following British-era dress codes which disregarded national clothing and costumes of various regions.

On 10 October 1987, musician Ananda Shankar, globally renowned for his innovative sitar renditions and his experiments with fusing eastern classical with western jazz and rock music, was stopped from going into a club in Calcutta for being attired in a kurta and pyjama ensemble. Interesting, because some three decades earlier, during the 1960s, his famous uncle, the sitar maestro Pandit Ravi Shankar, had the world's most iconic Brits, the Beatles, sit at his feet, cross-legged, Indian-style, clad in kurtas and pyjamas.

Yet, a few of the clubs during the colonial period came about as a reaction to the discriminatory practices of the British. The story goes that the Calcutta Club, which was set up in 1907, was instituted in order to accommodate non-whites who were barred from entering the other clubs. Its history is traced back to an interesting incident. The then Viceroy of India, Lord Minto, had wanted to invite the eminent Bengali industrialist Rajen Mookerjee to dinner at the Bengal Club. But he was informed that the rules disallowed it. The Calcutta Club thus came into being.

Of course, racism was not the only vice which these clubs were afflicted with. Male chauvinism, bordering on misogyny, was equally rampant. Most clubs barred women entry, forget extending membership rights. After the British were chased out, the clubs continued the legacy of exclusion. 'Brown sahibs', the Indian equivalents of the upper-class white men, now took over and stuck to the old rules of allowing only selective membership. It was as late as 2007, when after a bitter battle against gender discrimination by a few eminent citizens of Calcutta, that the Calcutta Club started to allow women as members.

A section of scholars argue that India was fertile ground for planting the seeds of flagrant discrimination. For one, the caste system, which ostensibly came into effect in order to create a perfectly functioning society in which division of labour was meant to ensure that different areas of work were divided among social groups according to ability and aptitude (and the idea that skills and knowledge would be passed down through generations), was in reality a mode of practising discrimination.

The 'club culture' clearly fired the imagination of the Bengalis because, over the years, people throughout the region have been getting together to form themselves into groups around a common cause or theme with the result that almost every neighbourhood in the state of West Bengal today has at least one club. These are mostly 'youth clubs' in which young, male members of a residential area get together to spend their spare time engaging in various activities including playing indoor games (cards, carom, chess, table tennis, etc.) or outdoor sports (cricket, football, etc.). Often, they carry out philanthropic work, especially social services like organizing blood donation camps. Almost all of these clubs conduct their own separate Pujas during the specific festival seasons, Durga Puja being an occasion for fierce competition between groups. Funds for these celebrations are collected from families in the neighbourhood, shops and even educational institutions like schools and colleges and other establishments. Called chanda (donation), this door-to-door method of crowd-collection has gained notoriety for the element of coercion often employed by the men (and women, who have increasingly become members of these youth clubs compared to the past). In innumerable instances, they have resorted to veiled and even open threats in order to extort money from involuntary donors. One of the commonest complaints of people who have to part with 'donation' is that the clubs quote arbitrary (read: exorbitant) figures rather than letting the payer decide how much to give. Others participate in the donation process willingly though it is debatable whether they do so of their own volition or they feel that there is no point in trying to get out of it.

Politics is discussed heatedly over hot tea or cold beer in these clubs. Often politicians generously donate to the clubs' funds in the hope that they will help campaign for their political party and 'influence' voters in the neighbourhood. There are also 'women only' clubs much like the 'ladies' clubs' of the colonial era in which British women, barred from the male exclusivity, got together, usually in the home of a member, for 'kitty parties' where they drank gin and played cards for money. Having said that, gambling is hardly the activity of today's women's clubs in Calcutta or the rest of Bengal, which are the loci of a great deal of significant work, especially in the area of gender issues.

The elderly has formed clubs too, in which members go for morning and evening walks together or participate in other 'health' and 'fitness' programs. There are 'laughing clubs', for instance, in which members gather, usually at a park or other open spaces and are guided by an instructor as they release stress through induced-laughter.

These clubs are ubiquitous. Not the esoteric colonial clubs in terms of the social strata that their membership represents. But they have stemmed from the same concept, which is the 'clubbing' together of a group of people who share a common trait to the exclusion of another. Clubs are often named after Bengal's icons though they do not strictly adhere to their philosophies. Vivekananda Club in southern Calcutta's Sonarpur, a tiny, one-storey, low-ceiling hut overlooking a lake, for instance is well-known in the locality for its wild parties late into the night, especially on New Year's Eve, and not for the study of the great leaders' philosophy.

A key feature of club culture, perhaps it goes without saying, was/is: food. Whether the exclusive colonial clubs or the ubiquitous local clubs across Bengal, eating (and drinking—both hard and soft drinks) was/is central to all or at least most of the activities.

And this brings us to the topic of Bengal's cuisine, without a discussion about which, no story or history of this land can be complete. Says Shiladitya Chaudhury, connoisseur of global cuisine, 'It has been said about Bengalis that while others eat to live, Bengalis live to eat, so great is this species' love for food.'

This can be attributed to the region's easy availability of food chiefly because of the natural resources accessible to it. The world's largest delta, the Sundarbans, is to its east and south. As is the sea, the Bay of Bengal. The globe's longest mountain range, the Himalayas, stretch majestically out along its north. The land, in different parts, is (or at least, was when humans settled in Bengal) covered in dense jungles. Rivers, nearly a hundred of them (not counting smaller rivulets, streams and brooks), flow through the land. Indian rivers that originate in other regions, including Ganga, Jamuna, Mahananda, Dwarka, Kalindi, Atrai, Damodar, Punarbhaba, to name a few, flow through Bengal to eventually merge into the sea. Hundreds and thousands of lakes and ponds dot the landscape.

It is not surprising, that with so many water bodies, fish, both saltwater and sweet, became the staple for people of this region ever since humans settled here (and had learnt to catch prey using hunting tools). Moreover, the fertility of the land, enriched by the many rivers which carry and inundate it with vitamins and minerals, make it abundantly cultivable. Crops of various kinds, especially paddy, which is supposed to have arrived in the land over 5,000 years ago from Southeast Asia, was grown in Bengal from the time that humans settled in the area and had learnt the art of agriculture. Fish and rice, therefore, has always been and is still, today, the primary diet of Bengalis in the mainland. In the hills and forests, dwellers (that is, the tribal folk) subsisted off the jungle produce, hunting down wild animals such as deer and boar for their meat or eating a variety of fruits and greens. Ants, till date, are eaten by the village folk in the jungles along the western border of the state of West Bengal. As are snakes in the non-vegetarian category and mushrooms and wild berries in the vegetarian. Furthermore, due to the large expanses of green pastures, where cattle, including buffalos, cows and goats could graze, dairy became another major food group for Bengalis in the mainland. Milk from these animals became part of the staple for Bengalis. Poultry, that is chicken farming for eggs and meat, however, would come much later and is considered an external influence, brought in by subsequent regimes, after political conquests, namely the Mughals and the British.

The easy accessibility to food, some would argue, would have turned Bengalis, (especially with their brains grown intelligent by the rich content of Omega-3 oil in fish), to other more challenging pursuits. But Bengalis turned the preparation of food, including cooking fish and rice in a variety of different ways, and enhancing the taste of the dishes with a host of condiments and spices, into an obsession. In the early days, it must be remembered, entertainment comprised mostly of religious celebrations and social festivities, in which meals were an integral part. The pursuit of education, including reading and writing was not for the common people, far less the study of sciences, mathematics or the humanities. People chiefly just concentrated on gathering knowledge pertaining to rudimentary existence, namely, the production of food, that is, agriculture. Art, various forms of it, including folk drawings and painting, such as on the walls of huts with indigenous colours culled from flowers, fruits, vegetables, leaves and even mud (red earth was a commonly-used decorator in Bengal's villages) was a hobby, of course, and not a career option. Music, including vocal and instrumental, which entrepreneurial individuals throughout and in different parts of Bengal, composed by virtue of their innate talents, too evolved as natural tendencies and compulsions and could be called 'hobbies' (to use a modern definition of such activities) of the early people rather than pursuits which were given importance in society. Having said that, of course, Bengali civilization evolved for thousands of years and the cultivation of culture and art took place simultaneously. Like food, dance and music too played a significant role in the entertainment of the early times whether in religious ceremonies or social festivities. Folk dance and music in Bengal is traced back to thousands of years and people did spend considerable time not just in innovation but also in improving on techniques and skills. Musical instruments such as the 'ektara' (one-stringed), 'dotara' (double-stringed), 'dugdugi', 'esraj', 'khomok', not to mention various varieties of flutes, originated in Bengal and were refined over the years and is still used by folk singers such as the Bauls and Sufis of Bengal. Other areas of indigenous innovation, which served functions of meeting basic needs such as clothing and bedding, were the production of jute and cotton for cloth, blankets, mats, ropes and other items and early Bengali society invested large chunks of time in honing their skills in these pursuits. Pottery and the creation of a host of other earthenware for utilitarian functions, including vessels for cooking or storing water too, developed over thousands of years. Terracotta and other clay art too go back hundreds of years indicating that the people of this region did consider pastime activity a vital part of life. However, culinary pursuits did take precedence and the cultivation of cuisine in Bengal is, arguably, unmatched when compared to the early Bengalis' other areas of interest.

Indeed, somewhere down the line, Bengali cuisine had transcended its utilitarian function as food, to have become a form of art.

And so, different areas of Bengal (now divided into the two countries of Bangladesh and India) competed with each other in producing dishes which were innovative and experimental.

While a seemingly endless variety of fish was at the disposal of the Bengali a few stood out for commanding the most attention as far as experimentation and innovation was concerned, perhaps, chiefly, due to its taste.

'Ilish' or hilsa, which is found both in the river and sea, was and still is, amongst the most favoured fish of the Bengalis. It has traditionally always been at the centre of a tug of war between the 'Bangals' (Bengalis from the eastern part of Bengal, now fallen mostly inside Bangladesh) and the 'Ghotis' (Bengalis from the western part of Bengal, now mostly in the Indian state of West Bengal), each of whom have claimed superiority of skill and technique as far as culinary preparations is concerned.

Each has subjected the hapless species to a variety of cooking techniques, including drying, frying, baking, boiling and grilling, to name just a few.

Lately, it has been claimed, though it is not known who, when, where, why or how that the war has ended and that it has been established that the Bangals were by far the more knowledgeable and talented in cooking 'hilsa'. The 'Ghotis', in this context, has reportedly been handed a compensation prize, having been offered the tag of being the masters of another Bengali favourite dish, the 'daabchingri' (prawns and shrimps cooked in the hollow of the unripe coconut, after draining it of its juice and water), which they have evidently gracefully accepted.

One can only conjecture that the decision was possibly based on the creation of a unique dish by the Bangals: 'ilish macher paturi'. The recipe goes something like this:

- take succulent pieces of fresh hilsa (washed, cut, sized) and dip them in a mixture (of mustard seed paste, poppy seed paste, salt, turmeric, curd and mustard oil) and turn them until both sides are coated in the batter
- wrap the individual pieces in banana leaves (which ought to have been washed and cut into small pieces), making sure to tuck in a tiny, green chilly before tying it with a string (preferably white thread from a clean spool) to hold it in place
- heat generous amounts of mustard oil in a pan and dip the pieces into it and cook until the banana leaf turns golden brown
- remove the wrappings when cool and eat with hot, white rice.

Tips: the Bangals prefer to crush/grind the mustard seed and poppy seed using a 'sheel' and 'nora' (a traditional stone pestle 'nora' is used as a crusher/grinder with a flat stone base as mortar or 'sheel') to prepare the poppy and mustard paste.

Rice too is eaten by Bengalis in different ways, not just in terms of the cooking styles including boiled, baked, fried, etc. but also in raw forms such as flattened, puffed and popped (known as 'cheera', 'muri' and 'khoi').

Indeed, research reveals that while fish is considered the primary source of protein (lentils for vegetarians) for the Bengalis, rice is considered the primary source of carbohydrates, calories and therefore, energy, for the Bengali. Paddy is cultivated during different times of the year with 'aman', which is always planted during the monsoon and harvested in autumn, being the most common. Other than the crop grown during the rainy season, in summer, that is, in the months of May and June, another type of paddy, known as 'aush' is planted, which is harvested during the months of August and September.

The topic of Bengali cuisine has been covered extensively (if not exhaustively) in literature throughout the ages and had often come up in ancient texts which sometimes delved into the subject to draw out detailed (and well, delicious) descriptions of the culinary customs of the land or at other times merely mentioned them in passing, referring to them while describing some religious or social occasion.

Some of the earlier references to Bengali food are found in the *Charyapada* which, composed between the tenth and twelfth centuries, were a set of mystical verses rooted in the principles of the Buddhist philosophy. Initially passed down as oral poems, which were sung or recited or otherwise rendered vocally, they were both spiritual and social, encompassing the religious and regular lives of the people spanning the entire region of what is now spread over Bengal, Assam, Bihar, Jharkhand, Odisha and parts of Bangladesh, like Chittagong and Sylhet. References to fishing and hunting are found in the *Charyapada*. The eating of rice and sweets made from sugarcane juice too finds mention.

These texts thereby, also give us a sense of the food items which were on the menu for Bengalis during different periods of time. Gradually, over the years, other edibles entered the growing list, some of which have come to be considered indispensable in Bengali homes. These changes, or rather new entrants, to the Bengalis' diet chart can be traced through the works of scholarship. For instance, fifteenth-century texts like the *Mangalkavyas*, discuss the cooking of different types of daal, though the earlier *Charyapada* do not, indicating that this grain was not indigenous to the land but had arrived later.

Indeed, today, a large number of food items which are essential commodities in the Bengali kitchen, have arrived to the land from distant shores, brought in by subsequent foreigners who invaded and ruled.

Potato, like daal, for instance, is an integral part of Bengali cuisine today, but was imported by the Portuguese in the sixteenth century, when they started to arrive in the land. 'Aloo bhaatey' (mashed potato) or 'aloo bhaajaa' (potato fries) to be eaten with ghee and daal as accompaniments to plain, white rice is considered to be as traditionally Bengali as say, fish and rice. Other foreign fruits, vegetables, grains and nuts, to have invaded the Bengali kitchen include brinjal, okra, tomatoes, carrots, beetroots, cucumbers, onions, garlics, cashews, litchi, pomegranate, poppy, to name just a few. These were mostly imported from Europe or the Americas.

Before them, of course, the Mughals had arrived with their elaborate and evolved cuisine, which is known to have first significantly altered the food habits of the people of the land. Their food, called 'Mughlai khana', which includes such famed dishes as biriyani (rice slowly baked together with different types of meat, fish or eggs in a technique called 'dumpuckt' and garnished with aromatic and colourful spices like saffron and cinnamon) or 'luchi-aloo-dum' (small, round pieces of flat bread made of flour, which are deep-fried in ghee and eaten with dumpuckt-style potato curry) are now inexorably intertwined with what is known as Bengali cuisine. In fact, Calcutta does not just house hundreds of restaurants specializing in 'Mughlai khana' but 'Calcutta street food', a concept which is considered one of the many charms of the ancient city for tourists, would be incomplete without the thousands of roadside and footpath eateries and stalls that sell biriyani and other dishes which arrived in Bengal during the Mughal period.

The process of assimilation, however, took time. It was unthinkable for Bengali Hindus, especially from the upper-castes, to eat such Mughlai food items as beef, which was one of the main meat dishes of Mughals. Moreover, Hindus followed strict regulations as far as cooking food was concerned, which went beyond basic cleanliness and hygiene and encompassed the idea that partaking food cooked by people of other religions was tantamount to eating food touched by 'untouchables'. Of course, intermingling, especially as far as eating together was concerned, was not common between Muslims and Hindus during the Mughal era. Households and families lived segregated and separate lives and the need to eat each other's food was rare, if at all. Though the taboo continued to exist, its intensity had greatly diminished over four centuries. Initially, lower-caste Hindus, especially the 'untouchables', who often rejected their religion of birth and embraced Islam and later, Christianity, the religion of the new rulers, for a variety of reasons (including opportunities in education or the need to escape the drudgery of the lowlife of 'untouchables'), began to partake of foods of the Muslims and British. Gradually, 'progressive' and educated youth from the upper-castes, especially during the British period, when the Bengali Renaissance took place and the younger generations of Bengalis wanted to do what they deemed was 'modern', started to foray into forbidden territory and gave in to the temptation of eating the food of the foreigners, both that of the Mughals as well as that of the Europeans. And to drink the beverages they introduced to the region, which included hard liquor like beer, brandy, gin, sherry, rum, whiskey and wine or non-alcoholic soft-drinks like lemonade.

A tongue-in-cheek account of how the older and younger generations of upper-caste Bengali Hindu families differed on the issue of eating the unfamiliar food or drinking, for that matter, the unfamiliar beverages of the foreigners is found in *Sattar Batsar (Seventy Years)*, the autobiographical journal of Bipin Chandra Pal, one of the pioneers and key figures of the Indian National Movement. He writes that while growing up in Sylhet (now in Bangladesh) and later, while living in the hostel of his college in Calcutta, where he was sent for higher education, he had broken the taboos of food and drink to the utter disapproval of his father.

A humorous description of how he was chided and thrashed by his father for drinking lemonade (which was made and sold by Muslims in a shop in Sylhet) reveals the attitudes of the older and younger generations to the changes in social and cultural (including culinary) lifestyles. Resistance was the usual response of the elder generation, set in their ways. Acceptance, even eagerness to embrace the new, was what characterized the younger generations' attitude to the colonial culture, including colonial cuisine.

And though these same men, like Pal, and women of course, would lead the movements to chase out the British, the food and drink that the colonizers introduced to Bengal stayed on, gradually getting so assimilated with the local cuisine that it has become hard to distinguish between pre- and post-colonial food.

One of the most important additions to the Bengali menu

during the British era, has been bread, a food item that caused considerable consternation in Bengali households when it was first introduced in the factories of Calcutta. Parents forbade their children, in vain, from partaking of what was considered an impure food item, as it was mixed with yeast, a fermented ingredient, which, with a few exceptions, was by and large excluded from the meals of most Hindu households. The other food item which, though an influence of the British, has become synonymous with Bengali snacking, is the biscuit. British-era bakeries are still to be found in some shopping areas in Calcutta's old neighbourhoods. Chops, cutlets, devils (in which meat, fish or eggs are dipped in egg and flour batter before being deep-fried), cakes, patties and pastries, thus slowly made inroads into the Bengali menu. So much so that, Bengali traditions such as feeding 'payesh' or kheer to children or adults on their birthdays, has now more or less been completely replaced with the cutting of cake.

But perhaps no other item of food or beverage of the British era has become more integral to Bengali cuisine and its culture really, than the idea of having 'cha bishkoot' (sipping tea and dipping dry biscuits into it). From dawn to dusk, the Bengalis' day is punctuated, at regular intervals, with sessions of 'adda' (chit-chat) over cups of chai.

Of course, Bengali cuisine has continued to evolve and experiments with fusing different foods did not limit itself to the cultural churning that was taking place during the British era. Not known to be content or complacent with status quo, Bengalis keep adapting in all aspects, not the least of which is in culinary matters.

An example of a recent and rather interesting, if not inevitable (because of the strong influence of western, especially American, culture that economic liberalism has ushered in) fusion foods to have emerged and entered the Bengali dessert menu is the 'chocogolla'. It is a chocolate-covered avatar of its more famous country cousin, the celebrated roshogolla, which needs no introduction.

Speaking of roshogollas (which, incidentally, translates roughly into sugary, syrupy shapes of roundness), a recent legal tussle with neighbouring state Odisha over its ownership demonstrates just how far Bengal and Bengalis will go to defend its claim as the rightful inventor of this sweet.

Though the actual origin of the feud is debated with some suggesting that it may be as old as the roshogolla itself, and as bitter as the dessert is sweet, but the current fight is supposed to have begun around 2015. Odisha had reportedly observed a 'rasgolla divas' (or roshogolla day) to mark celebrations of Rath Yatra dedicated to the deity, Lord Jagannath, with claims that the sweet was a part of the offerings made to the gods for centuries. Bengal, alarmed by the overtures of usurpation by their otherwise friendly neighbour, decided to stop it in its track. Bengal applied for a GI (Geographic Indicator) tag, which is an official registration of goods and products that allows Indian regions to patent items which originate from there. Odisha countered Bengal's claim to the GI tag and the matter was dragged to court. Bengal won the case when eventually, in November 2017, it was declared the rightful owner of the 'Banglar Roshogolla'. Two years later, in July 2019, Odisha too received a GI tag for its own variant of the roshogolla.

Bengal's purists don't mind at all. 'Justice has been served to us and the world knows that we are the original inventors of the Banglar Roshogolla,' said a descendant of Nobin Chandra Das, the nineteenth-century Bengali confectioner, who is credited with inventing the Banglar Roshogolla in 1868.

That's sweet.

XIII

THOSE WHO WENT TO JAIL SO THAT WE CAN BE FREE

'Freedom is not given, it is taken.'
—Netaji Subhas Chandra Bose

Four decades after 1857, on 23 January 1897, an infant was born who would grow up to carry forward the work left unfinished by the martyrs of the First War of Independence. Subhas Chandra Bose could have led the privileged life which the wealthy and westernized Indians of the time enjoyed. He belonged to a family, many of whose members were educated in Britain and held important positions and jobs in the civil services or administrative offices of the British government by virtue of the upper social and economic strata to which they belonged.

Subhas, the ninth of 14 children, himself was schooled in British and European academic institutions, like his brothers and sisters. When he was five years old, he was admitted to the Protestant European School, run by the Baptist Mission, in Cuttack in the present state of Odisha, which was, at that time, a part of the Bengal Presidency. He spent seven years there and in 1909 switched to Ravenshaw Collegiate School, from where, in 1913, he completed his Tenth Standard or Matriculation Examination, securing second position.

From childhood, however, Subhas was disturbed by and questioned the subjugation of his own people by foreign rulers and started to read the spiritual writings of Ramakrishna and Vivekananda for answers. By the age of 16, he was drawn to his own, that is, Bengal's ancient traditions, including its religion, history and culture and he rebelled against the British rulers' attempts to suppress the indigenous heritage of the land and superimpose its own. Though he had gotten admission to the prestigious Presidency College in Calcutta because of his high academic ranking in school, he was expelled for slapping a British instructor (Professor Oaten), who had insulted an Indian student and who was known to make derogatory comments against the Indians on a regular basis. Later, Subhas joined Scottish Church College in Calcutta from where he graduated with a Bachelor of Arts degree in 1918.

Concerned by Subhas's growing association with the radical nationalism which was building up and gaining momentum throughout Bengal and the rest of the country, and which threatened to land him in trouble with the British government, his father, though himself deeply committed to the cause of India's Independence, sent him to England to pursue higher studies. In 1919, Subhas did appear for the Indian Civil Services examination, as per his father's wishes, securing fourth place but he subsequently resigned, citing his unwillingness to serve the British. 'He was clear in his heart and mind that fighting to free India, his beloved motherland, from British rule was his sole goal in life,' says Madhuri Bose, Subhas' grandniece. 'During this time, he had exchanged many letters with my grandfather—his beloved elder brother Sarat Chandra Bose—in which he expressed this.' In a letter dated 6 April 1921, Subhas wrote to Sarat, explaining the reason for his decision to quit the lucrative and prestigious profession thus: 'Only on the soil of sacrifice and suffering can we raise our national edifice.'[93]

Indeed, during the 90 years since 1857, when the First War of Independence broke out and 1947, when the British were finally chased out, Bengal had become 'the soil of sacrifice and suffering'. Hundreds and thousands of men and women, young and old, came out in droves, daring to 'raise the national edifice'. Fears were shed. And so was blood. From 1857 to 1947 Bengal was a battleground.

The first uprising against British rule, the soldiers' mutiny of 1857, had erupted in Bengal, as we have seen. And after igniting the fire, Bengal became one of the main loci of the flames of revolution which spread throughout the country and continued to burn for the next 90 years.

Initially, the Indian Independence Movement, as the revolution came to be known, was a set of sporadic, often spontaneous rebellions which erupted in different regions across the subcontinent. It must be remembered that the idea of the Republic of India as a nation emerged over a period of decades and centuries really, and was consolidated gradually. The British East India Company's aggressive acquisitions throughout the entire land, which saw the annexing of independent kingdoms, princely states and fiefdoms, ironically, played a key role in catalysing a unity of the otherwise disjointed leaderships. While they revolted individually against British East India Company's aggressions and attacks, they also united, as was evident during the 1857 Rebellion, with the common goal of defeating the foreigners.

Attributing rebellions such as the one in 1857 to the interference of the British East India Company into the matters and affairs of the princely states, kingdoms and fiefdoms, Queen Victoria, after she was declared the empress of India, decreed

---

[93]Madhuri Bose, granddaughter of Sarat Chandra Bose and grandniece of Subhas Chandra Bose in an interview to the author.

that as far as possible, these individual rulers would be allowed independent reign and could control their own regions, albeit with certain riders. The British Crown thus ostensibly toned down the erstwhile policies of the British East India Company. For instance, the new regime did away with the former regulation called the Doctrine of Lapse, which allowed for British East India Company to takeover independently-ruled states in case the ruler left no biological heir after his or her demise. Despite these moves, however, British Crown rule was perceived to be as oppressive and exploitative as that of British Company rule, namely because the so-called redressed laws existed only in theory. In practice, the British Crown rule surpassed Company rule, treating the masses with contempt and disdain and unleashing on the people of India a brutal reign of terror, steeped in racial discrimination and flagrant violations of human rights. British Crown rule was an authoritarian regime during which time dissent was crushed ruthlessly.

The nine decades between 1857 and 1947 was marked by the attempt by the British at such crushing of dissent. But more importantly, these nine decades were marked by the resilience of the people of the land, which rose up, again and again, stronger and stronger, each and every time they were crushed. And as far as Bengal was concerned, the roots of the struggle for independence from British rule went deep.

The list of freedom fighters from this region is remarkable. Subhas Chandra Bose, who came to be known as 'Netaji' or the 'The Leader' was an undisputed leader amongst them. Arrested repeatedly by British police for his nationalistic activities, he became an active member of underground revolutionary groups of the time. He represented the progressive, dynamic youth of Bengal who, having been born into and educated in the British system, experienced first-hand the superciliousness and utter complacency of the imperialist invaders, who propagated the idea of racial, read—white—supremacy.

One of the earlier and most brutal incidents of crushing of dissent was the hanging of Khudiram Bose, a young, orphaned revolutionary. Khudiram, along with a fellow revolutionary, Prafulla Chaki, were sent on a mission by the underground organization, Anushilan Samiti, to which they belonged, to Muzaffarpur, now in the state of Bihar, to kill Douglas Kingsford, a magistrate notorious for his harsh judgments against revolutionaries. From ordering whippings to rigorous prison terms to corporal punishment, he stopped at nothing to try to crush dissent.

Anushilan Samiti was one amongst several radical nationalist groups which were founded during this time with the goal of driving out the British. Formed in 1902 by Satish Chandra Basu, a university student from Calcutta and patronized by Pramathanath Mitra, a barrister, it was a secret society, which was based on and took inspiration from a number of different ideologies, including the Hindu Shakta and Italian Nationalism, which advocated the idea that violence and force were the only means to overthrow oppressive regimes. Anushilan Samiti, literally, 'bodybuilding society' followed the ancient Hindu philosophy of perfecting body, mind and soul as the goal of human life and endorsed indigenous traditional systems such as yoga while simultaneously rejecting European, especially British, ways.

Anushilan Samiti and other radical revolutionary societies of Bengal became extremely active during what has come to be called the First Partition of Bengal, which took place in 1905, when Lord Curzon was the viceroy of India. It divided the Bengal Presidency into two separate units on religious lines, claiming that being far from the centre of power, the eastern part of Bengal, dominated by Muslim populations, was difficult to administer. The people of Bengal, however, saw in this move an attempt to divide and rule. The partition particularly angered the Hindus, who argued that it had turned them into a minority—not religiously but linguistically. Because under the new division or delimitation, western Bengal was clubbed together with Odisha and Bihar. This reduced the population of people who spoke Bengali by more than half.

Leaders of Anushilan Samiti comprised a group of bright, young men and women from the wealthy families of Bengal who, though most often educated in the western system, turned against the West, namely western imperialism. Aurobindo and Barin Ghosh, who had been born into a respected Bengali family living in England and who had embarked upon revolutionary nationalism when they returned to India in their teens and twenties, were a part of this. Aurobindo was associated with a publication called *Jugantar*, edited by Bhupendranath Dutt and wrote articles which aroused Indians' patriotic pride and the ire of the British rulers.

Khudiram was born into a middle-class family in the Bengal village of Mohobani in the district of Midnapore, where his father worked as a revenue collector. He was the fourth child after three elder sisters, writes historian S.K. Agarwal.[94] Khudiram was also the third son but his two elder brothers, all born after the girls, died soon after they were born. According to religious traditions of the time, in order to ward off bad luck so that the youngest boy would survive, the parents ceremoniously 'sold' their son to one of his elder sisters, who paid his father, Trailokyanath Bose and mother, Lakshmipriya Bose with three fistfuls of rice grains, called 'khud'. He was thus named 'Khudiram' and though he, their third son, did manage to live beyond infancy, when he was only six, his mother died, followed one year later by his father. Khudiram was brought up by his sister, Aparupa Roy, who took him away from their native house to live with her and her husband's family

---

[94]S.K. Agarwal, *Khudiram Bose*, Ocean Books, 2006.

in another village. Her husband, Amritalal Roy, took the initiative to enrol him in an English school in the district's main town of Tamluk, called Hamilton High School. When he was 13 or 14, he started to be influenced by the growing feelings of nationalism. Prominent personalities of the time who were leading movements against British rule often visited various villages, towns and cities and aroused passionate discourse against British misrule. Among those to have gone to his school to deliver speeches, were the iconic freedom fighter and later spiritual saint, Sri Aurobindo Ghose and Sister Nivedita, the European philanthropist, who was so enchanted by the teachings of Vivekananda when he visited her country, that she renounced the world, followed him to India and immersed herself in spiritual and philanthropic work.

Later Khudiram would join the underground revolutionary network, Anushilan Samiti. Another influential secret society was Jugantar which was formed by Aurobindo, his brother, Barindra Kumar Ghose and other prominent freedom fighters, including Bhupendra Nath Dutta, Jatindra Nath Mukherjee, who later became known as Bagha Jatin (literally 'like-a-tiger Jatin') for his bravery and of course, Khudiram Bose and his companion, Prafulla Chaki.

The eastern wing of Jugantar, headquartered in what is now Bangladesh, was led by the fiery freedom fighter and school teacher, Surya Sen, also known as 'Master da'. He engineered the daring Chittagong Armoury Raid two decades later in which police armoury lines were attacked and ransacked by the revolutionaries. Jugantar's fearless women warriors included among others, Kalpana Dutta and Pritilata Waddedar, who was martyred at the age of 21, when she committed suicide by consuming cyanide to avert arrest after she led an attack on a European club.

Leaders of Anushilan Samiti and Jugantar included journalists, lawyers, professors and others, who came from well-to-do families and were most often educated in the West. Aurobindo and

Barindra were sons of a respected surgeon, Krishna Dhun Ghose, who moved his entire family to England so that his children could study in English schools and eventually join the prestigious Indian Civil Service. Aurobindo not only succeeded but received a scholarship to study at King's College, Cambridge, where he secured eleventh position out of 250 competitors. However, uninterested in pursuing a career serving the British, he returned to India and took up employment at the estate of the prince of Baroda, Gujarat in western India, where he soon became a part of the growing movement for Independence from British colonial rule. He later came to Calcutta and began to write against British imperialism in Jugantar's magazine.

At this time, several editors of *Jugantar*, including Bhupendra Nath Dutta, were arrested and tried for writing articles against British rule. Douglas Kingsford, the chief magistrate of Presidency Court in Calcutta's Alipore, oversaw the trials and in most cases, handed out harsh and what can be called perverse, diabolic and sadistic punishments, sentencing these learned men to rigorous labour during imprisonment.

Shukla Sanyal writes:

> Bhupendranath Dutt, the editor, and proprietor of the *Jugantar* was arrested in July 1907 and charged under section 124 A; Bhupendranath was sentenced to a year's rigorous imprisonment. The *Jugantar*'s stance was typically defiant. The paper did nothing to tone down the rhetoric in its future editions...This attitude cost the paper dearly. It suffered five more prosecutions that, by July 1908, brought about its financial ruin. The trials brought the paper a great deal of publicity and helped greatly in the dissemination of the revolutionary ideology...testimony to the fanatical loyalty that the paper inspired in its readers and the deep impression that the *Jugantar* writings made on them...revolutionary

terrorism (sic)* as an ideology began to win if not overt, then at least the tacit, support of Bengalis.[95]

*(One must mention that the phrase 'revolutionary terrorism' was applied by the British rulers to the activities of India's radical freedom fighters and the author seems to have used it in that context and as a concept that prevailed during those times. However, instances of the continued and callous use of the phrase to describe the activities of the radical revolutionaries of the freedom movement even in the present day, has caused considerable consternation and outrage. In 2019, a member of the West Bengal Assembly, Pradip Saha of the Communist Party of India (Marxists) raised the issued in the house and expressed shock over the use of the phrase to pertain to Khudiram Bose and Prafulla Chaki in a school history textbook. Taking cognizance of the matter, the state government immediately initiated steps to redress the grave error and as per the recommendations of a review committee which was set up to look into it, the word 'terrorism' was struck out and the text books were republished.)

The crackdown on their editors and writers resulted in fellow Jugantar members descending on the streets to launch large scale protests, demanding the release of their comrades. What ensued were more arrests, more trials and more sentencing. Kingsford at this time ordered the whipping of Sushil Sen, a young Bengali revolutionary who participated in the protest. This earned him further wrath of the Bengalis. Indeed, the more the British put people behind bars, the more resolute and determined the nationalists grew to overthrow the tyrannical regime. Jugantar, Anushilan Samiti and the other secret societies meticulously planned armed attacks against the rulers. They often went abroad to receive training in a host of guerrilla warfare techniques,

---

[95]Shukla Sanyal, *Revolutionary Pamphlets, Propaganda and Political Culture in Colonial Bengal*, Cambridge University Press, 2014.

including manufacturing bombs. According to Richard James Popplewell,[96] Barindra sent Hemchandra Kanungo, a fellow freedom fighter to Paris, where he learnt to make improvised explosive devices (IEDs) from Nicholas Safranski, a Russian rebel living in exile there. On his return to Bengal, he and Barindra and other members of the secret societies, plotted a series of assassinations, including that of the notorious Kingsford. The first attempt to blow up the hated judge failed. Hemchandra had constructed a book bomb which was delivered to Kingsford's residence in Calcutta by Paresh Mallick, a member of the secret society. An empty tin can was filled up with a pound of picric acid and three detonators. A hollow was dug into a copy of Herbert Bloom's *Commentaries on the Common Law*. The IED was fitted into the pit. The tome was wrapped up in brown paper. The parcel was delivered. Kingsford reportedly didn't immediately open the packet but placed it in his bookshelf to read later.

In the meantime, British intelligence, suspecting that assassination attempts were being planned, warned Kingsford, who was promptly promoted and removed from Bengal, to what was considered a relatively safer place to work, Muzaffarpur in Bihar. The book bomb, along with his furniture and other household items, it is said, travelled with him to his new residence, but never went off. Another plan was devised and Prafulla Chaki and an associate were sent by Anushilan Samiti to Muzaffarpur for a recce. He returned to Bengal and recounted in detail Kingsford's new whereabouts, including where he lives, the clubs he attends in the evenings, the routes he takes to work and back, etc.

In the next phase, Prafulla, disguised as a traveller and assuming the name Dinesh Chandra Roy, went back to Muzaffarpur to carry out the assassination along with Khudiram, who took up the name

---

[96]Richard James Popplewell, *Intelligence and Imperial Defence: British Intelligence and the Defence of the Indian Empire, 1904-1924*, Routledge, 1995.

Haren Sarkar. For over three weeks, the duo put up at an inn run by a philanthropist named Kishori Mohan Bandyopadhyay without being suspected.

Though Bengal police intelligence had warned the superintendent of police in Muzaffarpur of the possibility of an attack on the life of Kingsford, no evidence could be gathered.

On 29 April, Khudiram and Prafulla, who had been observing the daily movements of their target ever since they arrived in Muzaffarpur, stationed themselves in a park near the British Club, which was frequented by Kingsford.

Kingsford and his wife had been playing bridge with the wife and daughter of barrister Pringle Kennedy. Around eight in the evening they decided to head home. The freedom fighters mistook the carriage in which the two women were travelling as that of Kingsford's and hurled the powerful explosive Hemchandra had prepared using six ounces of dynamite, a detonator and black powder fuse. The two women sustained injuries and died shortly afterwards. Kingsford escaped the assassination attempt unscathed.

Though the duo fled separately, Khudiram was later caught. He had walked barefoot for nearly 25 miles and by morning had reached a railway station called Waini. In the meantime, British police were deputed at every major railway station. Khudiram is reported to have asked for a glass of water at a tea stall, when a couple of policemen, Fateh Singh and Sheo Prasad Singh, who had been on the lookout, noticed him and were immediately suspicious. They asked him a few questions and convinced that he was the bomber, pounced on him. Khudiram tried to wriggle out of their grip and in the scuffle his pistol fell out. Eventually the policemen overpowered him.[97]

---

[97] According to the 1908 'Judgment in the appeal of Khudiram Bose vs. Emperor', available at https://indiankanoon.org/doc/1765978/. Accessed on 9 July 2021.

By some accounts, Khudiram is understood to have been listening to the conversation at the tea stall, in which the people gathered were discussing the attempted murder of Kingsford. When he realized he and Prafulla had missed the target, he blurted out in disappointment, 'Kingsford didn't die?' It is reported that Prafulla died after consuming cyanide to avert arrest.

When Khudiram, handcuffed, was brought back to Muzaffarpur the next day, writes Ritu Chaturvedi[98], virtually the whole town descended at the police station to take a look at him. The following day, *The Statesman* wrote in its editorial, 'The railway station was crowded to see the boy. A mere boy of 18 or 19 years old, who looked quite determined. He came out of a first-class compartment and walked all the way to the phaeton, kept for him outside, like a cheerful boy who knows no anxiety... on taking his seat the boy cheerfully cried "Vandemataram".'[99]

Khudiram's high profile trial swung Bengali, indeed Indian public opinion, already inflamed against British tyranny, completely in Khudiram's favour. Here was this scrawny, orphaned boy who fearlessly took on the task of eliminating a hated enemy.

The first trial took place on 21 May 1908 at the Sessions Court in Alipore, Kolkata. Defence lawyers, Kalidas Basu, Upendranath Sen and Kshetranath Bandyopadhyay refused to take fees for their service, claiming that it was their way of expressing solidarity with the cause of freedom. Subsequently, three other lawyers, Kulkamal Sen, Nagendra Lal Lahiri and Satish Chandra Chakraborty joined them, fighting the case without fees. Kishori Mohan Bandyopadhyay, the owner of the inn in Muzaffarpur, where Khudiram and Prafulla had put up and another freedom fighter, Mrityunjoy Chakraborty were tried simultaneously. However, Mrityunjoy (incidentally, whose name

---

[98]Ritu Chaturvedi, *Bihar Through the Ages*, Sarup & Sons, 2007.
[99]Editorial, *The Statesman*, 2 May 1908.

means, 'the defeater of death') died during the trial and Kishori Mohan's trial was separated from Khudiram's.

Two days after the trial began, Khudiram's lawyers convinced him to sign on a statement, denying his involvement in the bombing. Though reportedly initially he was reluctant to do so in spite of the fact that he was intimated that he faced a death sentence, he later agreed, after the defence told him that it was important for him to live on so that he could continue to serve his country. The declaration was submitted to the magistrate E.W. Bredhowd on 23 May 1908. Khudiram's lawyers built up the defence based on this and argued that Prafulla's suicide on the verge of arrest clearly indicated that he was the perpetrator. They further reasoned that Khudiram, by far the younger, thinner and physically weaker of the two could not have hurled the bomb. On 13 June 1908, the scheduled date of the verdict, the defence lawyers unexpectedly found additional fuel with which to fire the line of defence against Khudiram's culpability. Before the trial, the judge received an anonymous letter threatening to kill him, with the claim that this time Biharis and not Bengalis would carry out the act. As a last-ditch effort, the defence counsel argued that the letter indicated that other operators, and not Khudiram, were at play. In spite of the strength of their arguments, the judge delivered a death sentence.

An uproar of dismay and disappointment swept through the court premises, where crowds had gathered from across Bengal and beyond. The streets of Calcutta erupted in protest with demonstrators against the verdict descending on the streets in anger.

Khudiram, however, was calm as the verdict was read out. In fact, he smiled. Perplexed, the judge asked him whether he had fathomed the implications of the order. Khudiram said he did.

Though initially reluctant, Khudiram, on the urgings of his lawyers, agreed to an appeal. The second hearing, at the Calcutta

High Court, took place on 8 July 1908. His lawyers argued that on several counts Khudiram had not been given a fair chance at justice and pointed out, among other lacunae, the fact, that his statements were neither recorded in the accused's mother tongue, Bengali, as was the law, nor was it read back to him in the vernacular, as was the law. They made an impassioned appeal to the British judge and pleaded with him to consider that the British people prided themselves on an impeccable and just legal system. However, all reasoning fell on deaf ears. The death sentence was upheld.

A final plea was made to the Governer-General for reducing the sentence but it was turned down. In fact, he ordered that the hanging should be executed no later than 11 August 1908.

On the date of the hanging, before dawn, swelling crowds thronged the jail premises, with offerings of flowers and garlands for Khudiram, their hero. When he was taken to the gallows, he was smiling. He walked erect and appeared cheerful as the hangman drew the hood over his head and the noose around his neck. The mourners poured forth from far and wide, lining the streets and as the hearse carrying his dead body passed, they showered petals, with cries and chants of 'long live'.

Reporting the execution the next morning, one of Bengal's prominent dailies, *Amrita Bazar Patrika* wrote, 'Khudiram's execution took place at 6 a.m. He walked to the gallows firmly and cheerfully and even smiled when the cap was drawn over his head.'

In reporting the execution, the British newspaper *Empire* too could not help but observe the behaviour of the brave young man as he faced death. 'Khudiram Bose...was executed this morning,' it stated adding, 'It is alleged that he mounted the scaffold with his body erect. He was cheerful and smiling.'[100]

---

[100]Hitendra Patel, *Khudiram Bose, Revolutionary Extraordinaire*, Publications

Indeed, the black and white photographs of Khudiram Bose, from his days in jail, are testimony to the martyr's fearlessness. His eyes or face reflect no fear as he stands in a relaxed posture, in front of his prison cell, in one of the pictures. The two prison guards, one British and another Indian, who flank him, look more tense... and uptight.

Fearlessness was the characteristic of the times. It is as though the freedom fighters throughout India had transcended the boundaries of life and death and transported themselves psychologically into the realm of the eternal. Unafraid to be martyred for the cause of freeing their motherland from the British capturers, they seemed to have somehow been aware that their purpose in life was to ignite a fire and then get extinguished. Like a matchstick.

The poet Sukanta Bhattacharya, belonging to the early twentieth century, wrote a poem called, 'The Matchstick' which is perhaps, or can be interpreted to be, inspired by the lives of the freedom fighters of those times. Translated into English it reads like this, 'I'm just a tiny matchstick. So insignificant, you won't even notice me. But know this: a fire dwells in my mouth. And my heart is filled with the restless passion to ignite.'

Even after Khudiram's hanging, the trials continued and became known as the 'Alipore Bomb Case'. Aurobindo was arrested for his association with Anushilan Samiti, Jugantar and other secret revolutionary societies and charged with treason or more specifically 'waging war against the King'. The punishment, if proven guilty, was death by hanging. His brother Barindra and other freedom fighters too were tried.

During this time, in order to try to crush the freedom movement, British authorities indulged in some of the cruellest, most diabolic acts of torture, inflicting not just physical but

---

Division of Ministry of Information & Broadcasting, Government of India, 2008.

psychological pain during police and jail custody, illegally imprisoning the undertrials and often forcing them into solitary confinement.

Aurobindo was placed, during the entire duration of the trial, in a tiny cell at Presidency Jail, where, he later wrote, he had to fight daily with himself to retain his sanity. Alone, without recourse to either reading material or any other diversion, at one time, he engaged himself in observing a set of red and black ants which he found in a corner of the cell.

In, *Tales of Prison Life*, where he records his experience in solitary confinement, he describes the agony, thus:

> My prison-cell was nine feet long and about five or six feet wide. This windowless cage, fronted by a large iron barred-door, was assigned to me as my abode. The cell opened into a very small courtyard, paved with stones and surrounded by a high brick wall. A wooden door led outside. The door had a small peep-hole at eye-level, for sentries to keep a periodic watch on the convicts when the door was closed. The door to the courtyard of my cell was generally kept open. There was six such contiguous cells known as the 'six decrees'. The word 'decree' was a reference to the special punishment prescribed either by the Judge or the Jail Superintendent in the form of solitary confinement within these tiny, cramped cells.
>
> There were varying degrees of severity even in solitary confinement though. The first degree of severity consisted of keeping the courtyard doors shut to deprive the prisoner of all human contact. The tenuous link with the outside world was then preserved through the eyes of the vigilant sentries and the visits of fellow-convicts, who came twice a day to deliver meals. A still higher degree of severity consisted of having a prisoner's hands bound in handcuffs and feet

in shackles. One might assume that prescription of such a severe form of punishment would require a suitably grave offense like physical violence or disrupting the peace in jail. But that assumption would be incorrect. Even slackness in prison labour or repetition of mistakes in one's assigned work would often be adequate cause to invite such harsh punishment.

The legal system disallowed undertrial prisoners to be subjected to solitary confinement or to be held under such torturous conditions. But such niceties of law were dispensed with when dealing with those accused in affairs related to the Swadeshi (Independence) movement or 'Bande Mataram' and hence arrangements were promptly made for them as desired by the Police.[101]

The case, formally called, 'The Emperor versus Aurobindo Ghose and Others,' reportedly dragged on for nearly a year first with hearings at the Magistrate's court where 222 witnesses were interrogated and 1000 artefacts produced as evidence. This was followed by a hearing in the Session's Court, where 206 witnesses were called to testify and 1,438 exhibits were presented.

Finally, on 6 May 1909, the verdict was delivered. It must be pointed out here that during the period of trial, one of the accused, Naren Goswami, had turned approver and was subsequently killed by the other freedom fighters within the jail premises. Getting drift of Goswami's plans to reveal secrets of the Samiti to the police during cross-examination, Barin Ghose, Hem Chandra, Satyen Basu and Kanailal Dutta, along with the others who were incarcerated as political prisoners, hatched a plot. Dutta and Basu, pretending to be sick, got themselves admitted to the prison hospital. From there Basu sent word to the traitor Goswami, tricking him into believing that he wanted to join him in turning

---

[101]Sri Aurobindo, *Tales of Prison Life*, Sri Aurobindo Ashram Publications, 2018.

informer. Swallowing the bait, when Goswami came to visit him at the hospital, accompanied by a guard and a jailor, Dutta and Basu turned on him and chased him down the corridors with loaded guns, which had been sneaked in as part of a cache of weapons which Barin and the others were building up inside their cells. They were successful in pumping enough bullets into him to cause his death but could not kill themselves to avert being rearrested and were soon overpowered by the guards and jailors, who too incidentally had been injured during the shoot-out. Dutta and Basu were tortured, given a cursory trial and hanged but the murder of Goswami is believed to have resulted in saving the Society's secrets from spilling out into the public domain and more importantly, in preventing the final verdict from being as harsh as the British government in India would have liked it to be. The prosecution had depended completely on Goswami's testimony to nail several of the defendants, including and especially, the main accused, Aurobindo.

To the dismay of the British, Aurobindo was acquitted for lack of concrete evidence. Eventually the trial could not prove his involvement in the conspiracy, far less the degree of his culpability in the case. While reading out his judgment, Charles Porten Beechcroft pointed out that as no evidence could be found against him other than that he had written incendiary articles and speeches against British occupation of India, Aurobindo could not be held guilty of the conspiracy.

Barin, as well as Ullashkar Dutt, two of the four who had initially taken full responsibility of the bombing in order to protect the others from being prosecuted, however, were convicted and received the death sentence but it was later commuted to a life imprisonment and they were deported to the notorious Cellular Jail of the Andaman and Nicobar Islands, on the Bay of Bengal. They languished there until eventually released in 1920 under a general amnesty. The 36 other nationalists who had been accused in the case were handed different sentences and jail terms involving varying degrees of punishment.

The Alipore Bomb Case was a milestone in India's journey towards Independence. It did not just bring to the fore the resentment that was lurking in the hearts and minds of the native people of the land against the foreign invaders but it triggered the all-encompassing and all-engulfing nationalism which would eventually drive out the British.

The revolutionaries involved in the case may have been associated with Bengal and tried for their violent rejection of the partition of Bengal proposed by the British administration in 1905, but the strong sentiments of patriotism which the trials generated broke the barriers of local politics to sweep through and bring into its fold the entire country.

The trial, in general, and the hangings of the young revolutionaries, Khudiram Bose, Kanailal Dutta and Satyendranath Bose in particular, created a furore, with widespread protests that shook up the British administration, which, up until then, was largely complacent, taking for granted its power over the dissenting Indian people.

Another significant political development of the time which contributed to the growing revolutionary activity in Bengal and other parts of the country was the founding on 28 December 1885 of the Indian National Congress (INC). Though established by, or rather with the help of, a couple of retired British officers, Allan Octavian Hume and William Wedderburn, who were considered moderates in the British establishment and supporters of increasing Indian representation in the civil services and other administrative offices, it eventually grew to represent the defining movement of Indian nationalism.

It was a milestone in the emergence of movements which pitted Indian nationalism against British imperialism.

The INC, initially and ironically, however, was identified with the idea that it would strengthen British power in India. A section of British authorities, namely moderates like Hume, justified the establishment of such organizations (in which Indians would take part in political discourses and exchanges of ideas) to the hardliners with the argument that this would work in favour of the British. They argued that garnering the support of the growing class of English-educated and English-speaking elite, which INC comprised, in an atmosphere of increasing native animosity towards the British in India, was a method that would assist in quelling dissent and, therefore, would eventually augment chances of the British government's continued presence in the land.

However, INC gradually became instrumental in leading the movements that culminated in freeing India from British control.

Bengal played a key role in the INC and contributed to the organization taking on a complex characteristic. The Bengal unit, especially when INC was led by Subhas Chandra Bose, argued in favour of a radical approach to driving out the British from Indian soil. This clashed with the majority view in the party, set by Mohandas Karamchand Gandhi, its top leader, who was considered to have the 'last word' on issues. Gandhi advocated peaceful dialogue, rather than confrontation, as the only sustainable method. But Bose did not want to settle for anything less than an unconditional withdrawal of the British. For Bengal, there was a greater stake in driving out the British. Bengal, after all, was on the brink of being divided.

But the leadership of Bose, who was popular with INC's young and radical wing, was not supported by Gandhi and eventually Bose resigned. Later, he led the formation of an army, the Azad Hind Fauj or Indian National Army (with the help of Britain's enemies, namely Germany and Japan, convincing these nations to free Indian prisoners of war who had fought for the British during World Wars I and II and who had been languishing in German and Japanese prisons, for the purpose) and embarked on his goal of forcing the British out of India. He did this from outside India, of course. Repeatedly arrested by the British government in India and politically isolated by his Indian colleagues, Bose had realized that in order to launch any attack on the British, he would have to leave the country. In December 1940, he was released from jail on health grounds and kept under house arrest. He decided to, or rather pretended to, as a red herring, practice penance, the spiritual observation of solitude and silence during which he didn't even meet close family members. His food was served to him by pushing dishes under the door. However, secretly he was plotting his own escape. Among his few confidantes was his 21-year-old nephew Sisir Kumar Bose, who, eventually helped him flee. On a January night in 1941 he drove him, sitting in the backseat of his car disguised as another man, an insurance agent name Mohammad Ziauddin, out of the gates, past the watchful eyes of the sentries. They drove for hours, stopping over at the house of a relative from where they continued on to Gomoh Station in Dhanbad District in the modern state of Jharkhand. By some accounts, Subhas's decision to travel all the way to Dhanbad from where he caught a train, the Howrah to Peshawar Express, which originated from near his hometown of Calcutta, was influenced by his desire to hold several rounds of meetings with local revolutionaries in the forests along the railway lines. Finally, on 18 January, he boarded a train to Pathankot in Punjab, with his relatives bidding him an emotional, if inconspicuous farewell by staying ensconced in the confines of the car, as instructed by Netaji. Sisir, his nephew, however, insisted that he would accompany him to the railway platform. By the time the news of his disappearance spread in the media, Subhas had crossed over the western border and reached Afghanistan. Speculation about the reasons for his disappearance gripped Calcutta, with the theory that he had renounced the world and ran away to become a hermit being one of the most prominent. It reverberated not just with outsiders who fell for the red herring of Subhas's penance during house arrest, but also in sections of the media, the British government and even many members of his own family, who were in the dark about the escape. British intelligence, however, stepped up surveillance in the Bose household.

The Great Escape, as the episode has come to be called, is considered Bose's last contact with his beloved motherland. It is a widely held belief that Bose died in a plane crash on 18 August 1945 in Taiwan, though this theory is also hotly debated and dismissed by a large section of people, including parts of the extended Bose family, who claim that there is evidence to suggest that he lived on and had travelled to the Soviet Union. 'Netaji', which was the honorary title conferred on him by the soldiers of INA successfully managed to unite the troops into an organized and inspired army.

Chandra Kumar Bose, grand-nephew of Netaji, points out how difficult Subhas and his INA had made life for the British. 'The final onslaught on British imperialism was certainly the battle of the Azad Hind Fauj, under the leadership of Netaji Subhas Chandra Bose,' he says. He quotes British historian Michael Edwards to cite the kind of dread that Subhas and his army created in the mind of British rulers. Chandra Kumar Bose, quoting Michael Edwards, says, 'It slowly dawned upon the government of India that the backbone of British rule, the Indian Army, might now no longer be trustworthy. The ghost of Subhas Bose, like Hamlet's father, walked the battlements of the Red Fort, and his sudden amplified figure overawed the conferences that were to lead to Independence.'

Clearly, British historians themselves attribute to none other than Subhas, the creation of the conditions that eventually led to Independence. However, several factors, including opposition from within, namely that of his political detractors in the country, sabotaged his plans of using force to drive out the British. Bose and Bengal's revolutionaries had demanded that the British quit India unconditionally. Bose and Bengal's revolutionaries did not want India divided, because it entailed the division into two of their own beloved Bengal. But the betrayal of Bose by foes in his own land paved the way for Partition, which turned the story of Bengal into one laced with pain and despair.

When the British finally did quit India, it was not on terms that Netaji Subhas Chandra Bose and others of Bengal's great revolutionaries had fought for. Their beloved Bengal was divided by the British. In fact, Bose, who was completely against the division of India and Bengal, was not in the country when the British finally did leave India.

XIV

THREE HUNDRED AND THIRTY YEARS LATER

'Life without suffering is like a boat without a sailor in which there is no discretion of itself. The slightest breeze can rock it.'

—Ishwar Chandra Vidyasagar

It's a rain-lashed, storm-struck day at Sagar Deep, (literally Sea Island), three hours and 30 minutes by boat along the river route from Sutanuti, where 330 years ago, a British seaman anchored his ship and began the colonization of Bengal.

From Sagar Deep, situated at the southernmost tip of the Indian state of West Bengal, where the river Ganga finally flows into the Bay of Bengal, one can see how colonization had ended. By cutting up Bengal. It left its mark on the land, scarring it for life. Yes, the British bisected Bengal, before they finally left India on 15 August 1947. Bengal's revolutionaries, who had fought tooth and nail to stop them from dividing their beloved land, had been hanged, killed, silenced or chased out. One part of the divided land remained in India, because of the relentless struggles of a few revolutionaries like Shyama Prasad Mukherjee, who managed to convincingly argue against the whole of Bengal being given away, which too had been a consideration. The other piece was handed over to the newly formed country, Pakistan, created on the ostensible basis that Muslims of India, who were a religious minority, ought to have their own land after independence from Britain. Divided Bengal fell into East Pakistan, on India's eastern border. Punjab, on India's western border, was divided and went into West Pakistan.

From Sagar Deep, the vista opens up to the vast stretches of sea dotted with islands, which were once Bengal's own, India's own, but are no longer so. The sea from Sagar Deep extends eastward to the Sundarbans (the delta region at the northernmost mouth of the Bay of Bengal), so named because of the deep jungles of 'sundari' mangroves which cover it. The jungles of the Sundarbans, which at one time, stretched for hundreds of kilometres all around, but is now shrunk to less than a tenth of its original size, having been encroached upon by a host of intruders including deforestation, is of course, home to the ferocious breed of tigers which the British had named Royal Bengal Tiger. Hundreds of rivers and canals, infested with crocodiles, flow through the Sundarbans. From the banks of these canals, often narrow and black, and the rivers, with such wild and colourful names as 'Matla' (drunken) or 'Haldi', one can see, clearly, on the other side, the parts that once belonged to India. To Bengal. When Bengal was ripped into two, it divided the Sundarbans, half of which fell into the newly formed country, then Pakistan. Now, of course, Bangladesh.

On the topic of Bangladesh, it is important to point out that, as far as Bengalis are concerned, a semblance of justice came, 24 years after their land was sliced off and served up to another country when, in 1971, East Pakistan launched a bloody struggle for independence from West Pakistan, which was in control of governance and had for all practical purposes dominated and oppressed its eastern counterpart. In fact, right from its inception, Pakistan had declared that Urdu, the predominantly spoken language of West Pakistan would be the national language, even though the Bengali majority lived in East Pakistan. This effectively deprived the Bengali population of government jobs, higher education, representation in civil and military services and other benefits and privileges. Bengalis of East Pakistan rebelled but their protests were brutally crushed. The British had left but they clearly left behind their legacy of oppression. On 21 February 1952, students of the University of Dhaka, the capital city of East Bengal, who had been demanding official status for Bengali, gathered outside the East Bengal Legislative Assembly building, refusing to budge unless their demands were met. Pakistan police opened fire, killing four young boys, Abdus Salam, Rafiq Uddin Ahmed, Abul Barkat and Abdul Jabbar. This resulted in a countrywide strike and agitations which eventually culminated in a demand for autonomy and a separate country for themselves based on language rather than religion. After a civil war in which hundreds of thousands of men, women and children were butchered, Bangladesh was born. Bengal was still, and perhaps will always be hurt, but the fact that the land that they had to give up now belonged solely to Bengalis, irrespective of their religion, assuaged their battered emotions to a great degree.

The rivers and canals in most places of the Sundarbans double up as the natural borders between India's West Bengal and Bangladesh. On rain-lashed, storm-struck days, when the vast gray horizon stretches out for miles and sea merges with sky, the distinction of borders in the Sundarbans and at Sagar Island across the delta, blur considerably. And indeed, rain and storm are regular occurrences in this delta region. Cyclones that form in the Bay of Bengal gravitate towards this coastland before crashing into it. The Sundarbans, including Sagar Island, has witnessed as many as 11 cyclones in the first 20 years of the twenty-first century, which works out to be an average of more than one every two years. Bengal's ability to withstand, physically, psychologically and politically, the devastating impact of cyclones that have ripped through it seems to be symbolic of its ability to withstand the devastating impact of all that has transpired in this land, politically, socially, economically and culturally. Its geographic location has played a direct role in the way its story has unfolded. Indeed, geopolitics is at the centre of the Bengal story. The very fact that Bengal was the initial ground zero of British colonization was because foreign merchants could land there since it was accessible by sea and river. It is as simple as that. Bengal, rather than an area in the centre of the country, was divided partly due to the fact that it is positioned in the peripheral areas. The justification used to argue the decision was that Bengal (and Punjab) had some of the highest concentrations of Muslims in the country and was therefore the ideal locus of a new country for Muslims. But its geographical location was considered the main reason. It was only natural that it would be the chosen land. For Partition. It was the logical conclusion.

Divided, Bengal was. Into two parts. Eastern Bengal became East Pakistan, a province of the newly-formed country of Pakistan. Western Bengal remained in India, becoming the state of West Bengal. Later of course, East Pakistan declared independence from Pakistan and in 1971, after a bloody war which witnessed the butchering of hundreds and thousands of civilians in East Pakistan, it became the country of Bangladesh. Indeed, the story of Bengal is inextricably linked to the fact of its being where it is. Always in the eye of the storm, as it were. And Bengal, after Independence, was like a land left devastated after a storm.

The Partition of India triggered one of the biggest refugee crises in recent history with an estimated 14 million people displaced according to official figures. Over one million people were killed. Of this figure, the division of Bengal accounted for nearly half. Over five million Bengali Hindus living in East Bengal had no choice but to abandon their houses, property and other immovable assets and even movable assets, including livestock and other belongings and flee from the newly formed Islamic country. Likewise, nearly two million Muslims who had been inhabitants of West Bengal had to leave everything behind and migrate to East Pakistan. If statistics don't move anymore, inured as humanity has grown to tales of suffering, narrowing down to the individual stories would perhaps depict, to some extent, the sheer horror of what displacement meant.

The Dasguptas, a wealthy, landed and educated family living in East Bengal, had to flee during religious riots otherwise, in the words of a surviving member, 'We would have been butchered, chopped into pieces.' His father, a school teacher, his mother, a housewife, an elder brother and a sister boarded a train to West Bengal.

> My parents did manage to pack the jewellery and whatever cash was in the house and they thought that *that* would see us through when we landed as refugees in Calcutta. But at the railway station looters took everything, snatching away even the clothes that we were carrying. By the time we landed in Sealdah Station in Calcutta, my father had lost his mind.

Without money or moorings, they somehow made their way to a refugee colony, one of the many which had sprung up in the area. 'My mother worked as a domestic helper in nearby households to support us. My father never got his sanity back and died one day.' There were no tears in the eyes of the gentleman, who had, through grit and determination, become a high-ranking officer in the Indian Administrative Service, but a deep sorrow pervaded his words as he narrated his childhood memories of the Partition of Bengal. Hundreds of such stories, each more painful than the other, lurk in every corner of Bengal. For those who witnessed the Partition, if they didn't lose their minds or memories, the pain did not heal. In 70 years, many died—dissolved like waves in the ocean of time. Generations came and went. The scars did not go away.

Every aspect of Bengal, through the past seven decades after Independence, from its politics to its economy, from its literature to its culture, from its music to its art, from its science to its spirituality, can trace its roots back to this one event, the Partition or Division of Bengal. Political and economic turbulence marked the initial decades after Partition, with Bengal virtually crushed under the weight of the refugee crisis. The seeds of political dissent and protests that have subsequently germinated and flowered and continue to be an integral part of the political culture of the state had been planted during this time, born of utter desperation, despondency and desolation. Uprooted from their habitats, having lost their land, lifestyles and livelihood, the people who had arrived in West Bengal from East Bengal were at the mercy of the elements as it were, barely provided a roof over their heads in a 'colony'—a locus of temporary shelters comprising hundreds of shanties, set up in the peripheries or wastelands, to house the refugees. In East Bengal, they were often landed gentries, agricultural lords. The men (and, more tragically, as far as they were concerned, the women too), who had never worked earlier, had to find economic activity, often more 'lowly' than they could have imagined, in even their worst nightmares, to sustain themselves. These included anything from working as domestic helpers to doing a variety of odd jobs like helping in tending gardens, cutting grass, carrying luggage at railway stations and other menial activity. People of upper-castes and classes, for whom it was always taboo to engage in such work, had to abandon their consciousness of social strata and embrace the new jobs. It was a sociological phenomenon, a time of vast change, when an entirely new class of people, the middle class, came into being. They were 'in-between' the rural rich and the urban poor. Dr Ashok Mitra, former West Bengal finance minister, writes in an article, 'I had worked in West Bengal from 1947 to 1954 and observed the plight the East Bengal refugees were reduced to.'[102]

For the refugees of West Bengal, it was a downward mobility because it was a lifestyle for the worse: people used to living in lush green villages, surrounded by vast open spaces, blue skies, green ponds and red and brown earth roads, were now suddenly thrust into the colourless world of cramped slums, where they had to use community infrastructure to cook, bathe, live and love.

It was a time of complete economic instability, not just for the refugees, but entire Bengal and really the whole of the new nation, India. The transition from foreign rule to independence was accompanied by uncertainties in every field, including education and employment. The loss of East Bengal meant that hundreds and thousands of acres of land, whether agricultural, forested or riverine, was now no longer available for farming, fishing or other economic activity for the self-sustenance of hundreds and thousands of people. For the government, it meant a lack of access to resources, previously considered Bengal's own. With a hugely reduced agricultural income and no industry to speak of, not to mention the pressure to absorb millions of refugees, the overburdened Bengal exchequer was ready to collapse even before it could stand on its own feet.

The pain that Bengal suffered, however, had a profound effect on its literature, art, music and, eventually, cinema. Its people, jolted mercilessly out of the familiar rhythms of life, and with their known realities shattered suddenly, were thrown into psychologically (not to mention, physically) altered states of existence. It was a time of great creativity. Indeed, the flip side of displacement, desertion, desolation and depression was art. Pain produced poetry and loss gave rise to lyrical prose and literature.

---

[102]Ashok Mitra, 'Parting of Ways, Partition and After in Bengal', *Economic and Political Weekly*, Vol 25, No. 44, Nov. 3, 1990. Article also available online at https://www.jstor.org/stable/4396934. Accessed on 21 July 2021

The journey which culminated in the division of Bengal was so full of pain and loss that Bengalis, in heart, mind and soul turned to the escape routes of creativity.

Of course, the roots of Bengali literature are traced back earlier, to the first millennium, when between the tenth and twelfth centuries, the *Charyapada*, a collection of 47 mystical hymns of the Buddhist faith were composed. These were the works of various Buddhist monks. The manuscripts were discovered in 1907 by the Bengali linguist, Haraprasad Shastri, at the Nepal Royal Court Library, written on a palm leaf collection. The language, an early Bengali and a smattering of other ancestral forms of eastern languages, which could not entirely be deciphered, was classified by Shastri as a 'sandhyabhasha' or 'dusk language'. Indeed, the development of the Bengali language itself evolved over a period of time and it is considered that the current form of the language started to take shape about 1,300 years earlier when the Sanskrit scriptures started to be influenced by the local dialects of the region. The script that evolved was based on the classical language but took on symbols to phonetically represent sounds of the vernacular. The script became known as the Eastern Nagari script but according to a section of historians, Bengali has also been influenced by other scripts such as the Perso-Arabic and Sylheti Nagri. But the Bengali alphabet itself is supposed to have developed almost completely to its present form during a later period, known as the middle or medieval period of Bengali language and literature.

That brings us to the three categories into which Bengali literature is roughly divided. These are 'ancient' (650 CE–1200), 'medieval' or 'middle' (1200–1800) and 'modern' (from 1800 onwards). While the *Charyapada* and other extant religious texts are defined as Bengali literature's ancient or early history, the middle period saw a burst of cross-cultural influences reflecting the vast changes taking place within the region, including the Islamic invasions which ushered in Islamic literature in Bengal.

The advent of other religious orders than the already existing Buddhism and Hinduism, namely Vaishnavism, further influenced Bengali literature.

Vaishnavism or the Vaishnava tradition was followed by devotees and disciples of Prophet Chaitanya Mahaprabhu. Vishvamvar Mishra, nicknamed Nemai, was born on 18 February 1486, in a remote Bengali village by the river Ganga in modern-day Krishnanagar in the district of Nadia. He travelled to distant places throughout the eastern part of the land, preaching the idea of complete devotion as the means of achieving liberation to hundreds and thousands of his disciples before his death on 14 June 1533 in Puri in Odisha, when he was 47. Other than works of Hindu religious scripts such as the *Mangalkavya*s and Islamic epics (for instance, the works of Abdul Hakim and Syed Sultan) Vaishnava writing (including the poetic texts centred on the life and times of the Prophet Chaitanya Mahaprabhu as Nemai came to be called), had become an integral part of the literature of Bengal. It was also a time of great works of translations into Bengali from Arabic, Persian, not to mention, Sanskrit. Though religious or spiritual themes were the commonest, during this period, the secular works by Muslim poets, such as Alaol, became notable. Indeed, Bengali Islamic writing was exploring a host of themes other than religion which included love and longing, history and happiness, culture and cosmology. Hundreds of proverbs and rhymes, which are still in common use today, and which arouse much interest as far as their beginnings are concerned, is said to have originated in the one and a half century period, from around 1200 to 1350. Notable writers of the time were Ramai Pandit and Halayud Misra. The later part of the medieval period in Bengali literature is divided into the pre and post Chaitanya era and spans the nearly four and a half centuries from 1350 to 1800.

The beginning of the modern period of Bengali literature coincided with the Bengali Renaissance. Or rather, the Bengali

Renaissance ushered in the modern period of Bengali literature. It was distinct from the previous trends in literature in different ways, including a vast range of themes and its rendition in a variety of literary forms. The novel and short story genres were rendered in the Bengali language. One of the distinguishing characteristics of this literary period was the theme of nationalism and freedom that ran through the writings like a common thread and reflected the growing demand for independence. The key figures of the modern Bengali literary movement spanning 200 years, included, among other luminaries, Bankim Chandra Chattopadhyay and Sarat Chandra Chattopadhyay, whose short stories and novels dealt with complex themes and characters and, for the first time, delved into the dark areas of social and political commentary, taking on both the oppressive colonial rulers as well as the indigenous practitioners of oppressive traditions. Later generations of literary geniuses included Bibhuti Bhushan Bandyopadhyay and Manik Bandyopadhyay, whose works inspired a number of films, including Satyajit Ray's iconic *Apu Trilogy*, based on Bhushan's autobiographical novel. Other pioneers of the literary movement included Michael Madhusudan Datta, whose poem 'Tilottama Sambhab Kabya' is considered to be the first Bengali poem written in blank verse. Published in 1860, a year before the birth of one of the greatest literary geniuses of all time, Rabindranath Tagore, such great works by the early stalwarts of the modern Bengali literary movement seemed to have created an atmosphere of conduciveness for the next generations of literary luminaries. The horizon of the Bengali literary period of this time is studded with glittering stars, whose creative ingeniousness still continues to dazzle with their brilliance. But the one name that stands out, shining like the sun at the centre of it all, is that of Tagore. The thinker, philosopher, poet, dramatist, artist, writer and composer didn't just touch upon themes as wide-ranging as freedom and forbidden love, divine longing and death, but it has been said about him that his copious work has not left a single human emotion unexplored. In 1913, Tagore became the first Bengali, first Indian, first Asian and really the first non-European to win the Nobel Prize for literature.

Born on 7 May 1861, Tagore died six years before Independence, on 7 August 1941 at the age of 80. But his thinking and writing deeply and directly influenced the freedom movement. His songs, prose and poetry evoked, in a unique blend, both a transcendental spirituality as well as a grounded nationalism. He has the rare distinction of being the creator of the national anthems of two nations. The Indian National Anthem, 'Jana Gana Mana' and the Bangladeshi National Anthem, 'Amar Shonar Bangla'. Both of these songs, with their inspiring lyrics and elevating accompanying tunes, exemplify this extraordinary ability. Tagore infuses into the relatively narrow confines of the idea of an individual state the sense of an unlimited infinity. In the words, 'Bharat Bhagya Bidhata (the Supreme Decider of the destiny of Bharat)', national pride transcends into the realm of the divine. The versatility and genius of Rabindranath Tagore inspired and continues to inspire generations inhabiting the worlds of literature, music, art, philosophy and spirituality, eight decades after his death. Indeed, he had set the tone of the times and beyond. The generations that came into being in the decades following Partition were born with an innate sensitivity which reflected in the literature, art and music, not to mention education of the post-colonial era. Tagore had ushered in a cultural revolution in Bengal. One of his greatest contributions was in the sphere of education. He set up a centre of learning, called 'Shantiniketan' or 'abode of peace' in a remote village in Bolpur in Bengal's Birbhum District. He propounded the idea that the best education is imparted not through rigid, regimented, institutionalized or authoritarian instruction but by allowing the student to learn to identify their innate talents through freedom of thought and expression and by a constant connection with their natural environment.

Post-colonial literary work, spanning the decades of the 1950s, '60s, '70s and even to some extent the '80s and '90s, both reflected the churning that was taking place, politically, economically, socially and culturally, as well as refracted from it, like light, taking on a variety of colours and going off in different directions through a prism. The realities of the troubled times were *presented* in distinct ways in the novels, stories, poems, essays and journals of the era. They were also *represented* in distinct ways through allegory or satire, metaphorically and symbolically. Sometimes the troubled times were conveyed through the social realism of authors like Bonophool or, at other times, through the acerbic writings of authors like Premendra Mitra. Bengali works of translation too, through the use of the language in the vernacular, created a literary niche.

In the 1960s and '70s, Prasun Mitra, journalist, radio broadcaster and writer translated the works of national and international authors including the short stories of Munshi Premchand and the plays of Tennessee Williams. These captured the universality of prevailing human conditions and were as much a reflection of lives in Bengal as of those in the regions where the original works were set.[103] An interesting anecdote exists about Mitra's translation of Tennessee Williams' *A Street Car Named Desire*.[104]

Mitra translated the title as *Trishna Jajabori* (*The Thirsty Nomad*) but the publishers felt it was too aesthetic, and somewhat esoteric for mass marketing and replaced it with *Ruper Kheya* (*The Beauty Boat*). Mitra, livid that his classy title was compromised for the sake of crass consumerism called back the book but the publishers

---

[103]Munshi Premchand (translator: Prasun Mitra), *Premchander Golpo Guchho*, National Book Trust. India, 1974.

[104]Tennessee Williams, (translator: Prasun Mitra), *A Street Car Named Desire or Trishna Jajabori*, Mitraloy Publishers, 1965.

pleaded with him and eventually convinced him. However, Mitra crossed out the printed names in each copy of the book that he owned or was asked to autograph, and rewrote his own original title by hand with an ink pen. The Bengali works of translations of that era are often a reflection of this obsessive adherence to perfection in conveying the beauty of the Bengali language.

Along with literature, art, both visual and performing, that is, dance and theatre, was also evolving. Reflecting the times and refracting from it. The 'Bengal School of Art' was a leading endeavour, which had emerged, in the early 1900s, as a reaction to the predominance of British and European art forms, techniques and subjects. Led by Abanindranath Tagore, a nephew of Rabindranath, who widely popularized it through the classical art courses in the university he founded, it was an attempt to revive lost, indigenous art forms and themes. The movement, which is also referred to as 'the Indian Style of Painting' saw artists abandon English and European styles and influences and embrace traditional folk forms. The most renowned amongst them was Jamini Roy, whose paintings depicted the simplicity of rural, especially tribal people. His unique style, elongated lines in subdued colours, was inspired by the Kalighat 'patachitra' traditions, the ancient system of storytelling through scroll art. Post-colonial Bengali art has remained conscious of presentations that combine the realism of say, idyllic, open landscapes, with the idea that these depictions are also an 'ideal' and 'aspirational' at a time when cramped, city-living has been forced on a divided and displaced people. There are also the 'refracted' versions of reality, the modern art, which captures a state of mind or consciousness that is triggered by the outer realities.

Cinema too had arrived in Bengal. The first film shows date back to between 1896 and '97, a few months after the Lumiere Brothers' *Cinematographe*, which was also the first Indian film showing, was shown in Bombay (now Mumbai) on 7 July 1896.

Hiralal Sen, who started the Royal Bioscope Company, was one of the leading entrepreneurs of the film business in Bengal and started to make short films from the turn of the century. The golden era of Bengali filmmaking is considered to be the post-colonial cinema, which was, like the literature and art, often a realistic reflection of the times and often an escape route, an exercise in fantasy. The romantic films starring the hugely popular duo Suchitra Sen and Uttam Kumar steered the imagination of the Bengal public, still reeling from displacement and economic downturn, to the riveting chemistry of the young couple, generating feelings of fantasy, hope, love. There are stories galore of young men and women in Calcutta, sometimes alone and at other times together, sneaking off to catch a matinee, morning or evening show. 'It was a time of struggle. There were few jobs. There was not enough money for two meals a day. But that didn't stop us. We saved up for a ticket. The two and a half hours or so inside that dark hall took us away from all the troubles,' reminisces a Calcutta gentleman.

But while on the one hand, cinema provided a perfect escape, in the hands of a few master filmmakers, it was also a vehicle for the projection of a stark and harsh reality. In their films, Ritwik Ghatak and Satyajit Ray focused their sensitive lenses on human stories that evoked the sorrows and horrors of Partition. In the iconic *Meghe Dhaka Tara*, one of Ghatak's greatest cinematic works, a family, displaced due to Partition, living in a colony, is shown to be struggling to survive. The individuals are broken and their dreams shattered, as poverty and disease wreak havoc, becoming triggers for betrayal and heartbreak. Ray's *Ashani Sanket* is also an incisive portrayal of life torn by famine, due to the manipulations of greedy, oppressive colonial rulers, before Partition. Bengali cinema has gone through ups and downs with the 'art' or 'parallel' cinema as the genre of serious films were called, often finding it difficult to survive financially. 'Commercial' or 'popular' was comparatively more successful economically. However, the earlier, classier black and white versions gradually gave way to kitschier avatars, which were over-the-top. Technicolour films, depicting heroes and heroines in flamboyant, colourful costumes, spewing crass dialogue, became more common. In terms of a rough graph, 'parallel' films (such as those of the 1950s, '60s and '70s, when Ghatak, Ray and other greats like Tapan Sinha and Mrinal Sen were the luminaries), almost tapered off for a while. The 'popular' cinema of the '50s, '60s and '70s, as stated earlier, too underwent a kind of degeneration of standards, whether in terms of story, dialogue, direction, editing, camera, music and really, cinematic art itself. This can be attributed to the fact that 'parallel' cinema could not sustain itself economically. And 'popular' cinema, without a competitive market, became only about revenue generation rather than art and culture. If the earlier commercial cinema were 'tearjerkers', the latest could be categorized as 'jeer-inducers', for want of a better description.

The trend was to reverse again starting the late 1990s when filmmakers in Bengal achieved a kind of 'parallel is the new popular' approach. Directors like Gautam Ghosh, Aparna Sen and Rituparno Ghosh had already made art movies that were also commercially successful, including *Paar*, *36 Chowringhee Lane* and *Dohon*, respectively, to name just a few. The next generation included Aniruddha Roy Chowdhury, Mainak Bhaumik, Kaushik Ganguly and others. This revivalist art-cum-commercial cinema is marked by realism of treatment and theme like the earlier parallel films but are less likely to focus entirely on the subject of the 'downtrodden'. For instance, the clothes are more relatable than the outlandish costumes of the old popular cinema but not always as quintessentially tattered. 'Songs' which are, and have always been, staples of commercial cinema but were largely missing from earlier art cinema now entered as an essential, if not integral, ingredient. One of the best examples of the Bengali film industry's journey of change are the films of the three generations of Suchitra Sen's family. While Suchitra was the 'reigning queen of the silver screen', to use a much familiar phrase describing her during the early days of the golden age of popular cinema in Bengal, her daughter Moon Moon acted in a number of movies of the transitional phase and her two daughters, Raima and Riya are now part of the revivalist trend. Says Moon Moon, 'Bengali cinema has evolved tremendously in terms of themes, treatment and even technology. My mother's films were significantly different in all these different aspects than mine and my daughters' films, in turn, are different in all these different aspects.' Explaining that art and commercial cinema are no longer mutually exclusive, Aniruddha Roy Chowdhury, who started his career in cinema as an ad film maker, says, 'The division between art and commercial as far as cinema is concerned has blurred because the current crop of filmmakers don't feel that films which depict serious topics and which centre on deeper themes cannot be packaged attractively enough for them to be successful in the market. The attempt now is to try strike the right balance.'

Theatre, which is considered an integral component of the culture of Bengal (which itself is known as the cultural capital of the country), too flourished throughout this period. It originated during the British era initially as private entertainment in elite households and later developed as public entertainment with commercial productions held in the city's theatres. A number of theatres and auditoriums sprung up in and around Calcutta, a few of which still continue to exist like a testimony to the sheer grandiose of this medium that had gained tremendous popularity during that time. The Star and the Minerva were two of the earliest theatres that came into existence in the period from 1883 to 1888. Girish Chandra Ghosh was one of the pioneers of the genre and introduced the use of Bengali songs and local musical instruments in the productions. He was known both as a thespian par excellence and as an ascetic, devoted to Ramakrishna

Paramhansha. The rich tradition of folk theatre, called 'jatra', of course, existed in the land for centuries and continued to thrive in the rural areas throughout the British era. These were performed by travelling troupes and were marked by melodrama and exaggerated acting, expressions and gestures. Post-colonial theatre in Bengal is known for its strong political content, usually Left-leaning, and have been a medium of protest and critique. Anti-establishment, this theatre necessarily opposed the policies of the government. This form of theatre differed from the earlier avatar in the fact that it was driven by the conscious goal of awakening in the people of India a sense of cultural identity, which had eroded during colonial rule. This theatre was, moreover, organized and attached to an association of Indian thespians established just before Independence, in 1943, called the Indian People's Theatre Association (IPTA). Theatre has withstood the onslaught of competitive mediums like cinema and television and a number of production houses continue to put up plays, both traditional as well as experimental in terms of form and content both. Indeed, there has been a concerted effort by Bengal's renowned cinema directors and actors to ensure that the tradition of theatre does not whittle away. For them, theatre is the treasured representative of Bengali culture. Of those to have endorsed the supremacy of theatre was none other than legendary actor Soumitra Chatterjee, who himself has acted in nearly 300 films and received a number of prestigious international and national awards including, in 2018, the Knight of Legion of Honour, the highest French order of merit and in 2012, the Dadasaheb Phalke Award, India's highest award in cinema. Satyajit Ray's protégé, Chatterjee has acted in as many as 14 of the great director's films. Yet, he fondly remembered his roots as a stage actor before his first film (he debuted with Ray's *Apur Sansar* in 1959, which was to gain iconic status eventually). In fact, throughout his outstanding cinema career he kept in touch with theatre and returned to stage acting in 1978. Since then, along with his films, he continued to perform, until his death on 15 November 2020 at the age of 85, in different productions including his own plays, directed by him. 'The experience of performing live is incomparable,' Chatterjee said in an interview to the author. 'The energy of the audience is infectious for actors and the immediate interaction with the people present is gratifying. This does not happen in cinema.' Chatterjee also pointed out that theatre, being the older form, is more traditional. Chatterjee's daughter, actor Poulami Bose of the theatre group 'Mukhomukhi' (meaning 'Face to Face') is continuing the legacy of her father. Other renowned groups that carry forward the tradition of theatre in Bengal include, among others, Nandikar, founded by Rudra Prasad Sengupta and Swapna Sandhani, founded by Kaushik Sen.

A pioneering theatre endeavour was started in 2006 in Bengal, when an IPS officer named B.D. Sharma, who was then inspector general of the state's prisons, decided to introduce the inmates of the jails to play production. Explaining the evolution of what subsequently came to be known as 'Culture Therapy', Sharma says, 'In the year 2000, legislation was passed that did away with the idea that prisons were places of "punishment" and decreed that henceforth prisons and jails ought to be called "correctional homes" or places were the inmates could be "corrected" of the ills that caused them to commit crimes.' Sharma says that only one per cent of the prisoners were hardened criminals. Ninety-nine per cent had committed crimes at the spur of the moment, often in a fit of rage. 'I felt that in order to be a "correctional home" to the incarcerated people, it was necessary to induce in them a sense that here one could be educated and entertained and, in the process, they can live and learn.' Six years later, in July 2006, while on a visit to a correctional home, Sharma invited theatre director Pradip Bhattacharya to put together a cultural show with his troupe inside the jail for the entertainment of the inmates. Recalls, Sharma, 'I discussed the idea of bringing about "cure through culture" with Pradipda and it appealed to him.' Bhattacharya subsequently staged a play on rural literacy. Before the programme, some prisoners also sang songs and recited poetry. This set Sharma thinking about the possibility of training the inmates in theatre. Sharma approached Bhattacharya for the task, who readily agreed. After months of rehearsals, a group of 24 convicts—18 men and six women—staged *Tasher Desh* (Country of Cards), a dance drama, composed by poet laureate Rabindranath Tagore, at the iconic Rabindra Sadan auditorium in Kolkata on 1 May 2007. The drama, dealing with the theme of imprisonment of the mind and the idea of freedom, was the perfect choice to showcase Culture Therapy. One of the biggest successes of Culture Therapy has been the dance drama, *Valmiki Pratibha,* directed and composed by danseuse Alokananda Roy, whom Sharma had invited to join soon after the production of *Tasher Desh*. The Tagore masterpiece had a direct appeal in terms of the theme because it delineated the journey of Ratnakar, from the dreaded dacoit to the spiritual saint Valmiki. Roy has successfully trained hundreds of inmates in dance and says, 'it is fulfilling to witness their transformation.' Gradually Sharma extended Culture Therapy to include not just theatre but dance, art, jatra (folk theatre), poetry recitation, education and sports.

The music of Bengal too was influenced by the revolutionary changes taking place post-Independence. The first traditional Bengali songs were the religious chants in Hindu and Buddhist temples in the first millennium CE and was subsequently transformed by Vaishnavite music, the Bengali lyrics that sung the praise of Chaitanya Mahaprabhu. The arrival of the Islamic rulers introduced Bengal to the style of highly-developed songs, known as Hindustani classical music. Khayal (another name for the classical songs), rendered in Bengali lyrics, has been a lost tradition for nearly 100 years and currently, the musician Kabir

Suman is trying to revive it. But 'Bengali music' comprises a long list of traditions that include both spiritual and secular songs written in the Bengali language as well as a range of tunes and musical instruments indigenous to Bengal. The modern, colonial and post-colonial periods have been marked by the advent of patriotic songs and the songs of Rabindranath Tagore, known as Rabindra Sangeet as well as 'Nazrul Geeti', the songs of Kazi Nazrul Islam, one of Bengal's greatest poets, lyricists and composers of devotional, love and patriotic songs. 'Ucchhanga Sangeet' (literally higher music), which refers to the highly-developed classical tradition, has thrived in Bengal and Rabindra Sangeet, Nazrul Geeti and modern Bengali songs such as those of the poet-lyricist-composer, Salil Chaudhury, have all infused classical music into their compositions. The other Bengali tradition that has continued to thrive, like a common thread beading together every other musical genre through the centuries, are the songs of Ramprasad and Rajanikanto, exponents of 'Shyama Sangeet', the devotional and love songs dedicated to Goddess Kali. Atul Prasad too composed songs in this tradition as well as in the genre of patriotic music. One of the most modern musical groups which initiated an organized approach to creating a genre of Bengali songs to mark the changing times is the Calcutta Youth Choir. Started in 1958, a decade after Independence, by Satyajit Ray, Salil Chaudhury and the versatile film and theatre actress Ruma Guha Thakurta, it was a forum for the creation of songs of mass movements and folk forms. The lyrics were consciously inspiring and the tunes energetic. The rhythms were brisk and connoted an impatience to move forward and achieve.

Bengal, which had just come out of battle, was trying to march ahead and put its best foot forward. From literature to theatre, to cinema, to art and music, it was a conscious, vibrant effort to stay alive and thrive. This was also a time of the angst-ridden Hungry Generation with their iconoclastic poetry and prose of dissent.

They were trying to break every shackle of rule and regulation that held humanity back through their literature, art, music. Then there were the 'film songs' which was created for cinema, a genre that has survived the test of time and continues to thrive and evolve to this day. The cultural churning taking place in Bengal ran parallel to the political, economic and social changes.

Because of it. In spite of it. As a reaction to it.

The Indian National Congress (INC) was in power during the interim period in Bengal, between 15 August 1947 and 25 October 1951, when free India's first Parliamentary elections took place. It took four months to complete, finally concluding on 21 February 1952. The interim, also known as 'provincial' government, of course, was elected in 1946, by the Constituent Assembly, which was created to oversee the 'transfer of power' from British rule to Indian rule. In the Parliamentary elections INC was re-established in both the Centre as well as most of the states, including West Bengal. However, Bengal was a hotbed of opposition politics with the radical Communist parties playing a key role in moving the narrative forward. INC and the Centre was continually challenged in this land, the land which had been lacerated against its will, bleeding and seething. It set the tone for Bengal politics and through the past decades, the fire of discontent has been burning. Often just simmering. At other times erupting into flames. But ever lurking, right beneath the surface.

Governments have been replaced over and again. INC, which ruled for 15 years since Independence, had to make way for other political establishments including a United Front coalition government led by the Communist Party of India (CPI). Ajoy Mukherjee, leader of another political party, the Bangla Congress, was made chief minister.

Subsequently splits took place in the CPI, with factions differing on issues, which included anything from whether or not to participate in elections, to the permissible extent of radicalism.

The Communist Party of India (Marxists), which took different stances on issues such as Parliamentary Democracy and India's border conflict with China, came into being.

As did the 'ultra left' Communist Party of India (Marxists-Leninists), also known as the 'Naxals', which began with a violent peasant rebellion in the Naxalbari region of northern West Bengal, in the foothills of the Himalayas. The Naxal movement spread to the city of Calcutta, with Bengal's youth and intellectuals joining it in droves. As far as the idealistic were concerned, it was a cause worth espousing, because it pitted the have-nots against the haves. It was a revolution by illiterate peasants, exploited for generations by feudal lords, but was organized and provided leadership by urban intellectuals, educated in the history and philosophy of Lenin and Marx. Charu Majumdar, a college professor from Siliguri, in northern Bengal, was the brain behind the mass movement. However, the rebellion gradually grew to become a bloodbath, and got blamed for indiscriminate murders and killings. Calcutta and parts of Bengal in the early 1970s was like a war zone, often the stillness of night, even in perfectly 'respectable' residential premises, pierced with the sound of gunshots or bombs exploding, followed by the rush of running feet, possibly police chasing a suspect.

While hundreds of young men and women did join the movement as noted above, hundreds of others were picked up by police on mere suspicion, often locked up without trial, beaten, tortured and even eventually killed in fake encounters. 'Countless young boys (and girls) were killed at this time,' recalls an elderly Calcutta homemaker who was a college student then, adding, 'We were always scared when our brothers went out of the house and used to think, "Will we ever see him alive again?"'

Police was given order to shoot at sight.

Siddhartha Shankar Ray, who was the chief minister of Bengal at that time, had explained in an exclusive interview in 2009, 'It was a time when policemen were the prime target of the Naxals. They were being killed indiscriminately. They were given orders to shoot to defend themselves.'[105]

The Congress in Bengal was gaining unpopularity with the indiscriminate crackdown on youth when, in 1975, the Emergency was announced.

The Emergency quashed freedom of speech and imposed a host of other restrictions. With the jailing of many of Bengal's intellectuals, writers, journalists, columnists, academics and others who spoke out against the government, Congress was perceived to have breached the democratic tenets of the country and had lost its credibility. In the Bengal state elections of 1977, the Communists were overwhelmingly voted into power. Led by the CPI(M), the Left Front government, with its Left partners, CPI, Revolutionary Socialist Party (RSP) and Forward Bloc (traced back to the days of Netaji Subhas Chandra Bose) ruled Bengal for 34 years.

These three and a half decades was full of the proverbial 'good, bad and ugly'. The Communist government in the first decade of its rule in Bengal, initiated the revolutionary land reforms, which ensured that the nearly 80 per cent of Bengal's population, the poor villagers who were the worst hit by famines and starvation-deaths, got small plots of land which they could cultivate. This entitled them to the basics of food and shelter. For the urban poor, namely factory labourers, trade unions were instituted as organized support systems against exploitation by business owners. While the Left government's emphasis on looking after the interests of the working classes was lauded by the state's urban ideologues, intellectuals, academics and thinkers, it alienated an important sector, which was the industry-owners. While the lack of access to land for factories made it difficult for businesses to start, far less expand, repeated strikes and lockouts by the trade

---

[105]Siddhartha Shankar Ray in an interview with the author.

unions exasperated the existing ones. Indeed, gradually many of these workers' unions ceased to be vehicles of needful dissent and turned into weapons of disruption of work, endless strikes and violent agitations, often resulting in murder.

A number of industries shut down. Many owners fled. The lack of jobs meant that people left Bengal in search of employment. The economic downturn was exacerbated by the problem of 'infiltration'—a phenomenon that describes the state's granting of work and filling up government vacancies in every sector from education to police only with people belonging to the Left parties. With virtually no opposition (the Congress had become a weak force) election-time provided no alternative. Allegations of rigging, however, was rampant as was charges of corruption. The Communists grew complacent. When the liberalization of the economy took place in the early 1990s in India, initially Bengal was a reluctant participant. Then chief minister Jyoti Basu was not keen to disturb status quo. The rural constituency, which comprised 80 per cent of voters, had been loyal to the Communist government because its land policy did not allow interference of big industries, far less foreign direct investments (FDIs) that opening up the markets would entail. Basu's successor, Buddhadeb Bhattacharjee, who took over in the year 2000, however had a different vision. He wanted to industrialize the state and his motto was 'do it now'. He wanted to 'modernize' Calcutta and suddenly multiplexes and malls mushroomed in and around the city. Skyscrapers and swanky residential complexes cropped up as did a host of services associated with modernization, including the advent of old-age homes.

Two events eventually brought the Communists down in Bengal. The attempt by Bhattacharjee to set up a couple of industries, around 2006, on agricultural land and the simultaneous rise of an alternative political party, the Trinamool Congress, founded by a breakaway member of the Congress Party, Mamata Banerjee.

In 2006, Bhattacharjee invited industrialist, Ratan Tata to set up a car-manufacturing factory in Singur 39 kilometres from Calcutta. Almost 1,000 acres of what farmers claimed was fertile farmland was acquisitioned by the government for the purpose. Local farmers decried the move, with nearly half of them claiming that they were unwilling to part with their land. Banerjee, who was in the political opposition, had been on the lookout for an issue with which to topple the Communist government. She and her party took up the farmers' cause. A similar takeover of fertile farmland for the creation of a petrochemical unit in Nandigram, in the district of Midnapore, too was thwarted by the local villagers with support from Banerjee. She defeated the Left government in the Assembly elections of 2011. She promised 'Poriborton' or 'Change'—a clean-up of the system and a smooth-functioning state.

While her decade-long rule, so far, has fallen short of the promised overhaul, the populist programs she has instituted for the poor, especially in remote, rural areas, has made her popular with the downtrodden. These include providing employment and education, not to mention subsidized ration to families who live below poverty line (BPL). This played a significant role in her sweeping every state election since 2011. In the 2016 Assembly elections she returned to power with a thumping majority.

But it is the just-concluded 2021 Assembly elections that is likely to go down in history as a watershed moment in Bengal politics. Perhaps even more so than the historic Assembly elections of 2011, when Trinamool defeated the 34-year-old Communist regime. This is because, for the first time, 'Bengal' and 'Bengali' had become a campaign issue. The bitter battle for political power turned into a desperate attempt by each contesting party to highlight its Bengaliness. Banerjee's campaign projected her as the defender of Bengal against 'bohiragotos' or 'outsiders'. This was a direct dig at the top leaders of her chief political rival, Bharatiya Janata Party, who were not Bengali. The BJP, on the other hand, brought to the fore its Bengali roots by pointing out that Shyama Prasad Mukherjee, a Bengali, was the founder of the Bharatiya Jana Sangh, the predecessor to BJP.

The winning campaign, however, was Trinamool's 'Bangla nijer meye key chay' (or 'Bengal wants her own daughter'). Mamata Banerjee was reinstated as chief minister of West Bengal for the third consecutive term, with her party bagging 213 of the 294 Assembly seats, the highest of all three state elections she contested.

Reflecting on the phenomenon, psephologist and political scientist, Professor Biswanath Chakraborty says, 'For Bengalis, this became the decisive factor. It overrode BJP's big advantage as the only party in the fray which did not have an earlier background in ruling Bengal and therefore had a chance to.'

The chance to rule Bengal. It has been a dream, as we have seen, of rulers from the days of Alexander the Great. Geopolitically, Bengal is strategically located. Since ancient times it was considered an important political and economic port because of its vast natural resources. The Himalayan mountains stretch out across its north. The Bay of Bengal spreads out to vast horizons on its east and south and the Hooghly, a large part of the river Ganga, flows gently along its west.

Yes, the river flows through Bengal and like the river, the Bengal story too keeps flowing, endlessly, timelessly. The 2021 elections drove home another point. That nothing lasts forever in the timelessness of time. The Congress and the Communist parties, both of which were powerful rulers of Bengal in their heyday, did not win a single seat, even though they united and fought the elections together.

This transience dwells in the timeless story of Bengal.

XV

THE END

'Aaj tobey ei tuku thaak, baki kotha porey hobey.
(Let this be all for now. Let's talk another day.)'

—Salil Chowdhury[106]

No, the Bengal Story does not have endings. It is a continuing tale, each part of which, uncannily, begins on a rain-lashed, storm-struck day.

On the morning of 28 May 2021, a super cyclone called Yaas, which had formed in the Bay of Bengal, crashed into India's eastern coast. Vast parts of the delta islands of the Sundarbans drowned. The severe cyclonic storm had coincided with a full moon and lunar high tides breached river banks and dykes, creating flash floods.

This account by Dibos Mondal, an islander from Sagar Deep, gives glimpses into the suddenness with which waves crashed into the land and wiped out entire villages. He said,

> After the Indian Meteorological Department issued the cyclone alert, the state government had evacuated islanders to safer shelters. However, many returned to check on their homes, cattle and belongings. Most live in mud huts with

---

[106]From the Bengali song of the same name composed by Salil Chowdhury.

thatched roofs. From earlier experiences of cyclones and expecting extremely strong winds, we tried to tie down roofs and other structures with ropes and cords to prevent these from getting blown away. But what no one expected was that the sea would rise and engulf the islands, inundating our homes and everything in sight. Within less than 10 minutes of the cyclone making landfall, the water went from ankle-deep to knee-deep to hip-deep, to chest-deep, to nose-deep and then over our heads. We clung onto trees, clambered on to boats, clutching our loved ones and crammed into the houses in the vicinity, which had concrete rooftops, and waited to be rescued.

The Union and state governments deployed rescue teams which were on standby.

Since Cyclone Yaas ripped through the Sundarbans, environmentalists and scientists of Bengal have issued a clarion call for action to protect the delta from disintegrating and merging into the sea. Environment journalist and editor of climate news portal, *The Plurals*, Jayanta Basu initiated a movement entitled, 'Save Sundarbans NOW' which is a platform, comprising a coalition of villagers, engineers, environmentalists, scientists and other specialists, for planning, discussing and implementing a series of projects targeted at preventing the delta islands from eroding irrevocably. The group meets regularly (virtually during the Covid-19 pandemic) to chalk out sustainable solutions. 'The Sundarbans are an integral part of the heritage of Bengal and we ought to do everything in our power to try to protect it,' he says.

According to Kalyan Rudra, a river expert and chairman of the West Bengal Board of Pollution Control, rivers of the Sundarbans have been severely stunted and one of the ways of reviving the Sundarbans is by not restricting rivers from following their natural courses and by allowing adequate movement. He says that while the islands on the Indian side is on a degenerative phase, interestingly the delta islands on the Bangladeshi side are regenerative, possibly due to the pattern of silt formation from rivers. Two-thirds of the Sundarbans falls in Bangladesh while one-third is in West Bengal, India.

Experts warn that survival of the land, that is, Bengal itself is threatened when the Sundarbans is endangered. Joydeep Gupta, journalist and South Asia director of environmental portal, *The Third Pole*, points out that destruction of mangrove forests has contributed to the encroachment of the sea into the Sundarbans. He points out that mangroves act as natural buffers to cyclones by absorbing strong winds and waves from the sea, restricting the devastating impacts of severe storms. 'The importance of mangrove forests in preserving the delta cannot be overstated,' he says.

Indeed, experts warn that the gradual decay of ground in the Sundarbans could eventually extend to the mainland.

Fortunately, the administration has taken note of the seriousness of the situation. Dola Sen, Trinamool Rajya Sabha member says, 'West Bengal chief minister Mamata Banerjee has already announced plans of reforestation with plantation of mangrove forests in the districts along the coastline of Bengal being a priority.'

Bengal depends on it…to live through other rain-lashed, wind-swept and storm-struck days.

ACKNOWLEDGEMENTS

My mother, Jharna Mitra, sisters Mandira and Koli and my husband, Arijit Sengupta. My mother-in-law, Bijoya Sengupta and my little brother-in-law D2. Thanks for everything.

My journalism teachers in school Nancy Cox and Barbara Schramm. I remember their teachings every step of the way. Supriya Chaudhuri and Sukanta Chaudhuri, my professors at Jadavpur University. Clearly the lessons learnt from them were not limited to the riveting classes years ago. While writing this book, I found myself referring so often to the books on the subject of Bengal edited by Sukanta da. All I can say about Supriya di is that I thank my lucky stars that I had her as a teacher.

Gouri Chatterjee, my editor in *The Telegraph*, to whom I owe the privilege of being a reporter in Bengal. Rudrangshu Mukherjee, historian and former 'Opinions' editor of *The Telegraph*, from whose work I quoted extensively as I did from the many fascinating books he had given me to read and review. My former editors in *Outlook Magazine*, Krishna Prasad and Rajesh Ramachandran for letting me do the stories any reporter would die for.

Chandra Kumar Bose and Madhuri Bose, grandnephew and grandniece of Subhas Chandra Bose for all the insights on Netaji and the Bose family. I must also make special mention of Madhuri di's book, *The Bose Brothers: An Insider's Account*, to which I referred.

Thank you for the interviews and insight: Dr Debashis Ray, Dr Om Prakash Mishra, Professor Biswanath Chakraborty, Professor

Rangan Kanti Jana, Professor Maroona Murmu.

Joydeep Gupta (South Asia director, *The Third Pole*), Jayanta Basu (editor, *The Plurals*) and Dr Kalyan Rudra (chairman of West Bengal Board of Pollution Control).

Thanks to Jainarine Deonauth, Guyana academic and editor. Thanks also to Parasram Persaud, Gangadai Persaud and Rupa Seenaraine of Guyana.

I am grateful to all the experts in different areas whom I have quoted in this book but could not individually mention here. Their voices truly enriched the narrative of the story of Bengal. To my sources, primary and secondary, without whose wisdom I could not write this book.

At Rupa Publications, thanks Anjasi Nongkynrih Nyshadham for taking the time and trouble to read through the drafts and for your suggestions. Rudra Narayan Sharma, especially for such 'sweet' suggestions as including a paragraph on the delectable desserts of Bengal, namely the 'roshogolla' and coming up with the idea to begin each chapter with a quote from a Bengali icon. And thank you so much, Rajen Mehra for commissioning this book.

Here I must mention that in undertaking the daunting task of translating a few lines from the iconic works of Bengal's great philosophers, poets, dramatist, writers and thinkers, I took a few liberties when I felt it would help convey the spirit of the original better. The originals defy translation and I hope that the shortcomings would be forgiven.

People do a lot of things which don't get recorded in books of history. Great acts of goodness. Little acts of love and kindness. One can only thank them for these. I have a long list. Here is a short one: B.D. Sharma, Brinda Dalal, Shoma Bhattacharya, Soutik Biswas, Mark Butterworth, Sujan Dutta, Damayanti Dutta, Amit Dixit, Sheetal Dhandore, Sanjay Goenka, Chandrani Banerjee, Moshumi Banerjee, Sandipan Chatterjee, Jayanta Ghoshal, Indira Basu, Anuradha Sengupta, Joydeep Sengupta, Kumar Tiku,

Rashmi Pratap, Pragya Singh and S.B. Easwaran.

Finally, a thank you to Vinod Mehta, my former editor in *Outlook Magazine*, whom I really missed while writing this book. I will never forget his encouragement when I was writing my last book and his one-word review of it in his column, 'Delhi Diary'. He called it 'gripping' and I never got to thank him for that. Hope you can hear this in heaven: Thanks a lot, Vinod!